Rhythms of
Writing

Rhythms of Writing

Pamela Dykstra

South Suburban College

HOUGHTON MIFFLIN COMPANY   Boston   New York

Senior Sponsoring Editor: Mary Jo Southern

Basic Book Editor: Martha Bustin

Senior Associate Editor: Ellen Darion

Editorial Assistant: Danielle Richardson

Project Editor: Elizabeth Gale Napolitano

Editorial Assistants: Joy Park, Sarah Godshall

Senior Production/Design Coordinator: Sarah Ambrose

Senior Manufacturing Coordinator: Priscilla Bailey

Senior Marketing Manager: Nancy Lyman

Cover Design: Harold Burch Designs, NYC

Interior Design: Greta D. Sibley & Associates

Text credits appear on page 331.

Printed in the U.S.A.

Library of Congress Catalog Card Number: 99-71999

Student Edition ISBN: 0-395-91805-7
Instructor's Annotated Edition ISBN: 0-395-91807-3

1 2 3 4 5 6 7 8 9-WC-03 02 00 01 99

Brief Contents

Contents

PART 2   Writing Sentences   91

Chapter 6: Writing Core Sentences   93

Chapter 7: Writing with Verbs   102

Chapter 8: Writing with Irregular Verbs   117

Preface

Rhythms of Writing, appropriate for first-level developmental writing courses, gets results through the application of three premises. Each relates to how we learn language and how we learn to write:

- **The structure of writing is different from the structure of talking.** Writing and talking are interrelated but distinct forms of communication, each with unique structures and contexts. When students recognize the differences between written and spoken communication, their writing improves, often dramatically.

- **Language is processed and produced in phrases and clauses.** We understand and create language in phrases and clauses—that is, in bits or "chunks" of thought. In writing, we shape these bits of thought into written patterns. When the process is demystified and the patterns of writing are emphasized, students can effectively learn these patterns and advance in their writing abilities.

- **Language is acquired by internalizing patterns.** We learn to write in large part through exposure to the rhythms of written sentences. Most students are products of an oral culture and have not had a great deal of exposure to these rhythms of writing. When students have the opportunity to read and work with many short models and practices, they begin to internalize the varying sentence patterns and to write in well-developed, mature sentences. Again, the results are often dramatic and highly gratifying.

These premises all have relevance for the developmental writer, for writing well involves more than recognizing and avoiding errors: it involves understanding and internalizing how sentences work. This book helps students to hear the differences between spoken and written language and to capture for themselves the rhythms of writing.

Special Features of *Rhythms of Writing*

Developed over a seven-year period and extensively class-tested, *Rhythms of Writing* helps students to write and think more effectively. Here are some of its key features:

1. **Helps students understand the differences between spoken and written language.** Students build on what they know (talking) to learn how

written sentences are shaped and structured. By seeing, hearing, and internalizing how fragments of thought are patterned into written language, students develop a sense of their own options as writers. They become increasingly aware of sentence boundaries, more familiar with the flexibility of language, and more confident in handling a variety of writing assignments.

2. **Hundreds of short, well-placed examples and models to support instruction.** An abundance of brief models at the sentence, paragraph, and essay levels bring alive the book's instruction. They also give extra practice in reading and help students to internalize the rhythms of writing. These models are collected from both students and professional writers. A wide range of cultural backgrounds is represented, highlighting the common human experience.

3. **Varied and thought-provoking writing topics.** An extensive list of topics for journals, paragraphs, short papers, and essays include assignments such as responding to proverbs, poetry, and excerpts from literature, newspapers, and magazines. These prompts are a true resource for teachers and students, collected, developed, and class-tested over many years.

4. **Visuals.** Along with the book's illustrative sentence, paragraph, and essay models, diagrams and outlines reinforce the instruction at every step. These concrete aids to learning respond to a common request made by students: "Don't tell me; just show me."

5. **Punctuation as an integral part of writing.** Punctuation is presented as a system of signs enabling readers to understand writers' thoughts. Commas receive particular attention. As students practice the varying sentence patterns, they learn how commas set off introductory words and words interrupting the flow of thought.

6. **Sentence combining exercises and collaborative exercises.** A generous number of sentence combining exercises, modeling exercises, and other types of exercises (at the sentence, paragraph, and short paper levels) actively involve students in learning. Many are designed for collaborative as well as individual work, as indicated by unobtrusive in-text icons.

In addition, *Rhythms of Writing* gives special attention to common problems, includes helpful information for ESL writers, and has a relaxed yet respectful tone. It is the first book to show students how the parts of a sentence connect and are related, beginning not with abstract "handbook" definitions, but with the familiar: the words, phrases, and clauses of talking.

Organization

Rhythms of Writing is adaptable for varying levels of basic writers and basic writing courses. The parts and the chapters within each part can be used flexibly.

Part 1: Writing Paragraphs, Short Papers, and Essays

Chapters 1–4 on paragraphs and short papers introduce students to the writing process, with Chapter 2 highlighting the rhetorical modes. Chapter 5 moves to the brief essay.

Part 2: Writing Sentences

Chapters 6–10 help students to understand the core sentence and sentence boundaries; examine common problems with verbs; and cover the basic punctuation marks, especially the comma, in relation to sentence structure.

Part 3: Writing Sentences with Varied Rhythms

Chapters 11–20 guide students in writing with sentence variety and changing the rhythms of sentences. These chapters consider subordinating conjunctions, adverbs, prepositional phrases, relative clauses, and other additions to the core sentence.

Part 4: Focusing on Words and Punctuation

Chapters 21–24 focus on words and punctuation that cause difficulties for basic writers, such as pronouns, easily confused words, possessive nouns, and quotations.

Part 5: Additional Resources for Writing

To supplement suggested writing topics found in Part 1, Chapter 25 contains additional writing topics in three sections: Ideas for Journal Writing, Ideas for Paragraphs and Short Papers, and Ideas for Essays. Chapter 26 spotlights problem areas for ESL writers.

Chapter Elements

Chapters contain the following flexible elements:

1. **"Focus on Fragments"** and additional "Focus on" boxes highlight common problems and solutions.

2. **Collaborative activities** in each chapter encourage students to share ideas and learn from one another.

3. **Computer tips** for drafting, revising, and editing include helpful word processing strategies for the developmental writer.

4. **Review sections** summarize the main points of each chapter.

5. **Review Practices and Extra Challenges** conclude the chapters in Parts 2–4, reinforcing the chapter instruction.

Resources for Instructors

Available on adoption of the text, the following ancillaries provide the instructor with excellent support material.

Instructor's Annotated Edition

Test Package

Test Bank Data Disk (available in Windows and Mac)

Acknowledgments

Many have contributed significantly to the creation of this book. I am indebted to my students whose honest feedback was essential in knowing what worked, what didn't work, and why. In addition, the following colleagues served as helpful reviewers throughout the development of this book. I am grateful for their excellent advice.

Nancy Barlow, Brookhaven College

Claudia House, Nashville State Technical Institute

Patricia Malinowski, Finger Lakes Community College

Vivian Naylor, Meridian Community College

Julie Nichols, Okaloosa-Walton Community College

Linda Rollins, Motlow State Community College

Kathryn L. Skulley, Denver Technical College

Karen Standridge, Pikes Peak Community College

Jean M. Turcott, State University of New York at Buffalo

Linda Whisnant, Guilford Technical Community College

Jayne L. Williams, Texarkana College

Gary Zacharias, Palomar College

I am equally indebted to Martha Bustin, my developmental editor, for her gentle guidance, creative suggestions, and consistent support. I also thank Mary Jo Southern, Senior Sponsoring Editor, for supporting me and having faith in this project. Friends and colleagues, particularly Evelyn Sowell, Nancy Frazier, and Linda Matthews, have assisted me throughout the publishing process. Karin and Britta

Hillstrom, my daughters, were also instrumental, for they spent countless hours sitting on the floor helping me edit chapters. Finally, I thank my mother, Patricia Dykstra, who taught me the joy and wonder of life, and my father, Dean Dykstra, who taught me the power and beauty of words.

P. D.

Rhythms of Writing

Introduction

Exploring the Differences Between Talking and Writing

◆ Language Patterns

◆ Differences Between Talking and Writing

◆ Different Kinds of Talking and Writing

◆ Improving Your Writing

You have had many years of experience talking and writing. Perhaps talking is easier for you, or maybe you would rather write. No matter which seems more comfortable, though, you know that they are not the same thing. Talking and writing are different because they involve different structures and different situations.

Language Patterns

Early Language

Our brains are fascinating. They work without our awareness. One of the most complicated accomplishments of our brains is figuring out language. By the time babies are eight months old, they are exploring the sounds they can make as they babble. Their babbling soon turns into words, and at about age two, they are putting words together. We can see that exploration in Adam, a child whose language development was carefully recorded. Some examples of his talking are listed below:

2 years, 3 months:	Play checkers. Big drum. I got horn. A bunny-rabbit walk.
2 years, 11 months:	Why you mixing baby chocolate? I finish drinking all up down my throat. Look at that piece a paper and tell it.
3 years:	You dress me up like a baby elephant.

—Pinker, *The Language Instinct*

Adam not only knows what the words mean, he knows how to put the words together. He has picked up (*internalized*) the basic patterns of English. He said, "You dress me up like a baby elephant," not "Elephant up baby a me like dress you." Adam knows how to arrange the words without anyone telling him, "This is a verb. This is a prepositional phrase. This is where a subject goes." Adam absorbed it all unconsciously through listening. That is how we all learned our first language.

Babies and young children internalize the words and structure of whatever language they hear. This is why it is essential to talk and read to children. If a child hears no language spoken, that child will not speak. If a child hears Chinese, the child will speak Chinese. And if the child grows up in a bilingual setting, hearing two languages, the child will easily learn both.

By the time we are three years old, we have internalized the basic patterns of the language spoken around us. We know what the individual words mean, and we know how to put those words together.

A Basic Pattern

In English, words are usually arranged in a subject-verb-object pattern. The subject does the action; the verb is the action; the object receives the action.

       subject verb   object
       We   exchanged gifts.

No one explained this pattern to us when we were children. We simply listened to others and practiced the pattern we heard. Without consciously trying, we learned that subjects come first, verbs come second, and objects come last.

In English, the order of words gives us valuable information. For example,

       The dog bit the man.
       The man bit the dog.

Those are two entirely different situations. The same words, *dog* and *man*, are used, but changing the position changes the meaning; it changes who or what did the biting and who or what was bitten.

This subject-verb-object pattern is not the way all languages work. In Latin, for example, switching the words does *not* change the meaning. *Canis virum momordit* means *The dog bit the man*. If the words are rearranged as *Virum canis momordit*, the meaning remains the same: *The dog bit the man*. Scrambling the order of words in Latin does not change the meaning because the endings on words, not position, tell whether a word is the subject or the object. English is different; it relies on position to tell who did what to whom.

This textbook guides you in taking the patterns you already know and using them in your writing. We are used to talking in these patterns. But if we write exactly the way we talk, readers will be confused because the structure of writing is different from the structure of talking.

Differences Between Talking and Writing

 SMALL GROUP DISCUSSION Discuss your answers to the following questions:

- Which would you rather do: talk or write?
- Why?
- How are talking and writing different?

Different Structures

One of the most important differences between talking and writing is structure. We talk in chunks, but we write in sentences.

We Talk in Chunks

When we talk, we say things such as, "I went to the mall and bought these chairs on sale two of them and they'll go in the living room I think." We put our words together in groups, groups such as *I went, these chairs, in the living room*. People who study language have a name for these groups: *chunks*. We talk in chunks of information, stringing them together until we get our idea across.

Listen to yourself talk; listen to anyone else talk. You will hear chunks and chunks of information tied together by the words *and, so*, or *you know*. When we have said what we want to say, our voice goes down in pitch. The drop in pitch is the signal that we are finished, letting others know that if they talk, they will not be interrupting. This pattern of talking is seen in run-on sentences where one sentence "runs on" into the next. If you find yourself writing run-on sentences, you are probably writing the way you talk. You are stringing along chunks of information until you have communicated your idea and then placing a period where your voice goes down.

We Write in Sentences

Writing involves presenting the chunks of information in a different structure: a sentence. When we talk, people aren't likely to say, "There is a verb missing from that sentence." Unlike talking, writing demands a subject and a verb in every sentence.

Different Situations

Another important difference between talking and writing is the situation. When we talk, the listeners are right there with us. When we write, the readers are separated from us by both space and time.

When We Talk, the Listener Is Present

When we talk, we can see the listeners, and they can see us. We use gestures, facial expressions, and body language to communicate our meaning. We also watch the listeners' expressions and body language to see if they understand what we are saying or whether they agree or disagree. Often we don't even finish our sentences because we can see that others already understand our point.

Because listeners are present, the pitch and tone of voice can add important information. A falling pitch indicates that we have completed an idea; a rising pitch indicates that we are asking a question. People talking do not say "period" and "question mark." We also use tone to communicate information: we can whisper, yell, pause, or whine. Imagine the different ways someone could say, "I'm sorry." Someone could even say those words in a tone that meant "I'm not one bit sorry."

When we talk, others participate in the conversation. Conversation is a give-and-take process. Speakers and listeners create meaning together. Often we don't really know what we are going to say until we say it, and other people's input and questions help us clarify our thinking.

When We Write, the Reader Is Absent

When we write, readers can neither hear nor see us. The clues given in face-to-face conversation no longer work. We are dealing with a different situation, and it is important to be aware of the difference.

When we write, readers cannot see our body language or hear our voices change pitch, pause, and stop. If we write the way we talk—stringing along ideas—there will be nothing to separate one thought from another. Our writing will be one long mass of words. Readers will wonder where one idea ends and the other begins.

When we write, readers are not there to create the conversation with us and help us clarify our thinking. There is no discussion, no way of asking questions or getting feedback. If we write the way we talk, readers may become confused and conclude that we are disorganized and don't know what we think.

Writing has developed over a long period of time, and a system has evolved to communicate with readers. We use punctuation marks to show how ideas are separated or connected. We choose and arrange words carefully to create the effect we want. We spell words correctly so there is a common understanding of what words we are using. Writing is not better than talking; it is just different.

 SMALL GROUP DISCUSSION Read the following excerpt from a conversation and discuss your answer to the question that follows.

> So I put the key in the bottom lock of the door and it turned but the door wouldn't open and somebody was in there because there wasn't a key for the top lock so like somebody was in there already and they locked the bolt you know what I'm saying.

We all know that this is not good writing. Why isn't it?

Different Kinds of Talking and Writing

Not all speaking is the same, and not all writing is the same. What we say and write depends on the situation, on who is listening or reading, and on why we are talking or writing. Just think how many different kinds of talking there are. We talk with friends; we talk in one-on-one conferences and interviews; we may give speeches. When talking with friends, we are casual and relaxed, letting our ideas flow. Yet when speaking in an interview or giving a speech before a large audience, we are more formal and choose our words carefully.

Think of the different kinds of writing. We make lists of what to buy or what to do; we write letters to friends; we may write letters to apply for jobs. A list is just isolated words intended only as a reminder. Yet if we are writing a letter of application, our writing is formal and we concentrate on choosing the proper words, sentence structure, and format.

 SMALL GROUP DISCUSSION Discuss your answers to the following questions:

- How are a letter of complaint to a company and a letter of application for a job different? In addition to spelling and punctuation, how are they similar?

- Where do you think misunderstanding occurs more often: in letters or in conversation? Why?

The kind of writing used in college is relatively formal. Ideas are communicated in sentences, sentences are presented in paragraphs, and paragraphs are arranged in essays. This formality does not mean erasing our personality from our writing—not at all. It means we need to remember that writing and talking involve different structures and situations. When writing in college or the workplace, we need to keep the following advice in mind:

1. *Be clear.* We can't use readers' facial expressions as clues to whether they follow our line of thought. We need to imagine what will help readers understand our ideas.

2. *Organize ideas.* When we talk, other people participate in the conversation. We bounce from one idea to another, exploring and figuring out what we think. Because we are in the conversation together, listeners usually stay with us until our ideas become clear. Readers, however, are *not* with us. They lose patience if we jump from topic to topic, or they stop reading if our thoughts seem disorganized.

3. *Condense ideas.* Readers lose interest if we repeat ourselves and use unnecessary words.

4. *Let readers know how to make sense of the words they see.* Readers cannot hear us pause and stop. They cannot hear our voices change in pitch. Therefore, to let readers know how our ideas fit together, we rely on signs, such as periods, commas, question marks, and quotation marks.

5. *Use the correct word and spelling.* When we talk, we know which word we are using, but we may not know how that word is spelled. Writing involves not only choosing the right words but also spelling those words correctly.

Improving Your Writing

We learned how to talk by listening to others talk, by listening to what words they used and how they put their words together. We then practiced until we learned to communicate effectively. A similar process is involved in learning how to write well. We concentrate on the words writers use and on how they put those words together, and we practice until we communicate effectively. The skills you gain while using this book will be reinforced by the reading and writing you do for yourselves. Your involvement both inside and outside class is essential.

How This Book Works

This book provides the models, the guidance, and the practice necessary for becoming an effective and confident writer. Specifically, *Rhythms of Writing* guides you in the following ways:

Shows you models of writing

Sentences and paragraphs are highlighted as models of effective writing. Pay attention to the words these writers use, how they arrange words in sentences, how they connect their sentences in paragraphs, and how they use their paragraphs in essays. Reading and rereading these models will help you grasp their patterns and write in similar patterns. The more you study these models, the better writer you will become.

Guides you in writing your ideas in paragraphs, short papers, and essays

The chapters on paragraphs and short papers show you how to present your ideas so you are clear and convincing. The essay chapter explains how to apply to essay writing the skills gained in writing short papers.

Guides you in writing your ideas in sentences

Each section on sentences begins with spoken words displayed in a bubble. This sample conversation is there to connect with what you already know: the ideas of talking. The book then includes sentences from published authors to show you the various ways these ideas can be expressed in writing. Often there is a diagram of the sentence pattern to reinforce how this idea is presented in writing.

Helps you internalize sentence patterns

Because experienced writers have internalized sentence patterns, they hear their ideas in sentences when they write. This book, therefore, emphasizes sentence patterns. We begin with the core sentence and then explore how to use this pattern to change the rhythm of your sentences.

In addition, the following features are included to assist you with your writing:

1. Inside the front cover is a chart of sentence patterns. Check this chart to see if you are using correct patterns and to find different patterns for varying your sentences.

2. Easily confused words are listed alphabetically in Chapter 23. When necessary, you can look up words such as *your, you're, there, their,* and *they're* to find out how to use them correctly.

3. Inside the back cover is a checklist of questions to use with your classmates or friends when revising your papers.

Additional Ways to Improve Your Writing

Learning how to write well involves more than class participation. Internalizing the patterns of writing takes time and practice. Four additional ways you can improve your writing are listed below.

Read Daily

One of the easiest ways to improve your writing is by reading. When you read, you are immersing yourself in the language of writing. The more you read, the more your mind will absorb the patterns of writing.

Notice What Writers Do

Notice the words writers use—ordinary words used in creative ways as well as words that at first seem unfamiliar to you. Observe how writers express their ideas in sentence form, and reread these sentences until their rhythms remain in your mind. The more you study these models, the better writer you will become.

Write Daily

Keep a journal about what is going on in your life. Find a few minutes each day to express on paper what you are thinking or feeling. As you continue to write daily, you will sense that words come more easily and flow more naturally from your mind to paper.

Review What You Have Learned

People learn by repeating, reinforcing, and applying new information. Whenever we encounter new information, that information is stored in short-term memory. If it is not repeated or reinforced, it does not stay in memory. New information needs to be repeated in order to form neural (brain) pathways and become long-term memory. As you discover which areas of your writing you need to improve, review and practice them until the information becomes part of your long-term memory.

When you spend time reading, practicing, and reviewing, you are investing in your mind and your future.

Part 1

Writing Paragraphs, Short Papers, and Essays

Writing Paragraphs and Short Papers

Writing Essays

Writing Paragraphs and Short Papers

Paragraphs present ideas in manageable sections so readers can understand the writer's thinking. Without paragraphs, readers would be overwhelmed by pages of nonstop sentences. A paragraph is a package of thought that gets one main point across. When we are ready to make another point, we begin another paragraph.

The first word of a paragraph is indented to signal readers that a new point is being presented. If you are writing in longhand, start the first sentence of a paragraph about a half-inch from the left margin. If you are typing, indent with the tab key. In the following example, the student writer explains why she wants to become a registered nurse. Notice how she begins another paragraph to let readers know she is moving on to another point.

> I want to become a registered nurse in order to fulfill my childhood dream and to show my children the importance of an education. When I was about seven years old, I used to pretend I was a nurse and my little sisters were my patients. I used to take their temperatures, hit them on the knee with a stick to check their reflexes, and cure them of any sickness. I actually thought I had cured them and felt proud and fulfilled. Although years have passed, I have not outgrown my childhood dream.
>
> By becoming a registered nurse, I also hope to show my children, James and Sergio, the road to success. When looking at them, I see a part of me. I see them filled with energy and curiosity, unaware of the life that awaits them. Right now, life is easy for them. All they know is play. But as they grow older and face life's obstacles, I want them to know how to succeed. I want them to know that without education, life is not impossible but incredibly hard. Hopefully they will remember that I dedicated my time to completing my education, and they will follow in my footsteps. As my childhood dream becomes a reality, I hope I teach James and Sergio that education is the road to reaching their dreams.

—Student Writer

Paragraphs have varying lengths. In novels, they are often a half page long as authors describe scenes in great detail. In newspapers, they may be only two sentences long because newspaper editors have to squeeze their material into narrow columns. Most paragraphs written for college assignments are six to twelve sentences in length—long enough to get an idea across, yet not so long that readers get lost.

Paragraphs also have varying purposes. Most of the time, paragraphs are the building blocks of a longer piece of writing, such as a book, a magazine article, a business letter, or an essay. In these longer writings, paragraphs serve different purposes, depending on whether they appear at the beginning, the middle, or the end. We will begin here with shorter writings where the beginning, middle, and end are presented in one or two paragraphs. Later, in Chapter 5, we will develop ideas in greater depth by writing essays.

Chapter 1

Discovering Ideas and Finding Your Main Idea

- ◆ Understand the Writing Process
- ◆ Discover Ideas
- ◆ Find Your Main Idea
- ◆ Organize Your Details

Understand the Writing Process

Anything we see in print is likely to be a polished product. We don't see what went into making the product: all the crossing out and starting over, the crumpled-up and thrown-out pages, and the writer's frustration and confusion. All we see is the final copy. To produce it, the writer went through the writing process.

Recognize Writers' Frustration

Writing is not easy for anyone, anywhere. No one sits down and magically discovers clear and organized ideas. Even the most well-known writers struggle to figure out what they want to say and then how to say it.

Joseph Conrad, author of the novels *Lord Jim*, *Heart of Darkness*, *The Secret Sharer*, and *The Rescue*, talked about his frustration when writing:

I sit down religiously every morning, I sit down for eight hours every day . . . In the course of that working day of eight hours I write three sentences which I erase before leaving the table in despair. . . . Sometimes it takes all my resolution and power of self-control to refrain from butting my head against the wall.

Ernest Hemingway, author of the novels *The Old Man and the Sea, For Whom the Bell Tolls, The Sun Also Rises*, and *A Farewell to Arms*, gave this advice to writers:

Don't get discouraged because there's a lot of mechanical work to writing. . . . I rewrote the first part of *A Farewell to Arms* at least fifty times. . . . It's the hardest work there is.

Maya Angelou, author of the novels *I Know Why the Caged Bird Sings, Gather Together in My Name, All God's Children Need Traveling Shoes*, and *The Heart of a Woman*, explained the long process of writing:

After dinner I re-read what I've written. . . . Eight o'clock at night is the cruellest hour because that's when I start to edit and all that pretty stuff I've written gets axed out. So if I've written ten or twelve pages in six hours, it'll end up as three or four if I'm lucky.

Use the Writing Process

You have learned a lot about life; you have much to write about. Your mind is packed with memories, ideas, emotions, and questions. Feeling stuck, however, is *not* a sign of an empty brain! It is a sign telling you to go through the writing process. Writing is called a process because it does not happen all at once. There are different stages of writing:

1. *Discovering ideas.* Discover ideas by brainstorming, clustering, freewriting, and asking the reporter's questions.

2. *Finding your main idea.* Select ideas, arrange them in groups, and decide what point you want to make about your topic. Then write a sentence that names the topic and tells what point you will make about it.

3. *Supporting and developing your point.* Use specific evidence to develop your main idea. Then list the details in logical order and sketch a map or a simple outline.

4. *Drafting.* Write your ideas in paragraphs to see how those ideas connect to one another.

5. *Revising.* Read what you have written, checking to make sure your ideas will be clear to readers. Then, rewrite as necessary.

6. *Editing.* Check for spelling, grammar, and punctuation errors.

In this chapter, we look at discovering ideas and finding a main idea. In Chapter 2, we explore the various ways you can develop a main idea. Chapters 3 and 4 guide you in drafting, revising, and editing your papers.

Usually, discovering comes first and editing comes last. However, writers go back and forth. Writing is not a step-by-step, do-it-once-and-it's-done activity. While drafting, for instance, you may discover a new idea and return to freewriting to see what that idea looks like. Writing, like most creative acts, is messy. Be patient with the process.

Discover Ideas

Discovering ideas involves writing whatever ideas come to mind—without judging them, without deciding if they are good or if they will fit. Discovering ideas is similar to stocking the refrigerator or cabinets with food. Trying to write a paper without ideas is like feeling hungry and finding nothing in the refrigerator, nothing in the freezer, and nothing in the cabinets. The discovery process gives you something to work with, helping you avoid the blank-page panic known as writers' block.

We will review four methods for discovering ideas: brainstorming, clustering, freewriting, and asking the reporter's questions. The examples that follow each method are the work of students responding to this assigned topic: *Write about one of your goals. Choose an outside goal, such as a college degree or a job, or an inside goal, such as changing a personality characteristic. In your discovery writing, explore your goal, why this goal is important to you, or what you need to achieve your goal.*

Each of these four methods works differently for each person. Discovering ideas is an individual process that varies from writer to writer and from paper to paper. As you respond to a topic that has been assigned or explore the suggested topics listed throughout this chapter, try each method to see which works best for you.

Brainstorm

Brainstorming is often used in the business world when people meet to make plans or solve problems. The brainstorming begins with naming the topic or problem to be explored. Then every idea that is offered, no matter how foolish it may seem, is written on a chalkboard or a large piece of paper. There is only one rule for brainstorming: no idea is judged. The strangest ideas often trigger other ideas that spark a new direction or a creative solution for a problem. As you use brainstorming to discover your ideas, remember not to judge or discard any of them.

Steps in brainstorming:

1. Write your topic at the top of a piece of paper.

2. Jot down words and ideas as they come to you.

Here is one student's brainstorming about the topic "goals."

Goal: To get a college degree

set small goals that lead to my main one

stop procrastinating: "I'll do it later."

get priorities straight

keep out negative thoughts—stop saying, "I'm stupid. I can't."

take control of my life

have patience with myself

don't get frustrated with school and lose my motivation

organize time

bypass parties: put education before social life

would be nice to be qualified for a better job

need discipline—get up on time, don't miss classes, get homework done

need study skills

keep my goal in focus

not let other people get in the way of what I want

 DISCOVERY ACTIVITY Individually or in groups, use brainstorming to explore one of the following topics.

1. People go to movies because . . .

2. Someone should invent a . . .

3. Respond to a current issue, such as *Professional athletes are (or are not) paid too much.*

4. The biggest challenge the U.S. must confront is . . .

Cluster

Clustering is similar to brainstorming. While brainstorming involves putting ideas in a list, clustering involves putting them in circles. The center circle contains the topic, and spokes radiate from that center circle.

Steps in clustering:

1. Write your topic or key idea in the middle of the paper and circle it.

2. Concentrate on the idea in the circle. Around it, write other ideas that come to mind.

3. Circle each of those ideas and connect them with spokes to the main idea.

4. Concentrate on each new idea you have written and see what other ideas emerge. Write these ideas, circle them, and connect them with spokes to the circles they relate to.

See the student's clustering about the topic "goals" on page 15.

GOAL: TO BE A PHYSICAL THERAPIST

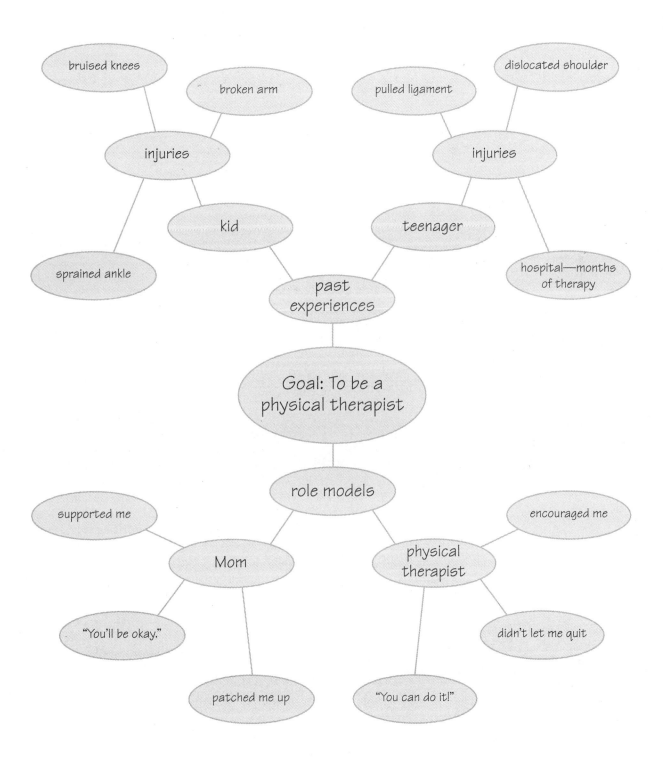

DISCOVERY ACTIVITY Individually or in groups, use clustering to explore one of the following topics.

1. A teacher, coach, or friend who inspired you

2. A movie, television program, or group that has a positive (or negative) effect on people

3. Your advice to future generations

4. A person Americans consider a hero

Freewrite

We often talk to figure out what we think or feel. Freewriting means writing as if we were just talking, without thinking about spelling and sentence structure. Many writers freewrite to explore ideas discovered in brainstorming and clustering. Other writers begin freewriting immediately. The choice is yours; do whatever works for you.

Steps in freewriting:

1. Think of your topic and start writing whatever comes to mind.

2. If a new idea emerges, start writing about that idea. Your writing does not have to make sense to anyone else. It doesn't have to be logical. Freewriting is experimenting.

This is a student's freewriting about the topic "goals."

> To let go of fear. Fear paralyzes me. Feel stifled. Only taking short breaths. Never breathing fully or deeply. Hands and face pressed tightly against the glass. Wanting to touch and not being able to feel. Regret. I'll regret this one day. I watch others move—they seem happy and free. I live controlled. What makes me like this? Why am I afraid to live. To breathe. Why do I feel like cement? Cemented in my tracks. I need to let go. Need to find me. I don't know. Find something I really want to do. Get confidence. Maybe getting good grades, maybe finding different job, maybe trusting that it will all work out.

 DISCOVERY ACTIVITY Freewrite or discuss in groups your responses to one of the following topics.

1. A good friend (or father, mother, boss, co-worker) is someone who . . .

2. If I had a magic wand, I . . .

3. Most of my friends value . . .

4. A current issue, such as *There should (or should not) be mandatory drug testing for employees working with the public.*

Keep a Journal

A journal is a notebook used specifically for freewriting. Use the journal on a regular basis to explore assigned writings or your own responses to life: what you think, feel, learn, and observe. Keeping a journal will help clarify the thoughts you have and discover thoughts you did not know you had. In addition, keeping a journal will improve your writing because the more you write, the more easily your ideas will flow from your mind to paper. See Chapter 25 for a list of topics for journal writing.

Ask the Reporter's Questions

Who? What? Where? When? and *Why?* are questions reporters use in covering a story. The reporter's questions are especially helpful in digging for additional details about an idea you have discovered through brainstorming, clustering, or freewriting. Not all questions may apply to the particular paper you are working on, and often the answers to the questions will overlap. That is fine. The reporter's questions are not rigid questions with rigid answers; there is no right or wrong. Use the questions creatively and see what they help you discover.

Steps in using the reporter's questions:

1. Write your topic on a piece of paper.

2. Ask each of the following questions and jot down your immediate response. If the question seems to open possibilities, explore further by freewriting.

   Who?
   > Who are the people involved? Who are they to you?
   > What are their values; what kind of people are they?
   > Who is affected, directly and indirectly?

   What?
   > Exactly what happened? What was going on beneath the surface?
   > What is the person, place, or thing similar to or different from?
   > What does the person, place, or thing look, smell, taste, feel, or sound like?

   Where?
   > Where did this event happen?
   > What about the place makes it significant?
   > How would things have been different if the event had happened someplace else?

   When?
   > When did the event happen?
   > Were there other events that triggered this event?

   Why?
   > Why is this event important?
   > What are the consequences?
   > I wonder why . . .

Asking a series of *Why?* questions about each answer you write will help you uncover additional details.

Here is one student's use of the question *Why?* to explore the topic "goals."

My goal is to save money.

Why do I want to save money ?
 I need money. Money is important.

Why is money important?
 I need money to pay bills, to buy necessities. I need money to buy things I want, not really luxury things but clothes that I like, things that make me feel good.

Why do I like clothes and things like that?
 I like looking good and feeling good about who I am. When I think I look good, I have more confidence.

Why will money give me confidence?
 I want to feel responsible, like an adult who is prepared for the future, not like a kid with his hand out, always looking for the next dime. I don't want to have to worry about where the next dollar is coming from, so I have security.

Why will money give me security?
 I want to know that I can take care of myself. I want to be able to take care of a family someday and know that I am a responsible parent. I want to have control of my future.

Why is all of this important?
 I want to feel good about who I am. I want to respect myself and have others respect me.

DISCOVERY ACTIVITY Individually or in groups, choose one of the following topics and explore your ideas about it by asking the reporter's questions.

1. A quality you admire (courage, determination, loyalty, kindness, etc.)

2. The best decision you ever made

3. What you learned about yourself or others on your first job

4. A current issue, such as *The U.S. should (or should not) have a national standard curriculum for elementary and high school.*

Find Your Main Idea

The Discovery Activities help you put ideas about your topic on paper. The next step is deciding what point you want to make about this topic. Readers need to know the point of your details: they need to know your main idea.

Select Ideas

Read your Discovery writing and look for ideas and details that have energy. When your response to something has been "I like that" or "Yeah, that's good," highlight or circle it. Then put those words or sentences on a clean piece of paper.

Group Ideas

Take the details you have accumulated and organize them into groups. Consider the analogy of a supermarket. Vegetables go in the vegetable section; meats in the meat section; frozen dinners in the frozen food section. Imagine the chaos of a store where everything was shelved in a jumbled fashion! Customers would be confused, wander around aimlessly, and eventually leave in frustration. Grouping details is equally important for writers. First, it will help you, the writer, organize your details so you can see what you have. Second, it will help your readers avoid confusion and stay interested.

Find Your Point

Look over your groups of ideas and think about the point you are making about your topic. You may not be able to use all the details in a group, and you may not use all the groups. Yet there will be at least one main idea tying most of your details together. These general-direction questions will help you find your point:

> How do these groups fit together?
>
> Does one idea lead to another idea?
>
> Is there a main idea here and details that support it?
>
> What do I need to add or delete to make my ideas and details connect smoothly?

PRACTICE 1 A student writer put his details in three groups: *parents*, *friends*, and *me*. Review his groups and answer the questions that follow.

Why I Want a College Degree

1. Parents
   Dad surprised. Mom will be proud.
   My parents didn't go to college. I will be the first in my family to graduate.
   Be a role model for my little brother. Show him he can do whatever he puts his mind to.

2. Friends
   Will show friends I succeeded.
   They think I'll quit and go back to hanging out.

3. Me
   Respect for myself. Say to myself, "I did this and didn't give up on my dreams."
   Well-paid job that will keep me financially secure.
   Live on my own, not have to live with others and live by their agendas.
   Put my goals first, not someone else's.
   Secure job market. Won't have to worry about losing my job.

---

1. The writer has grouped his details under the headings *parents, friends,* and *me.* The group about *parents* includes a detail that does not fit under the category of parents. What is it?

   _____

2. The writer can either delete that detail or change the name of the group. If he wants to keep the detail, what word could he use instead of *parents* to better summarize the details in this group?

   _____

3. Now that the details are arranged in groups, the writer can see what ideas have emerged. His groups offer him three options: he could write about all three groups, two of the groups, or just one of the groups. If this were your writing, which would you do?

   _____

Write the Main Idea in a Sentence

The main idea states the topic and the point about the topic so readers will know how to make sense of the details that follow. The student just described chose to write about all three groups. His main idea was *I want a college degree because I will gain my family's respect, my friends' respect, and self-respect.* The topic is *I want a college degree.* The point about the topic is *because I will gain my family's respect, my friends' respect, and self-respect.* The main idea tells readers the topic and answers the question *What about the topic?* The main idea of a paragraph is called a *topic sentence.* If your writing is more developed and covers a number of paragraphs, the main idea is called a *thesis statement.* Whether your writing is one paragraph or many paragraphs long, readers need to know your main idea.

Vague: I have a goal.

- We know the topic is *a goal,* but that is all we know. Make sure you include the point about the topic.

Clear: *My goal is to change my negative attitude toward my job.*

Vague: I am going to write about why I want a college degree.

- Words such as *I am going to write about* and *This paper is going to be about* give readers no new information. Omit empty words and make a direct statement.

Clear: *I want a college degree to gain personal satisfaction and a better job.*

Here are several main ideas. The topic is underlined once, and the point about the topic is underlined twice.

<u>topic</u>   <u>point</u>

<u>Marie</u> <u>taught me that some people can be trusted.</u>

<u>The most difficult decision I ever made</u> <u>was to work and go to college full time.</u>

<u>The elderly</u> <u>have wisdom to share with younger generations.</u>

PRACTICE 2   In the following main ideas, underline the topic once and the point about the topic twice.

1. Team sports teach people how to lose and survive.

2. Dr. Dunlap is a dependable doctor.

3. Mornings at our house are chaotic.

4. Living in a small town has advantages and disadvantages.

5. Maintaining a car is expensive.

PRACTICE 3   Read the following paragraph and answer the questions that follow.

> Drinking and driving is like playing Russian roulette. Last August, my younger brother drove out the driveway to pick up pizza. He only needed to go around the block, so when he didn't return, we went out looking for him. We did not need to walk far. The ambulance was already there, sirens screaming against the night. My brother was hit by a drunk driver and was pronounced dead on arrival. Drinking and driving is Russian roulette, and the drunk driver who hit my brother pulled the trigger.

—Student Writer

1. What is the topic?

_____

2. What is the writer's point about the topic?

_____

Organize Your Details

Once you have written your main idea, you need to find the best way of organizing the details that support that idea. The next chapter shows you a variety of methods for developing your main idea, such as giving examples or reasons. Regardless of which method you choose, your supporting details need to be specific and organized in logical order.

Use Specific Details

Often, when talking, we don't give much detail. First, whoever is with us can see what we see. If we point to an object, further description is unnecessary. Second, we usually know the person and share past experiences. When we mention someone we both know, all we need to say is that person's name. That is not the case in writing. We need to fill in the details.

Effective writing has specific and descriptive words, not big words. When the author John Updike saw an unfavorable review of one of his novels, he said, "My ears close up, my eyes go warm, my chest feels thin as an eggshell, my voice churns silently in my stomach." Those are not difficult words; Updike simply described how the experience felt. Powerful writing is bringing something to life for readers.

Make sure your details are specific. Using the reporter's questions will help you discover specific details. Another method of discovering details is to move into your imagination. Whenever we dream, our mind is seeing things, not our eyes. If you have ever had a vivid dream or a nightmare, you know how real mind-pictures are. When you are writing, re-create or create the situation in your mind and watch it as if you were watching a movie.

As you work on gathering specific details, keep this advice in mind:

1. *Use words that target the senses.* Write so readers can see, hear, touch, taste, and smell what you are describing.

2. *Create an experience for readers.* Use specific details that make the situation real. For example, if you want readers to understand that someone is jealous, you need to explain what that person specifically did and said. Writing the word *jealous* is merely the first step. It doesn't prove anything. The details will convince the readers.

PRACTICE 4   Read the following two paragraphs about a summer picnic and answer the question that follows.

Paragraph 1

The food at the summer picnic was delicious, especially the secret barbecue sauce. The ladies were really good cooks. They brought all kinds of very good cakes. The children liked sampling the icing.

Paragraph 2

The summer picnic gave ladies a chance to show off their baking hands. On the barbecue pit, chickens and spareribs sputtered in their own fat and in a sauce whose recipe was guarded in the family like a scandalous affair. However, every true baking artist could reveal her prize to the delight and criticism of the town. Orange sponge cakes and dark brown mounds dripping Hershey's chocolate stood layer to layer with ice-white coconuts and light brown caramels. Pound cakes sagged with their buttery weight and small children could no more resist licking the icings than their mothers could avoid slapping the sticky fingers.

—Maya Angelou, *I Know Why the Caged Bird Sings*

In paragraph 1, the writer tells us that the women were good cooks. In paragraph 2, Maya Angelou creates the experience. What specific details convince us that these women were good cooks?

_____

_____

PRACTICE 5   In the following sentences, replace the underlined word with specific details. You may want to replace the whole sentence with one or more descriptive sentences. The first one has been done for you.

EXAMPLE: My classes are <u>okay</u>.

I am overwhelmed by what my instructors seem to expect, but so far

they have been encouraging and supportive.

1. The weather is <u>awful</u>.

   _____

   _____

2. She is <u>nice</u>.

   _____

   _____

3. The dinner was <u>delicious</u>.

   _____

   _____

4. The movie was <u>great</u>.

   _____

   _____

List Details in Logical Order

Organize your details in a logical order so that readers can follow your thinking. As you order your details, consider three common arrangements: time, space, and importance.

Time Order

Begin with the events that took place first; then move toward the events that happened later. If you are writing about life events, you might begin with childhood and move to adolescence and then to adulthood. If you are writing about a good week, you can start with Monday and move toward Sunday. You might also arrange the details according to the hour of the day, seasons of the year, or months of the year. Words such as *first, second, next, then,* and *after* will help you indicate the passage of time.

PRACTICE 6   In the following paragraph, the writer orders the details according to life stages. What stages does he include?

_____

One of life's greatest gifts is having a best friend, and Carl Swann was mine. Living next door and born exactly one month before me, Carl was my first playmate, and our bond was as instant and natural as childbirth itself. As toddlers, we crawled together in the cool, moist grass of our backyards. As children, we conspired to lift the dark veil off such grown-up mysteries as matches, cigarettes, and girlie magazines. And as adults, we watched our families grow up and our children move on.

—Kweisi Mfume, *No Free Ride: From the Mean Streets to the Mainstream*

Space Order

Arrange your details according to the way they are physically placed, selecting top/down, left/right, north/south, far/near, or outside/inside. For example, if you are writing about your college campus, you might begin with the parking lot and move to the landscaping, the main entrance, the hallways, and then the classrooms.

PRACTICE 7   In the following excerpt, the writer remembers his childhood neighborhood and describes it for the reader. What kind of space order does he use?

_____

Our store was at an intersection at the edge of town on a long, sloping hill. If you stood in front of the store and looked right, you saw the town—the railroad tracks, the department stores like Leggets and Woolworth. If you looked straight ahead, you saw the courthouse, the jailhouse, the county clerk's office, and the road to Norfolk. To the left was the Jaffe slaughterhouse and the wharf where the Nansemond River met the Main Street Bridge.

—James McBride, *The Color of Water*

Order of Importance

Begin with the least important idea and move to the most important idea, or reverse the order and begin with the most important. Most writers choose to save their most effective point until last so they end with power. You can use words such as *just as important*, *equally important*, *more important*, or *the most significant* to introduce your ideas.

PRACTICE 8   In the following paragraph, the writer describes her embarrassment at her family's Christmas Eve celebration when her parents invited the minister and his son to share their traditional Chinese dinner. Does the writer begin with the worst detail or save the worst detail for the end?

Dinner threw me deeper into despair. My relatives licked the ends of their chopsticks and reached across the table, dipping them into the dozen or so plates of food. Robert and his family waited patiently for platters to be passed to them. My relatives murmured with pleasure when my mother brought out the whole steamed fish. Robert grimaced. Then my father poked his chopsticks just below the fish eye and plucked out the soft meat. "Amy, your favorite," he said, offering me the tender fish cheek. I wanted to disappear.

—Amy Tan, "Fish Cheeks"

Sketch a Map

After you have a list of your supporting details, arrange them in an outline or a map. In writing, a map is a sketch outline of your ideas. (See the paragraph map outline on page 26.) Travelers use maps to guide their way on the road. Writers use maps to guide their way on paper. Maps are essential to writing. First, the map will show you how to get where you want to go. Second, looking at the map while you are writing your draft will keep you on track.

COMPUTER TIPS FOR DISCOVERING IDEAS

If you are writing your paper on a word processor, the following tips may be helpful:

- Type your ideas as they come to mind. Don't be concerned about typing errors or spelling errors. As long as you can understand what words you intend to use, keep writing. You can return later to type the words correctly.

- Consider writing without looking at the computer screen. Ignoring the screen may keep you focused on ideas rather than on typing and spelling errors.

PARAGRAPH MAP

Where you plan to go and how you'll get there

Write your main idea in a topic sentence. Then list the details that support that idea. Put the details in order so that each detail leads logically to the next.

Main idea: Topic sentence

_____

_____

Supporting details

1. _____

2. _____

3. _____

4. _____

The paragraph map is flexible.

You may have fewer than four supporting details in your paragraph, or you may have more than four. Draw extra lines if you need them.

You may also find that your ideas are more developed, and your writing is more than one paragraph long. Draw extra lines for another topic sentence with its supporting details.

Review: Discovering Ideas and Finding Your Main Idea

- Discover ideas by brainstorming, clustering, freewriting, and asking the reporter's questions.

- On a clean sheet of paper, list the ideas that have possibilities and organize them in groups. Review your groups to see what main idea emerges.

- Write the main idea in a sentence that includes both your topic and your point about that topic.

- Check to make sure your details are specific and support your main idea.

• Decide on the best order for organizing your details: time, space, or order of importance.

• Sketch a map or an outline to see how your ideas and details fit together.

 REVIEW PRACTICE 1 Individually or in groups, read the following paragraph and decide what order the writer uses to arrange his details.

Before I was born, I went on the road. The road was U.S. 17, south from Jacksonville, North Carolina, through the Holly Shelter Swamp to Wilmington, where the hospital was. My father backed the Chevrolet out of its place in the hay barn next to the farm cart and helped my mother into the front seat on the afternoon of September 9, 1934. He made the trip in little more than an hour, barely slowing down for the stop signs in Dixon, Folkstone and Holly Ridge. I was born the next morning with rambling in my blood and fifty miles already under my belt.

—Charles Kuralt, "Wanderlust"

 REVIEW PRACTICE 2 Sebastian Junger begins his book *The Perfect Storm* by describing the fishing docks of Gloucester, Massachusetts. Individually or in groups, read the paragraph and point out details you think are most effective.

A soft fall rain slips down through the trees and the smell of ocean is so strong that it can almost be licked off the air. Trucks rumble along Rogers Street and men in t-shirts stained with fish-blood shout to each other from the decks of boats. Beneath them the ocean swells up against the black pilings and sucks back down to the barnacles. Beer cans and old pieces of styrofoam rise and fall, and pools of spilled diesel fuel undulate like huge iridescent jelly-fish. The boats rock and creak against their ropes, and seagulls complain and hunker down and complain some more.

Chapter 2

Developing Ideas

- ◆ Develop Your Ideas
- ◆ Description
- ◆ Illustration
- ◆ Narration
- ◆ Persuasion
- ◆ Cause and Effect
- ◆ Classification
- ◆ Process
- ◆ Comparison and Contrast

Develop Your Ideas

Often, after writing a main idea, a writer stares at it and wonders, "Now, what do I do?" The answer to that question is "Develop it." There are a number of ways to develop an idea. For example, if you wanted to write about a great time you had at a recent party, you could take any of the following approaches:

Describe it (description).

Describe the people, place, food, or music.

Give examples (illustration).

Select two or more specific events at the party that show you had a wonderful time.

Tell the story (narration).

Start at the beginning of the party and describe the exciting events in time order.

Give reasons (persuasion).

Argue why a party is the best way to relax on a weekend or why throwing a party is worth the time and money involved.

Name causes or effects (cause and effect).

Explain why you had a wonderful time: perhaps the previous week had been difficult, or you did not realize who would be there. You could also write about the effect the party had on you: your spirits were lifted, or you met interesting people.

Place things in categories (classification).

Look at the party through the focus of categories. You could write about the expected events and the unexpected events or about new friends and old friends.

Explain the process (process).

Give tips about how to throw a great party: explain, step by step, what to do.

Explore the similarities or differences (comparison and contrast).

Compare this party to another party you attended. You could explain how they were similar or different.

These methods can be used separately or combined to make your ideas vivid and clear. The following sections show you how professional writers and student writers have used them to develop their ideas.

Description

When you talk about a car you want to buy, the kind of person you would like to meet, or the weekend you just experienced, you are describing something or someone. When you are using description, choose words that will help readers see, hear, smell, taste, or feel what you are writing about. Do not include *every* detail; include only those details that make the impression you want. For example, if you want to describe how well the Lincoln Memorial is maintained, you don't have to mention that one brick at the edge of a walkway is crumbling.

Paragraph Models

PRACTICE 1   Read the following paragraphs and answer the questions that follow.

Paragraph A

Tim O'Brien describes his summer job at a meat-packing plant:

I spent the summer of 1968 working in an Armour meat-packing plant in my hometown of Worthington, Minnesota. The plant specialized in pork products, and for eight hours a day I stood on a quarter-mile assembly line—more properly, a disassembly line—removing blood clots from the necks of dead pigs. My job title, I believe, was Declotter. After slaughter, the hogs were decapitated, split down the length of the belly, pried open, eviscerated, and strung up by the hind hocks on a high conveyer belt. Then gravity took over. By the time a carcass reached my spot on the line, the fluids had mostly drained out, everything except for thick clots of blood in the neck and upper chest cavity. To remove the stuff, I used a kind of water gun. . . . Goggles were a necessity, and a rubber apron, but even so it was like standing for eight hours a day under a lukewarm blood-shower. At night I'd go home smelling of pig. I couldn't wash it out. Even after a hot bath, scrubbing hard, the stink was always there—like old bacon, or sausage, a dense greasy pig-stink that soaked deep into my skin and hair.

—Tim O'Brien, "On the Rainy River"

1. Tim O'Brien uses details that target our senses. Which of those details help us *see* the scene? Which details help us *smell* it?

_____

_____

_____

_____

2. Good writing affects the reader. What was your reaction when you read this paragraph?

_____

Paragraph B

Jack MacFarland couldn't have come into my life at a better time. My father was dead, and I had logged up too many years of scholastic indifference. Mr. MacFarland had a master's degree from Columbia and decided, at twenty-six, to find a little school and teach his heart out. He never took any credentialing courses, couldn't bear to, he said, so he had to find employment in a private system. He ended up at Our Lady of Mercy teaching five sections of senior English. He was a beatnik who was born too late. His teeth were stained, he tucked his sorry tie in between the third and fourth buttons of his shirt, and his pants were chronically wrinkled. At first, we couldn't believe this guy, thought he slept in his car. But within no time, he had us so startled with work that we didn't much worry about where he slept or if he slept at all. We wrote three or four essays a month. We read a book every two to three weeks, starting with the *Iliad* and ending up with Hemingway. He gave us a quiz on the reading every other day. He brought a prep school curriculum to Mercy High.

—Mike Rose, *Lives on the Boundary*

1. What was the students' first reaction to Jack MacFarland? What details give you that impression?

   _____

   _____

2. How do you think the students felt about MacFarland at the end of the year? What details give you that impression?

   _____

   _____

   _____

   _____

Ideas for Discussion and Writing

 SMALL GROUP DISCUSSION Complete one or more of the following sentences and share your experiences.

1. The best (or worst) job I have ever had was . . .

2. My favorite family tradition is . . .

3. Taking exams is . . .

4. The strangest (or best, or worst) place I have lived is . . .

5. The best part of last weekend was . . .

Writing Idea 1

Use an idea from the small group discussion for a paper. Begin with the completed sentence as your main idea and support it with description.

Writing Idea 2

Describe a place. Select one of the areas listed in the following unfinished sentence; then complete the sentence and use it as the main idea for a paper. *Anyone who looks in my (car, garage, living room, closets, kitchen cabinets, refrigerator, wallet) will realize that I am. . . .* Support your point by describing the area.

Writing Idea 3

Leo Buscaglia writes, in *Born for Love*:

> Happiness is difficult to define. It's a very personal thing. For some it comes rarely and is only brought on by extraordinary circumstances. I, on the other hand, am most happy with ordinary things: a dinner with friends, a walk in a park, a good conversation, a hug.

Buscaglia states that it is the ordinary events of daily life that bring him happiness. What ordinary things make you happy? Select one and describe it so that readers can imagine the experience.

Writing Tip

Use details that appeal to one or more of the senses. Ask yourself:

What does it look like? (Foggy, muddy, fluorescent, glossy, grimy)
(Does it look like anything else?)

What does it sound like? (Blaring, soothing, piercing, creaking, hissing)
(Does it sound like anything else?)

What does it smell like? (Sweet, rotten, moldy, clean, greasy, fresh)
(Does it smell like anything else?)

What does it taste like? (Bitter, bland, salty, sugary, metallic, spicy)
(Does it taste like anything else?)

What does it feel like? (Rough, smooth, grainy, tingling, numb, clammy)
(Does it feel like anything else?)

Illustration

If we are talking about someone and say that he or she is generous, our listener may respond, "What do you mean by generous? Give me one example." Examples (illustrations) make our general statements specific and concrete. Including examples is a convincing way to make your main idea real for readers.

Paragraph Models

PRACTICE 2   Read the following paragraphs and answer the questions that follow.

Paragraph A

Education is the great engine of personal development. It is through education that the daughter of a peasant can become a doctor, that the son of a mineworker can become the head of the mine, that a child of farmworkers can become the president of a great nation. It is what we make out of what we have, not what we are given, that separates one person from another.

—Nelson Mandela, *Long Walk to Freedom*

1. What is Nelson Mandela's topic sentence?

_____

2. What three examples support this topic sentence?

_____

_____

_____

Paragraph B

Inventions that we now take for granted were once but an individual's dream. For example, we have telephones because of one man's dream. Alexander Graham Bell, when teaching deaf children, imagined an instrument that would communicate sound over wires. Through trial and error, through disappointing failure and creative thinking, he eventually invented the telephone. The improvement of the lock and key is another example of one person's persistent dream. Jeremiah Chubb was determined to find a way to protect people's possessions. Although most people lacked confidence in his work, his invention was finally accepted when a burglar serving his sentence on an English prison ship was unable to pick Chubb's lock. Today, whenever we pick up a phone, we honor Alexander Graham Bell. Every time we lock doors to our houses or cars, we honor Jeremiah Chubb. We seldom think about inventors and their dreams. However, all the conveniences we now consider necessities started out as no more than an idea, relying solely on an individual's dedication and perseverance. We should not underestimate the power of dreams.

—Student Writer

1. What is the writer's topic sentence?

   _____

   _____

2. What two examples support his point?

   _____

   _____

Ideas for Discussion and Writing

 SMALL GROUP DISCUSSION Discuss one of the following quotations. Share experiences that support the statement. For each statement, list examples that could be used as support.

   1. There are a million excuses for not paying the price.

      —Michael Jordan

   _____

   _____

   _____

   _____

2. Gambling: The sure way of getting nothing for something.

—Wilson Mizner

_____

_____

_____

_____

3. Hard work spotlights the character of people: some turn up their sleeves, some turn up their noses, and some don't turn up at all.

—Sam Ewing

_____

_____

_____

_____

4. Any fact facing us is not as important as our attitude toward it, for that determines our success or failure.

—Norman Vincent Peale

_____

_____

_____

_____

5. Be kind. Everyone you meet is fighting a hard battle.

—John Watson

_____

_____

_____

_____

Writing Idea 1

Use the ideas from the small group discussion for a paper. Begin with the quotation, explain in your own words what it means, and finish by giving one or more examples as support.

Writing Idea 2

Write about someone who has one of the following traits: he or she is honest, faithful, determined, willing to listen, forgiving, kind, sensitive, courageous, trustworthy, dependable, creative, energetic, loyal, optimistic, or patient. Choose someone you know well or choose yourself. Write a main idea that includes the person and the quality. Support your main idea with one or more examples.

Writing Idea 3

Complete one of the following sentences, use it as your main idea, and support it with one or more examples.

1. _____ has made a difference in my life.

2. My strongest quality is _____ .

3. _____ still exists in America.

4. With modern technology, it is now easier to _____ .

5. I am investing my time wisely (*or* wasting my time) by

_____ .

Writing Tip

Make sure you use specific details in your examples. Replace vague and general words with specific words.

Vague	Specific
mad	irritated, offended, annoyed
nice (person)	encouraging, supportive, attentive, honest
great weather	clear, sunny, low humidity, in the low 80s
street	Dixie Highway
birds	migrating red-winged blackbirds
building	the apartment complex

Narration

Imagine that you want to convince a friend that volunteer work can lead to a paying job. You can tell a story of your own experience or someone else's. Telling the story (narration) involves explaining events, usually in time order. You have a wealth of knowledge gained from your own life and from observing life around you. Sharing those real-life stories is an effective way to prove your point.

Paragraph Models

PRACTICE 3   Read the following paragraphs and answer the questions that follow.

Paragraph A

I admire Bob for his cool, calm demeanor. Regardless of the pressure he is under, he never loses control. A prime example of Bob's cool under fire came at work when we were printing a major advertising campaign for a multi-million-dollar customer. We had to print millions of coupons and ship them to cities across the country by a specified deadline. Because Bob had been on vacation, his assistant made the shipping and distributing arrangements with national airline carriers. But the printing of the material ran into several snags and was delayed. Consequently, we faced a head-on collision with our deadline, and the carriers said they could not deliver our orders to the designated cities on time. We stood to lose our best client. Bob could have easily stood back and let his assistant, who had made the contact with the carriers, take the fall for not making alternative plans. But instead, Bob calmly got on the phone and contacted local distributors across the country, who helped us make the necessary deliveries on time. He saved our company a major customer, not to mention a few jobs, and he was never fazed.

—Student Writer

1. What words let you know that the writer is going to give us an example or a story?

   _____

2. What words in the last sentence refer to the topic sentence?

   _____

Paragraph B

My life went numb when I heard my father had died. I had just walked into the house, feeling good about my sixth-grade report card, unaware of the news that awaited me. As usual, I went straight into the living room. Unfamiliar faces stopped and stared at me. I looked at my mother, who seemed swollen, and my aunt announced, "Well, God likes to take those he loves to heaven. He liked Jesus and took him away. He liked Paul and took him away. . . ." As she continued, the bubble gum in my mouth grew stronger as my bones went numb. The chewing stopped; time stopped as she continued, "And God liked your father and took him away."

—Student Writer

© 2000 Houghton Mifflin Company

1. The topic sentence states that the writer's life "went numb" when he heard that his father had died. What details in the story indicate that the writer felt numb?

   _____

   _____

2. The writer includes the aunt's exact words. He could have omitted the exact words and just written a summary, such as *My aunt told me that my father had died*. What do the exact words add to this writing?

   _____

   _____

Ideas for Discussion and Writing

 SMALL GROUP DISCUSSION Share stories from your experience to support two of the following sayings.

1. What goes around comes around.

2. Money can't buy happiness.

3. Prosperity is a great teacher; adversity a greater.

   —William Hazlitt

4. People may doubt what you say, but they will always believe what you do.

   —Thomas Carlyle

5. A journey of a thousand miles must begin with a single step.

   —Lao Tzu

Writing Idea 1

Use the discussion as support for a paper. Begin with the saying as your main idea. Rewrite the saying in your own words; then support it with a story.

Writing Idea 2

Write about an occasion when things did not turn out the way you expected. Perhaps there was a time when you expected to be praised but were criticized—or a time when you were convinced you would fail but succeeded. Present your details in time order, beginning with what happened first.

Writing Idea 3

Complete one of the following sentences and use it as your main idea supported by your story.

1. The most difficult decision I ever made was _____

   _____.

2. A teacher (or coach, or friend) who inspired me was _____

_____.

3. I wish I had listened to _____

_____.

4. I was frightened when _____

_____.

5. I felt like an outsider _____

_____.

Writing Tip

As you remember an event, many details will come to mind. Although all of them are true, include only those that prove the point you stated in the main idea. If you include details that do not support your point, readers will feel confused and wonder why you have included them.

Persuasion

When we try to convince others by explaining why we believe, want, or deserve something, we are using persuasion. One of the most effective ways of using it is by giving reasons. People are convinced of the strength or truth of a position when we provide them with logical reasons.

Paragraph Models

PRACTICE 4   Read the following paragraphs and answer the questions that follow.

Paragraph A

The United States government should set term limits for senators and representatives. We have term limits for the president; we now need term limits for members of Congress. First, term limits would make elections fairer. Senators and representatives who are already in office have many advantages that new candidates lack. They have the benefit of name recognition and experience that make them a safe bet for voters. They also have financial privileges for campaigning, such as the free use of postal stamps, that put them one step ahead of newcomers. Term limits would level this uneven playing field. Second, term limits would give others with new insights and fresh approaches to the country's problems a chance to serve. Currently, many senators and representatives are professional politicians. Because they make a career out of being a politician, they are not living with the real problems and not thinking about realistic solutions. If we limit the number of terms members of Congress are allowed to serve, we would increase the number of newcomers in Congress. A steady flow of new individuals with fresh ideas and creative approaches would give us a more dynamic and effective government.

—Student Writer

1. The writer states a position in the topic sentence. What does the topic sentence say this paragraph will be about?

_____

_____

2. What two reasons does the writer give in support of this position?

_____

_____

_____

Paragraph B

Violence as a way of achieving racial justice is both impractical and immoral. It is impractical because it is a descending spiral ending in destruction for all. The old law of an eye for an eye leaves everybody blind. It is immoral because it seeks to humiliate the opponent rather than win his understanding; it seeks to annihilate rather than to convert. Violence is immoral because it thrives on hatred rather than love. It destroys community and makes brotherhood impossible. It leaves society in monologue rather than dialogue. Violence ends by defeating itself. It creates bitterness in the survivors and brutality in the destroyers.

—Martin Luther King, Jr.,
"The Ways of Meeting Oppression"

1. Martin Luther King, Jr., announces in the topic sentence that he will make two points about violence. What are they?

_____

2. What reasons does he provide to support each point?

_____

_____

_____

_____

Ideas for Discussion and Writing

 SMALL GROUP DISCUSSION The following letter from a mother asking for advice appeared in "Dr. Laura," a weekly newspaper column by Dr. Laura Schlessinger. Read the letter and discuss an appropriate response.

Question:

My son is 18 years old and graduating from high school. He will be starting a technical school soon and will still be living at home. (My husband and I will be paying for school.)

My son wants us to end all curfews. We told him we would do this after graduation. However, I would still like him to let me know where he will be and if he will be coming home very late or not at all. (We told him we could reinstate curfews if his school-work suffers.)

My husband and son feel I am being overprotective. I love my son very much. Am I acting overprotective?

—*Chicago Tribune*

Do you agree with Dr. Laura's response below, or do you disagree?

Answer:

Whether you are or not is not the point here. What you are stating is simply reasonable. Family members should always treat each other with the courtesy of letting each other know where they are, etc. Don't you and your husband do that with each other?

Your son is not a boarder—he's a family member, and the rules of courtesy apply.

Now, as to the curfew: Since you are investing in his education, your son owes you certain returns—i.e., commitment and accomplishment. If he's unwilling to uphold his end of the bargain, you are no longer obligated to uphold yours.

Your husband may be feeling a "guy thing" with your son—envying his youthful freedom. Watch out for that—your son is still a growing child who needs direction.

—*Chicago Tribune*

Writing Idea 1

Using the ideas from the small group discussion, write a response to the mother, stating your opinion and your reasons for having it.

Writing Idea 2

Imagine that you have been elected mayor, governor, or president. What is the first policy you will enact? Finish the sentence *I propose that.* . . . Then support this claim with reasons.

Writing Idea 3

Try to convince an instructor that you deserve an A in the course—or try to convince an employer that you deserve a raise or extended vacation time. Imagine that your grade, raise, or vacation will depend solely on how well you explain your reasons.

Writing Tip

As you decide what reasons you will use to support your argument, keep your readers in mind. In order to convince readers of the soundness of your point, you need to include and develop reasons that they will accept, respect, or at least consider seriously.

Cause and Effect

Why won't the car start? Will my college degree help me get the job I want? Our questions about the causes and effects of an action are part of making sense of the past and preparing for the future. Writing about causes involves exploring the reasons why something happened. Writing about effects involves exploring either what happened as a result of a previous event or what might happen as a result of an action.

Paragraph Models

PRACTICE 5   Read the following paragraphs and answer the questions that follow.

Paragraph A

When my mother and father divorced, everything in our lives fell like dominoes. During and after the divorce, my mother gave up her responsibilities as our mother. I was left to care for my three siblings and still try to continue school. My mother tried to escape by choosing a life of drugs. But even worse, one by one, the four of us followed her example. I, the first to fall, lived on the streets and became trapped by the streets. I was afraid to leave the bad friends and bad places. That was all I knew. The life of drugs and crime was my family for almost eight years. The day that I finally got the courage to do something about my life was the day I escaped from the prison of the past. Today, I am in college. It took me four years to make this decision, a decision still plagued with fear, but a decision I know is right because my life is only what I make of it.

—Student Writer

1. What were the effects of the divorce?

   _____

   _____

2. In the topic sentence, the writer uses the image of dominoes to describe the effects of divorce. Later, in the fifth and sixth sentences, she refers back to the dominoes idea. What phrases refer to dominoes?

   _____

   _____

Paragraphs B and C

Violence in language has become almost as casual as the possession of handguns. The curious notion has taken hold that we cannot communicate effectively unless we use four-letter words. Some screenwriters openly admit that they include foul language because they don't want the movie classified with a G (general) rating. They prefer the R (restricted) rating, probably on the theory of forbidden fruit. Therefore, writers and producers have every incentive to include violent language and gory scenes.

The effect is to foster attitudes of casualness toward violence and brutality, not just in entertainment but in everyday life. People are not as uncomfortable as they ought to be about the glamorization of human hurt. The ability to react instinctively to suffering seems to be shrinking. Youngsters sit transfixed in front of television or motion-picture screens, munching popcorn while human beings are battered or mutilated. Nothing is more essential in education than respect for the frailty of human beings; nothing is more characteristic of the age than mindless violence.

—Adapted from Norman Cousins,
"The Decline of Neatness"

1. In his first paragraph, Norman Cousins argues that movies include violent language and scenes because violence sells. The next paragraph begins with a topic sentence that tells us how this paragraph connects to the previous one. What word in that topic sentence indicates the purpose of the second paragraph?

   _____

   _____

2. What example does Cousins include in the second paragraph to prove that people are numb to violence?

   _____

   _____

Ideas for Discussion and Writing

 SMALL GROUP DISCUSSION   Holmes and Rahe, authors of "The Social Readjustment Rating Scale," have named and rated the life events that produce the most stress, events that demand the most difficult changes in how a person lives and adapts to life. The list that follows shows the top ten of these events, from most stressful (1) to least stressful (10). Discuss the items on the list and give each of them your own rating. Do you think any other items should be included on the list? If so, add them and rate them.

Life Events	
1. Death of a spouse	6. Major personal injury or illness
2. Divorce	7. Marriage
3. Marital separation from mate	8. Being fired from work
4. Detention in jail or other institution	9. Marital reconciliation with mate
5. Death of a close family member	10. Retirement from work

Writing Idea 1

Choose one of the life events on the list and explain the effects of this event on someone you know.

Writing Idea 2

Write a humorous explanation of one of your shortcomings, such as why you stay up too late, why you turn in homework or papers late, why you procrastinate, why you eat junk food. . . . Begin with a main idea that announces your shortcoming. Support your statement by explaining the cause(s) or reason(s) for this fault.

Writing Idea 3

Write about the positive or negative effects of an experience in your life or in the lives of one or more people you know. Consider the following possible topics.

1. The effects of a positive mental attitude

2. The effects of a religious faith

3. The effects of dropping out of school

4. The effects of drug abuse

5. The effects of the gain (or loss) of small businesses in a community

Writing Tip

When you are considering effects, the following categories may help you discover and clarify your ideas. If you are writing about *who* is affected, consider *yourself, family, friends,* and *community*. If you are writing about *how* people are affected, consider *emotional, physical,* and *financial* effects.

Classification

Whenever we make a monthly budget and sort expenses into categories such as food, transportation, clothes, and utility bills, we are *classifying*. When you support your main idea by classifying, announce the categories and then discuss each one separately. The categories you choose can vary. For example, if you were writing about cars, you could group cars according to their size: compact, sedan, coupe, and sport-utility vehicle. You might also group them according to other categories, such as cost, repair record, resale value, and safety record.

Paragraph Models

PRACTICE 6   Read the following paragraphs and answer the questions that follow.

Paragraphs A and B

When you are hit by adversity or have your life disrupted, how do you respond? Some people feel victimized; they blame others for their plight. Some shut down; they feel helpless and overwhelmed. Some get angry; they lash out and try to hurt anyone they can.

A few, however, reach within themselves and find ways to cope with the adversity. They eventually make things turn out well. These are life's best survivors, those people with an amazing capacity for surviving crises and extreme difficulties. They are resilient and durable in distressing situations. They regain emotional balance quickly, adapt, and cope well. They thrive by gaining strength from adversity and often convert misfortune into a gift.

—Al Siebert, *The Survivor Personality*

1. Al Siebert groups people according to how they respond to adversity (hard times). He presents four different ways people respond. What are they?

   _____

   _____

2. You have just read the opening paragraphs of Siebert's book. One group of people is developed more fully because this group is the subject of the rest of the book. Which group receives the most detail?

   _____

Paragraph C

It fascinates me how differently we all speak in different circumstances. We have levels of formality, as in our clothing. There are very formal occasions, often requiring written English: the job application or the letter to the editor—the darksuit, serious-tie language, with everything pressed and the lint brushed off. There is our less formal out-in-the-world language—a more comfortable suit, but still respectable. There is language for close friends in the evenings, on weekends—bluejeans-and-sweat-shirt language, when it's good to get the tie off. There is family language, even more relaxed, full of grammatical short cuts, family slang, echoes of old jokes that have become intimate shorthand—the language of pyjamas and uncombed hair. Finally, there is the language with no clothes on: the talk of couples—murmurs, sighs, grunts—language at its least self-conscious, open, vulnerable, and primitive.

—Robert MacNeil, *Wordstruck*

1. Robert MacNeil groups language according to level of formality, beginning with the most formal and ending with the least formal. He compares language to clothing. What does he mean by *darksuit, serious-tie language?*

_____

_____

2. What do you think MacNeil means by *bluejeans-and-sweat-shirt language?*

_____

Ideas for Discussion and Writing

 SMALL GROUP DISCUSSION Bring to class a college catalog, a television guide, a cookbook, and the Help Wanted section of a Sunday paper. For each publication, discuss the ways information is arranged in categories. Then discuss other ways the information could be categorized. For example, the jobs listed in the Help Wanted section could be categorized as part-time and full-time jobs.

Writing Idea 1

Write about two or three kinds of people or things. For example, you could write about types of friends, teachers, jobs, attitudes, lies, restaurants, movies, pets, employers, salespeople, shoppers, clothes, or neighbors.

Writing Idea 2

Write about types of college students. Consider grouping them according to their response to stress, response to other students, attitude, attendance, or participation.

Writing Idea 3

Write about types of dangerous drivers. You could group them as angry drivers, reckless drivers, absent-minded drivers, or preoccupied drivers (talking on the phone or to others in the car).

Writing Tip

As you think about possible categories for your topic, use the same organizing principle in grouping them. For example, if your topic is "vacations," you could use the organizing principle of *price* and write about three kinds of vacations: expensive, moderate, and inexpensive. Or you could use the organizing principle of *effects* and write about two kinds of vacations: relaxing and exhausting. Stay with just one organizing principle. In other words, don't write about two kinds of vacations, relaxing (effect) and inexpensive (price).

Process

Whenever we give someone directions about how to use something such as a cellular phone or a VCR, we are explaining a process. Explaining the process involves describing the steps in a logical order, which is usually time order.

Paragraph Models

PRACTICE 7   Read the following paragraphs and answer the questions that follow.

Paragraph A

Research has shown that excessive noise exposure is a leading cause of ear damage. Any noise level with a decibel count of over 85 attacks the inner ear's 16,000 hair cells, the tiny workhorses that transport airborne vibrations to the brain. Cells that are damaged are permanently damaged; they cannot repair themselves. There are three practical steps you can take to prevent ear damage. First, recognize dangerous noise levels: a gunshot has a noise level of 140 decibels, a jackhammer has 130, a rock concert has 120, a video arcade has 110. Second, when in noisy environments, wear ear plugs made of foam, silicone, or wax. It is not only the intensity of the noise but the length of exposure that causes damage. Third, give your ears a rest. For example, after several hours in a boisterous stadium, it's wise to wait a day before heading to a rock club. William Clark, a senior scientist at the Central Institute for the Deaf in St. Louis, warns that 75 percent of hearing loss in the typical American is caused by "what you've done to your ears throughout your lifetime."

—Adapted from Claudia Kalb, "Our Embattled Ears"

1. The writer gives three steps we can take to prevent ear damage. What are they?

   _____

   _____

2. In order to help readers recognize the different steps, writers announce the steps with *transition words*, words that connect ideas or serve as bridges between them. Some of the transition words for writing about a process are *first, second, third . . . , following, next*, and *finally*. What three transition words does the above writer use to announce the steps?

   _____

Paragraph B

Before signing an apartment lease, make sure you know what you are leasing. There is no three-day grace period where you can change your mind, so tenants should not sign a lease until they have taken the following steps. First, turn everything on and wait to make sure everything works. Run the shower and faucets, flush the toilets, and turn on light switches, the stove, and other appliances. Second, write the results down. Record any items that seem to be damaged or in need of repair. Third, ask for a heat estimate. The landlord must supply you, as part of the lease agreement, an estimate of utility costs based on the prior tenant's usage. Fourth, check the common areas. Take time to walk through the basement, hallways and other areas of the building that you'll have access to. Look for telltale signs of disrepair and check to see if the trash or recycling areas are neat and organized. Fifth, talk to tenants, asking about the neighborhood, the heat in their unit, and the responsiveness of the landlord to problems. Finally, if there are repairs to be made, have them written into the lease. Leases can be negotiated, and it is important that you are satisfied with what is in the lease you sign.

—Adapted from Brian Edwards,
"Look Before You Lease"

1. What is the topic sentence?

_____

_____

2. The writer lists six steps to take before leasing. Why are these steps important?

_____

_____

Ideas for Discussion and Writing

 SMALL GROUP DISCUSSION How should a person present himself or herself at a job interview? Discuss, in time order, the important things to do. Begin with how to prepare for the interview. Then talk about the beginning, the middle, and the end of the interview, discussing such things as handshakes and attitude.

Writing Idea 1

Use the discussion ideas as support for a paper about how to make a favorable impression at a job interview.

Writing Idea 2

Explain how you accomplished something you are proud of.

Writing Idea 3

Choose one of the following items and explain the process, step by step.

1. How to buy a car, a TV, or a cellular phone

2. How to avoid doing something you know you need to do

3. How to choose qualified daycare

4. How to break a bad habit

5. How to respond to an angry person

Writing Tip

Answering the reporter's questions is especially helpful when you are writing about a process. You should include not only the *who, what, where,* and *when* of the process, but also the *why*. Readers need to know why the steps are important.

Comparison and Contrast

Before we vote, we compare candidates' positions on issues that are important to us. Before we buy clothes, furniture, or any kind of equipment, we compare that item with similar items. Our daily decisions are made by comparing (looking at similarities) and by contrasting (looking at differences).

Paragraph Models

PRACTICE 8   Read the following paragraphs and answer the questions that follow.

Paragraph A

If you are shopping for a printer for your home computer, you need to know the difference between an ink-jet's and laser printer's performance. Ink-jets and lasers now print equally fast. The best ink-jets and most lasers can print 3 ½ pages of single-spaced text per minute. Although the speed of these printers is the same, their ability to produce color prints differs. Color ink-jet printers can print greeting cards, banners, T-shirt iron-ons, and images from CD-ROM encyclopedias. On the other hand, laser printers for home use are strictly one-color machines. They print only in black and white. Finally, the quality of reproduced photographs differs. The best ink-jets print deep black and colors with smooth gradations. None of the laser printers match these ink-jets for printing photographs. *Consumer Reports* concludes that an ink-jet is the best type of printer for most households.

—Adapted from "Better, Faster, Picture-Perfect,"
Consumer Reports

1. What two items is the author comparing and contrasting?

_____

2. The writer mentions both similarities and differences. How are these items similar?

_____

Paragraph B

The Uniform Time Act of 1966, which established daylight-saving time, should be repealed. Daylight-saving time confuses millions of Americans every spring and fall. Spring, when we lose an hour, is the most difficult time change. Adults who have to work or get children ready for school struggle to crawl out of bed at the cruel hour of five a.m. Children are also negatively affected by this artificial shift in the hour. They are not hungry at lunch time and refuse to go to bed at their normal bedtime. Our pets are equally surprised when we feed them an hour early, and they are not ready for their usual evening walk. Fall, when we gain an hour, has the opposite effect. Adults find themselves not oversleeping in the morning but dozing off before the ten o'clock news at night. The kids' stomachs are growling before lunch, and they are crabby earlier in the evening. Furthermore, the dog is jumping around, howling way before his feeding time, and begging to go out earlier than his scheduled walk. The additional daylight hour during the already grey skies of winter is not worth the annual frustration of confused adults, children, and pets.

—Student Writer

1. The writer gives details to prove that the time change in spring is confusing. What three groups are affected by this change in time? Which group is presented first? second? third?

_____

_____

2. The writer also gives details to prove that the time change in fall is confusing. What three groups are affected by this change in time? Which group is presented first? second? third?

_____

_____

Ideas for Discussion and Writing

 SMALL GROUP DISCUSSION Before going to college, you probably heard from friends and relatives what college life was like. What stories were you told? What expectations did you have? After talking about your expectations, compare them to the realities of college life. Did you encounter anything unexpected?

Writing Idea 1

Write about the similarities or differences between your expectations and your experience of college.

Writing Idea 2

Write about an experience where two people had different responses to the same event, such as a movie, a party, or someone's words or actions.

Writing Idea 3

Write about two different ways of doing something. For instance, you could write about two ways of responding to obstacles, two ways of looking at one's past, or two ways of interpreting a compliment.

Writing Tip

When you are comparing or contrasting, you will be looking at two persons, places, or things, which we will call A and B. Your two options for organizing your details are the block format and the point-by-point format.

When you use the *block format,* you present first all the details about A; then you present all the details about B. The student writer's paragraph about spring and fall time changes has this format. The writer first described the spring time change and then described the time change in the fall.

When you choose the *point-by-point format,* you move back and forth between A and B, dealing with each point separately. The *Consumer Reports* paragraph about computer printers is organized in a point-by-point format. The discussion of the two kinds of printers first compares and contrasts their speed, then their color printing, and finally, their photo reproduction. If the block format had been used, the paragraph would have first presented all the details about the ink-jet printer and then all the details about the laser printer. As you compare and contrast, use either the block format or the point-by-point format.

Review: Developing Ideas

- Decide how you will develop your idea. Will you be describing, including examples, telling a story, persuading with reasons, exploring causes or effects, placing items in categories, explaining a process, and/or comparing and contrasting?

- Whatever method you use, make sure you include enough specific details to convince readers of your point.

 REVIEW PRACTICE In your small group, discuss how the following general topics could be developed by the various methods of development described in this chapter.

1. A specific person's attitude

2. Dropping out of school

3. Community pride

4. Drug abuse

Chapter 3

Drafting and Revising

◆ Draft Your Ideas
◆ Revise Your Paper

Draft Your Ideas

After you have decided how you will develop your main idea and have arranged the supporting details in a sketch outline, it's time to write these ideas in paragraph form. A first draft is a practice paper where you explore and experiment.

Anticipate Readers' Questions

Writing is effective only if readers understand the writer's ideas. As you write your draft, keep in mind readers' needs and expectations. The following chart will help you anticipate readers' responses and recognize what readers need to understand your ideas.

Readers' responses	What you as a writer need to do
1. What's your point?	Begin with your main idea and stick to it.
2. Can you prove it?	Give adequate specific evidence.
3. I don't get it.	Connect your evidence.
4. So what?	Write a conclusion.

Readers respond: What's your point?
BEGIN WITH YOUR MAIN IDEA AND STICK TO IT

When you begin with the main idea, readers know what your topic is and what point you will be making about that topic. Make sure you don't wander from that point. When we talk, we take all kinds of side trips. Often one idea reminds us of another, and it is easy to end up on an entirely different topic, wondering how we got there. In writing, we ramble by freewriting. By the time you have finished drafting, though, you need to make sure every detail supports the main idea. When all your details support the main idea, your writing will have *unity*.

PRACTICE 1   The following paragraph has a detail that does not support the topic sentence. Find that detail and cross it out.

> Although I quit smoking a few months ago, I am still struggling with the desire to smoke. Every time I see someone puffing and exhaling, I see that light blue smoke as little blue ghosts laughing in my face, trying to pull me back into their lamp, into their ashtray. Although the cravings are weaker, they have not disappeared. They are like ghosts waiting to trap me. These ghosts remind me of my uncle in California. But I have will power. I am not about to let the little blue ghosts win.

> —Student Writer

Readers ask: Can you prove it?
GIVE ADEQUATE SPECIFIC EVIDENCE

Support your point with adequate specific evidence. When writers don't have enough evidence, they often try to make their writing longer by padding it with empty words and phrases. Do not confuse wordy writing with good writing. Paul Roberts, in "How to Say Nothing in Five Hundred Words," gives examples of ineffective and effective writing:

The worst

> In my humble opinion, though I do not claim to be an expert on this complicated subject, fast driving, in most circumstances, would seem to be rather dangerous in many respects, or at least so it would seem to me.

A bit better

> In my opinion, fast driving would seem to be rather dangerous.

Better

> In my opinion, fast driving is dangerous.

Best

> Fast driving is dangerous.

The first example says in forty words what the last example says in four. If you need more evidence to support your point, don't pad your writing with empty words and phrases. Instead, use the following three methods to discover additional ideas and specific details:

1. Freewrite.

2. Ask the reporter's questions: *Who? What? Where? When?* and *Why?*

3. Talk about your ideas with a friend or classmate.

PRACTICE 2   Read the following two drafts of a student paragraph and answer the questions that follow.

First draft

Watching football games at home is more enjoyable than watching games at a stadium. Many people enjoy the spectacle of a football game at a stadium. I, on the other hand, prefer to watch the games at home. It's cheaper. I save a lot of money by staying at home because I do not have to pay the prices they charge at the stadium. Although it is just a matter of opinion, I would rather watch the excitement and suspense of these games at home.

Second draft

Watching football games at home is more enjoyable than watching games at a stadium. First, I save money because I do not have to pay for expensive tickets, overcrowded parking lots, and bland food. It is also more comfortable sitting on my soft, warm couch than on hard stadium bleachers in pouring rain or driving snow. Finally, my television gives me quality control. The stereo speakers bring in the action-packed sounds without the crazy crowds, and my wide-screen TV gives me a better view than a ticket right on the fifty yard line. The price, comfort, and quality control of my living room make every game a home game for me.

1. Describe your impressions of (a) the first draft and (b) the second draft.

   _____

   _____

2. What specific evidence does the writer include in the second draft to support the main idea?

   _____

   _____

   _____

   _____

Readers respond: I don't get it.
CONNECT YOUR EVIDENCE

You know how your evidence is connected, but readers cannot ask you questions or read your mind. Therefore, it is important to arrange your ideas logically and to connect them so readers understand how one idea is leading to the next. Otherwise, readers see a string of unrelated sentences and cannot follow your train of thought. When you connect your evidence, your writing will have *coherence*, which means that the ideas stick together. To connect your ideas, use transition words or repeat key words.

Use Transition Words

You can connect ideas by using transitions, words or sentences that show the relationship between ideas. For example, if you were giving three examples to prove your point, you could introduce those examples with the transition words *first, second,* and *third.* These words are signals that you are moving from one example to the next. If you were writing about the effect of an event, you could use transition words like *consequently* and *as a result* to make your meaning clear.

Here are some of the most commonly used transition words:

Transition Words

When including examples:

To introduce your example	To connect examples
for example	also, as well as
for instance	another example of, furthermore
specifically	next, in addition, similarly
	not only . . . but also

When telling a story or explaining a process:

after	during	last	since
as	eventually	later	soon
as soon as	finally	meanwhile	then
at last	first	next	when
before	following	now	while

When persuading with reasons:

To introduce your reasons	To conclude your argument
first (second, third)	consequently, hence
another, in addition	therefore
because, since	in conclusion
last, finally	clearly, above all

When writing about effects:

as a result	hence	then	thus
consequently	so	therefore	because

When comparing or contrasting:

To indicate similarities		To indicate differences	
similar to	equally	on the other hand	different from
like	also	on the contrary	but
just as	too	instead of	although
		unlike	whereas

When concluding your paper:

in conclusion	evidently	clearly	finally

PRACTICE 3   Read the following paragraph and answer the question that follows.

> When interviewing for a job, respond to the interviewer's questions in a positive manner. Responding positively rather than negatively will increase your chances for employment. Four tips are included here as guides to a successful and positive interview. First, do not refer to your present or past employer with negative words. "Don't sound like a complainer," urges Vincent Chiera, who supervises JWCharles Financial Services' recruitment efforts and interviews some 250 job applicants each year. Even if you have legitimate complaints about a past employer, find something positive to say or avoid the topic completely. Second, Chiera advises, replace negative images with positive images. For example, rather than say how "bored" you were in your previous job, assert that you are "looking for a new challenge." Another tip for turning the negative into the positive involves your response to a question about your job search, a question such as, "Are you interviewing anywhere else?" This is a difficult question. If the answer is no, does that indicate that you have no idea of where else to look for a job? If the answer is yes, does it mean you are not sincere about wanting to work for this particular company? The best way to handle the question is to simply and quietly say, "Yes, of course I am. I am on a serious job hunt, but your company is first on my list." Finally, if the questioning continues with "Has another company made a job offer?" deflect the question by replying, "Not yet." Responding positively to an interviewer's questions will help you present yourself in a positive light and consequently enhance your status as a job candidate.

> —Adapted from Carol Kleiman,
> "Avoid Negative Thoughts for Positive Results"

What transition words introduce the tips and conclude the main idea?

_____

Repeat Key Words

Another way to connect your ideas is by repeating key words or using words that refer to your main idea. For example, if you were writing about an obstacle, you could occasionally repeat the word *obstacle* to keep readers on track. You could also use other words that refer to the obstacle, such as *the difficulty* or *the problem*.

PRACTICE 4   In the following paragraph, the writer orders his details according to time. He helps readers understand the time connection by using the transition words *then* and *now* and by using words that refer to time. Circle the words that refer to time.

> Three centuries ago, a Dutch mathematician named Christiaan Huygens invented a new religion. He didn't mean to. All he did was build a pendulum clock that allowed people, for the first time in history, to keep track of hours and minutes accurately. But over the decades, this power

attracted millions of followers. In the 1850s, people started strapping clocks around their wrists. Then came the school bell and, with the Industrial Revolution, the punch clock for shift workers and the standardization of time zones for the railroads. Now the idol of the West, the clock hangs in nearly every office. Its worshipers look into its face several times a day, waiting for signs that it is time to go to work, to eat, to sleep.

—Alan Zarembo,
"What If There Weren't Any Clocks to Watch?"

Readers respond: So what?

WRITE A CONCLUSION

Conclusions bring a piece of writing to a definite, satisfying end. Effective conclusions refer back to the main idea to create unity, coherence, and a sense that the writing has come full circle. Conclusions also focus readers' attention on the significance of what has been written.

Note the following suggestions:

Writing a Conclusion: Three Possibilities

Read your paper, pay close attention to the main idea stated at the beginning, and consider one of these possibilities:

1. Include an insight that readers would not have understood before reading your paper. To find an effective insight, read your paper, ask yourself, "So what?" and then answer that question.

2. Repeat a key word from the main idea.

3. Restate the main idea in different words and from a slightly different angle or point of view.

Writing a Conclusion: Three Cautions

As you draft your conclusion, follow these three guidelines:

1. Do not repeat the main idea word for word. That kind of repetition is boring for readers and suggests that you don't see the significance of your point.

2. Do not simply tell readers what they have just read ("As you can see from what I have written . . ."). This approach is unnecessary and can offend readers' intelligence.

3. Do not conclude with an idea that has not been previously mentioned or suggested. An entirely new idea confuses readers.

PRACTICE 5   Each of the following paragraphs has several possible conclusions. Circle the letter of the best conclusion.

Example 1

I love being around children because they are innocent in their approach to real-life problems. For instance, a three-year-old boy was told in his Sunday School class that the Lord is able to do all things but fail. He went home and heard his parents talking about not having money to pay the rent. So the boy told his parents innocently, "The Lord is able to do all things but fail." His parents were at first shocked, but they soon began to look at their problem from their child's perspective.

—Student Writer

1. What is the best conclusion for this paragraph?

   a. Now you can understand why I really love being around children.

   b. Seeing the innocence of children helps me gain a fresh perspective on life's problems.

   c. Children are not only innocent, they are also sensitive to other children and take care of one another on the playground.

Example 2

I never thought of myself as a college student. When I was in high school, I was an average student with barely average grades. Because I thought I was not college material, I never pushed myself. As my senior year began and my friends talked about the colleges they wanted to attend, I wondered what college would ever accept me with my grade average. One day in my English class, Bill Jeffries, a recruiter from one of our state universities, came to talk to us. He told us, "Any one of you can go to college if you set your mind to it. You don't have to be a straight A student to be college bound." He gave us important information to guide us through the application process and described a program that provides support for freshmen. I took a chance, and I applied. Surprisingly, I was accepted.

—Student Writer

2. What is the best conclusion for this paragraph?

   a. I am in college today because Bill Jeffries' encouragement changed my mind.

   b. In conclusion, that's why I went to college.

   c. Now you can understand from what I wrote that I changed my mind.

Consider a Title

Titles can catch readers' attention and interest them in your writing. Be careful about titles, though. One common error is putting the main idea in the title and then failing to include that main idea in your opening paragraph. Whether you use a title or not, your first paragraph must contain a sentence stating the main idea of your paper.

Be Patient: Helpful Hints

As you draft your ideas, consider these hints on the drafting process:

1. *Catch thoughts as they fly through your mind.* As you write, you will find yourself getting an idea about what to say next. It might be just a glimmer of an idea. If you wait to find the exact words, you'll lose it. Get your thoughts down on paper quickly, in any way you can. Jot down key words or use abbreviations. Later, you can go back and expand that idea.

2. *Give yourself a break.* Complete your draft early enough to give you time to set it aside, at least overnight. A break from it will clear your mind: you can then recognize which ideas need to be deleted or developed and which ones need additional support.

3. *Wait until the end of the writing process to edit.* When you are putting your ideas on paper, don't interrupt the flow of ideas to correct sentence structure or punctuation. Do that later, before writing the final draft.

4. *Have someone else read your paper.* All writers benefit from constructive feedback on their writing. Showing your paper to someone else allows you to find out how well you have communicated what you had in mind. If you look at the beginning of any book, you are likely to see a page where the author thanks one or more—sometimes many more—people for their assistance in writing that book.

COMPUTER TIPS FOR DRAFTING

If you are writing a paper on a word processor, the following tips may be helpful. (Commands may vary, depending on the word processing application.)

- Remember to save your material often.

- Type single-spaced. You'll want to see as much of your writing as possible on screen so you can watch the flow of ideas. Then, before printing, go to *Format* and select double-spacing.

- Try not to be sidetracked by easily correctable errors. You can correct those later when you revise.

- Do not be concerned about the order of your ideas. Later, when you revise, you can easily rearrange sentences and paragraphs by using the *Cut* and *Paste* commands.

- Check to see if your computer has an *Undo* command. Most word processors have an icon or function key that lets you "undo" your most recent error.

- When you are finished with your draft, save it before you print or close the document.

Revise Your Paper

After you have completed your first draft, it is time to *revise*. Revising involves seeing your writing through the eyes of your readers and making sure they will find your ideas convincing and easy to follow. You may discover a need for more details to support your point. You may need to delete details that wander away from your point, and you may decide to move sentences so your details connect logically and smoothly.

One valuable way to see your writing through readers' eyes is by sharing your paper with classmates for their feedback. One form of this peer review process is called the Author's Chair, which is included on the inside back cover of this book. In addition to the Author's Chair, the following questions will help you improve your draft.

Guidelines for Revising Short Papers

1. What is my main idea? Does it include my topic and the point I make about that topic?

2. Are my details specific? Have I included sufficient details to convince readers of my point?

3. Do the details support the main idea? Are there any details that do *not* fit the point I am making?

4. Have I arranged my details in logical order?

5. Are my ideas and details smoothly connected? Are there any places where I need to use transition words or repeat key words, so readers will understand how my ideas are related?

6. Does my conclusion give readers a sense of completion?

When Ernest Hemingway told an interviewer that he had rewritten the ending of *A Farewell to Arms* thirty-nine times, the interviewer asked, "Was there a problem there? What was it that stumped you?" Hemingway replied, "Getting the words right." Putting ideas into words and having those words express your ideas successfully will take more than one draft. Be patient.

COMPUTER TIPS FOR REVISING

If you are using a word processor, the following tips for revising may be helpful. (Commands may vary, depending on the word processing application.)

- When you have finished your draft, print it; then you can see the whole paper at once. Read it through and mark where you want to delete, add, or move material. Then return to your document and make the changes.

- *Delete.* Place the cursor before the word you want to delete and press the *Delete* key until each letter is gone.

- *Add.* Computers allow you to insert text anywhere. Place the cursor where you want to add words and begin typing. The previously typed sentences will automatically move forward.

- *Cut and Paste.* You can cut and paste both sentences and paragraphs. The process involves selecting, cutting, moving, and pasting.

  1. *Select.* Selecting means letting the computer know which material you want to move. To select, put the cursor at the beginning of what you want to move. Hold down the left mouse button and keep holding the button

down as you drag the cursor over the material. When you get to the end of the material you want to move, release the mouse button. The selected material will now be highlighted.

2. *Cut.* Find the *Cut* icon on the top scroll of your screen. Click on it. Most computers also recognize *Control X* as the cut command. Hold down the *Control* button and push the letter *X*.

3. *Move.* Move the cursor to the place in the document where you want the selected material to appear. Click the left mouse button so the cursor is securely there.

4. *Paste.* Click on the *Paste* icon on the top scroll. Most computers also recognize *Control V* as the paste command. Hold down the *Control* button and push the letter *V*.

5. If your move was successful, click the *Save* button.

- You can experiment without permanently changing your document. First, make sure the document is saved. Then start experimenting. If you find that these revisions are not at all what you want, close the document. When the computer asks if you want to save, answer *no*. Finish closing the document; then reopen it. Your original draft will appear on the screen.

Review: Drafting and Revising

- Sketch a map or an outline to arrange your evidence in the most effective order.

- Using your map as a guide, write the first draft. Keep in mind what information readers need to understand your ideas.

Readers' responses	What you as a writer need to do
1. What's your point?	Begin with your main idea and stick to it.
2. Can you prove it?	Give adequate specific evidence.
3. I don't get it.	Connect your evidence.
4. So what?	Write a conclusion.

- After you have finished the first draft, use the Guidelines for Revising Short Papers on page 59 to help you decide how to improve the second draft.

- Share your paper with a friend or classmate, using the Author's Chair guidelines on the inside back cover of this book. Having others read your paper will help you look at it from a reader's point of view.

 REVIEW PRACTICE 1 Individually or in groups, read the following two drafts and evaluate them by answering the questions that follow.

First Draft

The instructors just handed out a syllabus in the beginning of the semester and expected students to follow it. Not one of my instructors encouraged the class to do the homework, reminded us

when papers were due, or announced tests. I did not even know
that there was a midterm math exam until I walked into class on
exam day. Instructors also do not give students a running tab on
how many absences we have. It's as if they do not care. I chose to
sleep in once in a while and found out too late that I missed important information. No one told me, so how was I to know?

—Student Writer

Second Draft

My first semester at college taught me to be responsible.
The instructors just handed out a syllabus in the beginning
of the semester and expected students to follow it. Not one
of my instructors encouraged the class to do the homework,
reminded us when papers were due, or announced tests. I
did not even know that there was a midterm math exam
until I walked into class on exam day. Instructors also do
not give students a running tab on how many absences we
have. It's as if they do not care. I chose to sleep in once
in a while and found out too late that I missed important
information. No one told me, so how was I to know? I
learned quickly. My midterm grades taught me that in college, individual responsibility is the name of the game.

—Student Writer

1. Put a check mark (✓) next to the sentences that the writer added to the
second draft.

2. What difference do those additions make?

_____

_____

_____

_____

 REVIEW PRACTICE 2 Individually or in groups, read the following paragraph
from *No Ordinary Time*, a biography of Franklin and Eleanor Roosevelt. Franklin
Roosevelt was president of the United States and was also paralyzed by polio. In this
paragraph, the author describes how Roosevelt relaxed by imagining a time when
he was not paralyzed. The writer concludes the paragraph by repeating key words
used in the topic sentence. What are those key words?

_____

On nights filled with tension and concern, Franklin Roosevelt
used his imagination to fall asleep. He would close his eyes and
imagine himself at Hyde Park as a boy, standing with his sled in the
snow atop the steep hill that stretched from the south porch of his

home to the wooded bluffs of the Hudson River far below. As he accelerated down the hill, he maneuvered each familiar curve with perfect skill until he reached the bottom. Then, pulling his sled behind him, he started slowly back up until he reached the top, where he would once more begin his descent. Again and again he replayed this scene in his mind, blocking out the awareness of his paralyzed legs beneath the sheets, undoing the knowledge that he would never climb a hill or even walk on his own power again. Using his imagination to free himself from paralysis, the president of the United States would fall asleep.

—Adapted from Doris Kearns Goodwin,
No Ordinary Time

Chapter

4

Editing

◆ Condense Your Words
◆ State Your Meaning Directly
◆ Correct Errors in Grammar and Usage

Condense Your Words

Once you have taken your paper through several drafts, look closely at the smaller details of writing, such as word choice, grammar, and punctuation. Talking and writing have different styles, and *editing* often involves changing talking style to writing style.

In casual conversation, we say what we think just as the words come to us. In writing, we need to express thoughts as clearly and concisely as possible. Our writing ought to sound like writing, not like talking. As you edit your writing, delete the following talking-style words and phrases.

Do Not Repeat the Subject

When we talk, we often announce the subject first and then immediately repeat the subject by using the pronouns *he, she, it, that, we,* or *they*. For example, we might say: "My brother, he is there when I need him." We announce that the subject is *brother,* and then we immediately repeat that subject with *he*. When we write, we need to condense and write one clear subject.

My brother ~~he~~ is there when I need him.
My friends ~~they~~ count on me.

PRACTICE 1   Correct the following sentences taken from students' drafts by omitting the subject repetition. The first one has been done for you.

EXAMPLE   The New Year's Eve party ~~that~~ was an experience I will never forget.

1. My father he is on his feet from six o'clock in the morning until six o'clock at night.

2. The computer I use in the computer lab it does not print.

3. My grandmother she wants to celebrate her birthday by going out for dinner.

4. Having a baby it was a turning point in my life.

5. Working and going to school they are both important to me.

Delete Unnecessary Words

Effective writing has no wordy phrases or unnecessary words. Weeding out unnecessary words and replacing wordy phrases can take time, but the result is worth the effort. Here are some common wordy phrases and their more straightforward versions.

Wordy	Concise
in spite of the fact that	although
the question as to whether	whether
he is a man who	he
until such a time as	until
at this point in time	now
nowadays; in this day and age	[omit]
kind of	[omit]
because of the fact	because
due to the fact that	because
the reason why is that	because
the reason being	because
in the event that	if
owing to the fact that	since

PRACTICE 2   Condense the following sentences from students' drafts by deleting unnecessary words and stating each thought concisely. At times, you will have to reword the sentence. The first one has been done for you.

EXAMPLE   My father ~~is the kind of person who~~ never misses work.

1. Arriving late infuriated me because of the fact that it was avoidable.

2. The nurse seemed kind of irritable.

3. I understand my sister. The reason why is because we grew up in the same environment.

4. At this point in time, we are trying to make the relationship work.

5. In spite of the fact that I left early, I learned what I needed to learn.

State Your Meaning Directly

When we talk, listeners can see our gestures, hear our tone of voice, and understand what we say from the context of the conversation. When we write, readers are absent and do not have the clues given in conversation. All they have are the words we write. Therefore, every word counts. Every word must be written for a specific purpose and mean what we intend it to mean. Writing is direct and to the point.

Get to the Point

The thing is . . . you know . . . you know what I'm saying . . . well . . . like I mean . . . anyway . . .
   (Omit these talking-style words.)

I am going to write about . . . Let me give you an example.
   (Don't write what you are going to do. Just do it.)

As you can see from this paper . . . I guess you can tell that . . .
   (Omit. If you have included good details, readers will understand your point.)

Needless to say . . .
   (Omit. If it is needless to say, there is no reason to say it.)

I could go on and on about this.
   (These words give no new information. Omit.)

Like I said . . .
   (Readers will remember what you just wrote. Move on to your next point.)

Avoid Using You to Mean People in General

When we talk, we often use *you* to mean people in general. This generality is fine for talking, but not for more formal writing. As you edit your writing, look for places where you use the pronoun *you*. Ask yourself whom you really mean by *you*. For example, this textbook often uses *you* because the writer is addressing *you* specifically, the student writer. As you edit your writing, ask yourself if you are addressing the reader specifically. If you are not, replace the *you* with *people, I, we,* or whomever you specifically mean.

PRACTICE 3   In the following sentences, the writers have used *you* to refer to people in general. Replace the *you* with the specific pronoun the writer needs. The first two have been done for you.

EXAMPLE   When people work hard, ~~you~~ *they* usually get the recognition ~~you~~ *they* deserve.

EXAMPLE   From where we stood, ~~you~~ *we* could see four states.

1. When people lose their jobs, you may lose emotional stability.

2. We work at a store where you don't get paid overtime for holidays.

3. When high school students begin college, you have to start making new friends all over again.

4. When friends make a promise, you should keep it.

5. I prefer stores to catalogs because you can see the merchandise before you buy it.

Omit the Double Negative

In mathematics, two negatives become a positive. When they are multiplied together, the negative aspect is canceled out. The same cancellation works with words. Two negatives become a positive. Therefore, do not use two negatives close to each other to express a negative point. Negatives are words like *not, hardly, barely, scarcely,* and *nothing* and contractions like *didn't* or *couldn't.*

Incorrect: Nobody did nothing.

Correct: *Nobody did anything.*

Incorrect: I didn't hear nothing.

Correct: *I heard nothing* or *I didn't hear anything.*

Incorrect: She couldn't scarcely breathe.

Correct: *She could scarcely breathe* or *She couldn't breathe.*

Incorrect: He can't hardly think straight.

Correct: *He can hardly think straight* or *He can't think straight.*

Correct Errors in Grammar and Usage

Editing is essential because you want readers to pay attention to your ideas, not your errors. Although we have focused in this chapter on writing concisely and directly, other elements of editing are equally important. These elements, which we will cover in later chapters, are included in the following guidelines. Throughout the writing course, use these guidelines as you edit your papers.

Guidelines for Editing

1. Go back over your past drafts and papers, review the errors you made, and look for these errors in all future writings.

2. Read your writing *aloud, slowly,* exactly as you have written it, or have someone else read it to you. This essential practice lets you see what you actually wrote, not what you think you wrote. Reading aloud will help you to

   - hear when a sentence is confusing.
   - find words you have left out.
   - hear where your sentences end.
     Check to see if you say each sentence exactly as you punctuated it. If not, correct the punctuation error.

3. Check to make sure you have used correct words. Look particularly for

   - correct forms of irregular verbs (Chapter 8) and helping verbs (Chapter 7).
   - correct verb endings, including *-s* on present tense verbs when the subject is a singular noun and *-ed* on past tense verbs (Chapter 7).
   - subject-verb agreement (Chapter 9).
   - correct pronoun choice (Chapter 21).
   - correctly marked possessives and contractions (Chapter 22).
   - easily confused words (Chapter 23).
   - correct spelling (Chapter 23).

4. Look for general words that could be replaced with more exact or creative words.

5. Omit unnecessary words and look for places where you can condense a group of words into one word.

6. Review your sentence patterns. If all your sentences have the same pattern, refer to the chart of sentence patterns on the inside front cover of this book. Then return to your writing to find sentences that can be more effectively written in one or more of these varied patterns.

COMPUTER TIPS FOR EDITING

If you are writing your paper on a word processor, the following tips may be helpful. (Commands vary depending on the word processing application.)

- *Spell check.* Use the spell check function to correct your spelling errors. Spell check will find misspelled words and list suggested spellings. From the list of suggestions, select the spelling you want; the computer will automatically insert the word you selected. Be aware that spell check will not find all spelling errors. Because spell check ignores anything it recognizes as a word, it will not find words you have used incorrectly. It will not find easily confused words, such as using *there* when you need to use *they're*. It will also not find words that do not make sense, as in "The hikers walked three *moles*."

• *Find and Replace.* The *Find and Replace* command, usually listed under the *Edit* menu, will find any word or series of words you ask it to find. Say you have written a paper about applying for a job and want to see if you have included the word *résumé*. Go to *Find and Replace* and type the word *résumé* in the *Find* box. The computer will find the word if you have used it in this document.

• *Find and Replace* will also replace words. You can include a replacement if you want the computer to replace one word(s) with another word(s). For example, say you decide you want to replace the word *friends* with the words *Cynthia and her brother.* Go to the *Find and Replace* command. In the *Find* box, type *friends.* In the *Replace* box, type *Cynthia and her brother.* The computer will find every *friends* in the document and replace it with *Cynthia and her brother.*

• Check for fragments and run-ons. Use the *Enter* key to place each sentence on a separate line. Then read each sentence individually.

• When you have completed your final draft, print it out and read it slowly as you look for errors. A computer-generated paper looks perfect and professional. Do not let the professional appearance of your paper fool you. Read your paper carefully.

• Keep an error file. Create a document called *Errors.* Every time a paper is returned, type any errors and their corrections into the *Errors* file. Refer to this file when you edit to avoid repeating the same mistake.

Review: Editing

• Imagine that you are seeing your paper for the first time. Read it aloud slowly and make sure you have used words correctly.

• Omit talking-style words and unnecessary words that carry little meaning.

• State your meaning directly; get straight to the point.

• Use the Guidelines for Editing on page 67 as a checklist for editing your papers.

• Write the final paper.

• Give your paper one final reading—a proofreading. Read it aloud and look for words you left out and for handwriting or typing errors.

 REVIEW PRACTICE   Individually or in groups, edit the following paragraph for talking style by correcting errors and crossing out unnecessary words and sentences.

Math comes easily to my brother Johnny. The thing is that he gets

an A on every math test without studying. His ability to make sense

out of numbers amazes me. When I took algebra, all I saw was a mass of confusing *x*s and *y*s and equal signs. Yet, my brother he can make sense of it all. He does not need to scribble out answers for equations because the answers are clear in his mind. Well, when I took geometry, I struggled to pass. But Johnny he can look at pencil marks on paper and see three-dimensional figures that have volume. I could go on and on about how smart he is in math. Like I said, my brother doesn't need nothing that he does not already have: a natural ability to make sense out of numbers.

—Student Writer

Writing Essays

An essay is a series of paragraphs about one main idea. You already know a great deal about essay writing because paragraphs and essays have much in common. The parts of a paragraph correspond to the parts of an essay. The topic sentence of a paragraph is similar to an essay's thesis statement: each presents a main idea. The supporting details in a paragraph are similar to the supporting paragraphs in an essay: both support the main idea. A paragraph's concluding sentence is similar to an essay's concluding paragraph: each focuses readers' attention on the significance of what the writer has written.

When you write an essay, use the same process you used for writing a shorter paper.

1. Begin by discovering your ideas.

2. Group your evidence and find one main idea.

3. Write the main idea in one or two sentences.

4. Develop your main idea.

5. Sketch a map that outlines how you will support your main idea.

6. Draft your essay.

7. Revise to make sure your evidence is connected and will be clear to readers.

8. Edit for spelling and grammatical correctness.

This chapter will guide you through the process of writing an essay.

Chapter 5

Writing a More Developed Paper: The Essay

- ◆ Understand Essay Form
- ◆ Discover and Organize Your Ideas
- ◆ Draft Your Essay
- ◆ Revise Your Essay

Understand Essay Form

> I write entirely to find out what I'm thinking, what I'm looking at, what I see and what it means.
>
> In many ways writing is the act . . . of saying listen to me, see it my way, change your mind.
>
> —Joan Didion, "Why I Write"

Joan Didion, a well-known American writer, points out that writing gives us the chance to explore our ideas and to connect with readers. Essays give us a way to discover what we think and share that understanding convincingly with readers.

Ideas are more developed in an essay than in a one-paragraph paper. Therefore, the parts of an essay are presented in separate paragraphs. The main idea, the *thesis*, is stated in the introductory paragraph. The supporting evidence is given in the supporting paragraphs. The conclusion is given in the concluding paragraph. The following diagram shows how the parts of an essay work together.

DIAGRAM OF AN ESSAY

Thesis statement at the beginning
or the end of the paragraph

INTRODUCTORY PARAGRAPH

Provides background information or catches readers' interest.

Presents the thesis statement.

Topic sentence
Specific evidence

SUPPORTING PARAGRAPHS

Each begins with a topic sentence.
Each supports that topic sentence.

Topic sentence
Specific evidence

An essay can have as many supporting paragraphs as necessary.

Topic sentence
Specific evidence

Conclusion

CONCLUDING PARAGRAPH

Helps readers understand the significance of the writer's ideas.

From Bertrand Russell: An Example of Essay Form

The following essay is an excellent example of how the introduction, supporting paragraphs, and conclusion work together. Bertrand Russell was born in 1872 and lived until he was 97 years old. Orphaned at three, he was raised by his grandmother. He became a famous lecturer and author of books about mathematics, science, sociology, history, religion, politics, and ethics. In 1950, he was awarded the Nobel Prize in literature. In this passage from his autobiography, Russell reviews the complex topic of his life in only five short paragraphs:

"What I Have Lived For"

Three passions, simple but overwhelmingly strong, have governed my life: the longing for love, the search for knowledge, and unbearable pity for the suffering of mankind. These passions, like great winds, have blown me hither and thither, in a wayward course, over a deep ocean of anguish, reaching to the very verge of despair.

I have sought love, first, because it brings ecstasy—ecstasy so great that I would often have sacrificed all the rest of life for a few hours of this joy. I have sought it, next, because it relieves loneliness—that terrible loneliness in which one shivering consciousness looks over the rim of the world into the cold unfathomable lifeless abyss. I have sought it, finally, because in the union of love I have seen, in a mystic miniature, the prefiguring vision of the heaven that saints and poets have imagined. This is what I sought, and though it might seem too good for human life, this is what—at last—I have found.

With equal passion I have sought knowledge. I have wished to understand the hearts of men. I have wished to know why the stars shine. And I have tried to apprehend the Pythagorean power by which number holds sway above the flux.* A little of this, but not much, I have achieved.

Love and knowledge, so far as they were possible, led upward toward the heavens. But always pity brought me back to earth. Echoes of cries of pain reverberate in my heart. Children in famine, victims tortured by oppressors, helpless old people a hated burden to their sons, and the whole world of loneliness, poverty, and pain make a mockery of what human life should be. I long to alleviate the evil, but I cannot, and I too suffer.

This has been my life. I have found it worth living, and would gladly live it again if the chance were offered me.

Paragraphs are like the cars that make up a train. If the cars are not connected, the train will not go anywhere. If paragraphs within an essay are not connected, your essay will lose its power. Readers will not be able to follow your thinking; they will not understand how your ideas are connected. Russell connects his paragraphs well. He begins with a thesis, develops the thesis in the supporting paragraphs, and completes the essay with a conclusion. Each part is linked to the others.

---

*Apprehend means "to understand." *Pythagorean power* refers to the power of mathematics to explain how everything from music to astronomy works. Russell may mean that he has tried to understand what holds planets, stars, and galaxies together.

Introductory Paragraph

Three passions, simple but overwhelmingly strong, have governed my life: the longing for love, the search for knowledge, and unbearable pity for the suffering of mankind.

- Russell states his thesis: *Three passions . . . have governed my life.* He then names those passions: the longing for love, the search for knowledge, and unbearable pity for the suffering of mankind. He is indicating that the first section of his essay will be about love; the second, about knowledge; and the third, about pity.

Supporting Paragraphs

Russell covers the three sections in the same order presented in the thesis statement. He also ties these sections together by repeating the topic of the previous paragraph.

Paragraph 2

*I have sought **love**. . . .*
- Russell lets us know that this paragraph will be about love.

Paragraph 3

*With **equal passion** I have sought **knowledge.***
- *With equal passion* refers back to love. Then he states that this paragraph will be about knowledge.

Paragraph 4

***Love and knowledge,** so far as they were possible, led upward toward the heavens. But always **pity** brought me back to earth.*
- Russell refers back to the second and third sections by repeating the words *love* and *knowledge.* Then he indicates that this paragraph will be about pity.

Concluding Paragraph

This has been my life. I have found it worth living, and would gladly live it again if the chance were offered me.

- Russell's last paragraph refers to the whole essay as he summarizes his evaluation of his life.

Ideas must be connected within paragraphs as well as between them. In the essay we have been examining, for instance, Russell connects ideas within his paragraphs. Notice how he uses the transition words *first, next,* and *finally* to help readers follow his train of thought and understand his three reasons for seeking love.

> I have sought love, *first,* because it brings ecstasy—ecstasy so great that I would often have sacrificed all the rest of life for a few hours of this joy. I have sought it, *next,* because it relieves loneliness—that terrible loneliness in which one shivering consciousness looks over the rim of the world into the cold unfathomable lifeless abyss. I have sought it, *finally,* because in the union of love I have seen, in a mystic miniature, the prefiguring vision of the heaven that saints and poets have imagined. This is what I sought, and though it might seem too good for human life, this is what—at last—I have found.

Discover and Organize Your Ideas

We have looked at the form of an essay and concentrated on how the parts work together. Now that you know what you are aiming for, we will look at what will get you there: the writing process. You are already familiar with the writing process as discussed in Chapter 1. This section tailors the same stages to developing an essay.

Discover Ideas

Because essays give you a chance to explore an idea in depth, it is important to spend time discovering ideas so you have sufficient evidence to support your thesis. If an essay assignment involves interviewing others or doing research, you can use outside sources for information. If the essay is supposed to focus on your ideas, find a topic that interests you and one that you know enough about. As you consider your topic, ask yourself two questions:

1. Does it interest me?
2. Do I know enough about it to give specific details?

Group Your Details and Find a Main Idea

After using the Discovery Activities, select the details that have energy and put them into groups. Review the groups and ask yourself:

How do these groups fit together?

Does one idea lead to another?

Is there a main idea here and points that prove it?

What do I need to add or delete to make my ideas and details connect smoothly?

Organizing ideas is similar to putting a jigsaw puzzle together, but it is more complex for two reasons. First, you may have pieces that will not fit in this essay. Second, you may need to create pieces to fill in empty spaces. Organizing ideas involves deleting pieces, adding pieces, and rearranging pieces. Be patient; discovering how the pieces fit together takes time.

Write a Thesis Statement

The thesis statement sums up the main idea of an essay. The statement introduces your topic, states the focus you will take on that topic, and often includes a forecast of the points you will make. Let's review Bertrand Russell's introductory words as an example.

Three passions, simple but overwhelmingly strong, have governed my life: the longing for love, the search for knowledge, and unbearable pity for the suffering of mankind.

- Russell states his topic: *three passions.*

- He states his focus on the topic: *have governed my life.*

- He forecasts the points he will make by naming the passions he will write about: *the longing for love, the search for knowledge, and unbearable pity for the suffering of mankind.*

PRACTICE 1   Read the following thesis statement and answer the questions that follow.

Example 1

Becoming a parent taught me to be responsible for both myself and my child.

—Student Writer

1. The writer includes the topic, the focus on the topic, and the forecast in one sentence. What is the topic?

   _____

2. What is the writer's focus on this topic?

   _____

3. The writer includes a forecast of the two points she will make. What are they?

   _____

Make Sure Your Thesis Statement Is Clear and Complete

The thesis statement needs to include both your topic and your focus on that topic.

Incorrect: How dropping out of school affects a person's future.

- The previous group of words does not make a direct statement. The word *how* needs to be deleted.

Better: Dropping out of school affects a person's future.

- That sentence makes a direct statement. It includes the topic, *dropping out of school,* and the focus on the topic, *affects a person's future.*

Best: Dropping out of school limits a person's career choices.

- This thesis statement is less vague than the previous example. The writer has replaced the vague words, *affects a person's future* with a specific effect, *limits a person's career choices.*

PRACTICE 2   Read the following three potential thesis statements and label them as *incorrect, better,* or *best*. One of them is incorrect because it is not a statement. One is better because it includes both a topic and a focus. One is a clear, direct statement that lets readers know the direction the essay will take.

    a. How to be successful.

    _____

    b. Successful people ask questions, search for answers, and learn from their mistakes.

    _____

    c. Successful people have three traits.

    _____

Make Sure the Thesis Fits Your Essay

In the beginning stages of writing an essay, the thesis is called a *working thesis*. This name suggests an important fact about writing: our ideas change in the process of writing. As you draft your essay, which we discuss later in the chapter, you may begin to write about one point and then realize you have started writing about something else. That is fine. Follow your energy. Then, when you revise your essay, change the thesis to fit the body of your essay or change the body to match your thesis. By the time you hand in your paper, the thesis statement must fit your essay. You must cover the points stated in your forecast and cover them in the same order.

PRACTICE 3   Read the following thesis statement and forecast; then answer the question that follows.

Playing basketball gave me valuable job skills. I learned to win without cutting down the loser, to lose without blaming the winner, and to work as a team.

—Student Writer

The writer states that he or she will make three points. Which do you expect to find discussed first? second? third?

_____

_____

Develop the Thesis Statement

The supporting paragraphs develop the thesis statement. Because your readers don't know what you know, you need to develop your ideas with specific evidence and present that evidence so readers can follow your train of thought.

Develop with Specific Evidence

You could develop your thesis by giving examples or reasons, discussing causes or effects, describing specific incidents, placing items in categories, explaining a process, or comparing your topic to something readers will understand.

Present Supporting Points in Topic Sentences

Begin each supporting paragraph with a sentence that tells readers what point you will make in that paragraph. Once readers know what the paragraph will be about, they can make sense of the details.

Sketch a Map

Outline your thesis and your supporting points in an Essay Map. (See Essay Map below.) Under each supporting point, list details that prove that point. If you need additional details, use the reporter's questions (*Who? What? Where? When?* and *Why?*).

   Listing specific details is necessary for two reasons. First, you will be able to see if you mistakenly repeat details. Second, you will be able to see the best order for presenting the details. Knowing the order before you begin drafting will save time: you won't have to rewrite the draft simply because the order is ineffective.

ESSAY MAP

1. Focus the main idea of the essay into one or two sentences, the thesis statement.
2. Write the supporting points as topic sentences.
3. Under each topic sentence, list the details that support that section.
4. Make sure the details are in logical order.

Thesis statement

_____

_____

Topic sentences and the details that support them

   1. Topic sentence _____

       detail _____

       detail _____

       detail _____

(*Essay Map continues on page 79.*)

2. Topic sentence _____

    detail _____

    detail _____

    detail _____

3. Topic sentence _____

    detail _____

    detail _____

    detail _____

The map is flexible. You may have fewer than three—or more than three—topic sentences. Draw extra lines if you need them.

PRACTICE 4   Read the following student writer's map and answer the questions that follow on page 80.

A STUDENT'S ESSAY MAP

Thesis statement

    Courage is a quality I have been building through three stages of my life.

1. Topic sentence: *As a child, my life was not easy.*

    detail: *Needed courage because my mother was working.*

    detail: *My father was absent.*

    detail: *I was stuck with the responsibility of being a sister and a mother.*

2. Topic sentence: *In my adolescence, the need for courage increased, not decreased.*

    detail: *Responsibilities at home increased.*

    detail: *Schoolwork added more pressure.*

    detail: *Little time to party and enjoy friends.*

3. Topic sentence: *Now that I am an adult, I have the courage I need to go to school even though the problems in my family continue.*

    detail: *I handled high school and home, so I know I can handle college and home.*

    detail: *Problems at home—still bad.*

    detail: *Surviving taught me I am strong.*

1. What is the thesis statement?

   _____

2. Read the first topic sentence. What stage of life will the writer discuss in this paragraph?

   _____

3. Read the second topic sentence. What stage of life will the writer discuss in this paragraph?

   _____

4. Read the third topic sentence. What stage of life will the writer discuss in this paragraph?

   _____

Draft Your Essay

Drafting is a trial run. All writers write many drafts—it is part of the writing process and is to be expected, not dreaded. The goal is to get your ideas and details on paper, then to work on making them increasingly clear, well developed, and logically connected.

Begin drafting after you have sketched a map or an outline and use it as a guide when writing your draft. While drafting, you may find that your ideas take a different direction from what you have listed on your outline. If the new direction seems right, follow your new train of thought. Sometimes the most creative insights occur during drafting. After you are through exploring the new direction, reread what you have written to see if your ideas flow smoothly and fit your thesis.

Sometimes ideas fall into place easily, and the connections are smooth. At other times, you will find yourself stalled, totally confused. Your ideas may feel clumped and stuck together, and you can't figure out how to put them in order. When that happens, remember that other writers go through the same experience. American poet Anne Sexton (1928–1974) explains what happens:

> It might take me ten pages of nothing, of terrible writing, and then I'll get a line, and I'll think, "That's what I mean!" What you're doing is hunting for what you mean, what you're trying to say. You don't know when you start.

Drafting is a process of discovering what we think. It is often a difficult process. Yet when you have found words for your ideas and have communicated those ideas to readers, you will feel a tremendous sense of accomplishment. Listed below are tips for getting past the difficult spots and on toward an effective essay.

Be Patient: Helpful Hints

1. Do not worry about how you will begin your essay until you have finished drafting. It is difficult and often impossible to introduce a main idea when you are not yet sure what that idea will be.

2. If one section of the essay is giving you difficulty and you are stalled, work on another section. Follow your energy and write whichever part is easiest. Often, after you've been working on something different, ideas fall into place, and you know more clearly what you need to do in that confusing section.

3. When you're stuck, when you're totally confused about what to do next, choose one or more of these options:

   - Leave your essay and pick up a blank sheet of paper. Ask yourself, "What am I trying to say?" Then, in short sentences, list what you want to say. Keep it simple.

   - Reread what you have written and take a break: do some chore that doesn't require much thinking or take a walk. Let your ideas simmer on the back burner of your mind. Then, when some insight comes, jot it down—wherever you are.

   - Talk your ideas out with someone else or talk to yourself. Often, just hearing our words spoken aloud helps clarify ideas.

4. When your mind is blank and you need more ideas, use these methods for discovering them:

   - Go back and read what you have already written to see what new ideas emerge. Reading what you wrote helps generate the energy to move on.

   - Dig. Keep asking yourself, "Why? Why is this important?" Keep pursuing the answers until you have exhausted the question.

   - Talk with someone else. Often others ask us questions, and in the discussion that follows, we uncover important ideas and details.

5. At some point during the drafting process, reread the assigned topic to make sure you are following the assignment.

Connect Your Evidence

As you draft your ideas, weave your thesis throughout your essay, so readers understand how your points support the thesis and how one point leads to the next. There are three ways you can connect your paragraphs:

1. *Use transition words.* You could "number" the separate points you are making, introducing the first point with *First,* the second point with *Second* or *Next,* and so on. Keep numbering and use *Finally* to indicate the last point.

2. *Refer to the previous point.* Tie your paragraphs together by mentioning the point you covered in the previous paragraph.

3. *Repeat key words from the thesis statement.* Connect your topic sentences to the thesis statement by repeating one or two of its key (significant) words.

Develop the Introduction

Once you have completed the first draft, it is time to plan your introductory paragraph. The introduction accomplishes two goals: it interests readers in your writing and presents your thesis. You can build interest in your thesis in a number of ways;

a list of them follows. These methods can be used alone or combined; just make sure that the introductory material leads naturally to the main idea of your essay.

1. *Begin with a general idea.* Then narrow it to a specific thesis. A general idea presents a larger perspective and sets the stage for your thesis.

2. *Describe the situation, scene, or person.* Description creates a vivid picture that readers can visualize.

3. *Begin with a short quotation.* A quotation catches the interest of readers who are then curious to see how the quotation is connected to your essay.

4. *Make a comparison.* Compare the situation you will write about to another situation, one that is familiar to the readers. When they recognize one part of your idea, they will be interested in discovering the other part of your comparison.

5. *Begin with common ground.* Referring to something that you and your readers have in common helps them identify with you.

6. *Begin with a question.* Because a question needs an answer, readers are curious and want to continue reading.

Write the Conclusion

When you can see where your points are leading, consider your conclusion. A conclusion creates a sense of completion and helps readers understand the significance of your ideas. When you are ready to write the conclusion, do two things: reread your draft and then reread your introductory paragraph. Write a conclusion that circles back to the beginning and ties your essay into a unified whole. You could use any of the following tactics:

1. *Share an insight.* Reflect more thoroughly on all you have written and conclude with an observation, reflection, or understanding that readers are now able to understand because they have read your essay.

2. *Return to an idea in your introduction.* If, for example, you began your essay with a question, your conclusion is an effective place to answer that question. If you began with a problem, the conclusion is a good place to summarize the consequences or suggest a solution.

3. *Use a quotation.* Quotations and familiar sayings are effective if they apply to what you have written. If you find an appropriate quotation or saying, make sure your writing builds toward it. You could include words from that quotation earlier in the writing, so that when readers read your conclusion, they realize you have been building toward it.

PRACTICE 5   Read the following sketch outline of a student writer's essay and answer the questions that follow.

Introductory Paragraph

After we struggled through the first ten years of marriage, life began to settle down for us. But the security and peace lasted for only a short season. The financial floodgates soon opened.

Paragraph 2

The first floodgate opened when my husband decided to add an addition to our home.

Paragraph 3

The second floodgate opened when at forty-two, I was pregnant with child number six.

Paragraph 4

The third floodgate opened when I called a company to fix the furnace.

Concluding Paragraph

These were the main floodgates. Other debris rushed through the opened gates: plumbing, medical, and maintenance problems. Yet, through it all, there was also a bright side. We have a bigger house. We now have another laughing, bubbling voice to fill our bigger home. And we have a new, more energy-efficient furnace to keep us warm. The floodgates seem to have closed, and we are hoping for a long settling-down season.

—Student Writer

1. The writer includes two sentences of background information on her marriage and then presents the thesis statement. What is the thesis statement?

   _____

2. Paragraphs 2–4 support the thesis. What key words in the topic sentences connect these paragraphs to the thesis statement?

   _____

In the conclusion, the writer includes an insight that readers would not have understood before reading the essay: the bright side of the floodgates. In summarizing the bright side, she refers to previous paragraphs.

3. To what paragraph does *bigger house* refer?

   _____

4. To what paragraph does *laughing, bubbling voice* refer?

   _____

5. To what paragraph does *new, energy-efficient furnace* refer?

   _____

Revise Your Essay

After you have written your first draft, it is time to imagine that you are a stranger reading your essay for the first time. Looking at your essay from your readers' point of view will help you decide what improvements to make with the next draft.

Revising is often confused with editing. Revising and editing are two different ways of improving your essay. *Editing* is finding and correcting the smaller details: spelling, word choice, and punctuation. *Revising* involves looking at the big picture: your ideas and how they are developed and connected.

When your ideas are well developed and connected, your essay will have the three elements of effective writing: unity, coherence, and support. These three elements are explained here, followed by a checklist to use during your final revision.

Revise for Unity

The word *unity* comes from the prefix *uni* which means "one," as in *unit* and *union*. When your essay has unity, all the parts are united. The points and details are related to your thesis statement.

The thesis is one of the most important parts to check. When you began drafting, you began with a *working thesis*. We have noted that often, during the process of drafting, the direction of the essay changes. If that has happened, you may need to change the thesis to match the body of your essay or change the body to match the thesis.

A thesis makes a promise of what the essay will be about. If you state that you will make three points, make sure you cover those three points. Also, make sure your supporting paragraphs follow the same order presented in the thesis statement. For instance, suppose you state that you will cover points 1, 2, and 3. As you draft these points, you may find that the best order is 2, 1, and 3. That's fine. Simply go back and change the order in your thesis statement to match the order in the essay.

Your essay will have unity when

1. your thesis fits the body of your essay.

2. the main point of each supporting paragraph develops your thesis.

3. the details in each paragraph support the topic sentence.

4. your conclusion refers back to your introduction.

Revise for Coherence

The word *coherence* comes from the word *cohere,* which means "to stick together." When your essay has coherence, the ideas and details "stick together" because the connections are clear. Make sure you have connected your evidence in one or more of these ways:

Use transition words.

Refer to the previous point.

Repeat key words from the thesis statement.

Revise for Support

Readers are convinced by specific evidence. Make sure you have made your points vivid and concrete by developing *enough* evidence, such as examples and reasons, and by including *specific* details.

PRACTICE 6 Individually or in groups, read the following essay and discuss your answers to the questions that follow.

Credit Card Plague

1   In our culture of convenient credit, credit card companies rake in billions as they encourage us to "Charge now, pay later." I bought into their slogan and took it to new heights. I charged today, tomorrow, and the day after. I lived to "charge now" and disregarded "pay later." Credit card debt soon became a major obstacle in my life.

2   Credit card debt became an obstacle the day I went searching for credit. I first applied for department store cards and was turned down. Then, when walking past a local bank, I spotted an encouraging sign for credit card applications. It was downhill from there. The bank took a chance and gave me a card, but they also gave me a twenty-one percent annual rate. I was young, naive, and eager to spend. Before my urge to spend was gone, I had spent $400.00 over my $1,400.00 limit. Other credit cards began arriving in the mail, and I pursued their promises too. My debt grew.

3   Buried in debt, I put my initial goal of being financially independent on hold. Each month I set aside a certain amount of money for rent, food, and credit card debt. There was little left for clothes and entertainment. My debt was stifling me.

4   After living this lifestyle for a few years, I finally made a decision to take charge of my life and get out of debt. I knew how to get into debt. Now I had to learn how to get out of debt. The first key is to exercise common sense. I realized that my $30.00 shirt actually cost $37.00 by the time the bank added their charges. The second key is to exercise discipline. I eliminated all unnecessary expenses, made a budget, and closely monitored my spending habits. The last key to getting out of debt is to escape the heavy interest charges. I started making large payments on my debt, which lowered my monthly finance charges. Using common sense, setting limits, staying within those limits, and paying now instead of later have helped me achieve my goal. I am finally financially independent.

5   For many years, I allowed credit card debt to plague my life. I went searching for the easy way out and found trouble. It has been an uphill battle, but I have made it. I have learned an important lesson: Pay now; charge later.

—Student Writer

1. The writer begins with four sentences of background information that lead to the thesis. What is the thesis statement?

_____

2. Two common ways of connecting the topic sentences are repeating a key word in the thesis and mentioning the point made in the previous paragraph. In paragraph 4, which method(s) does the writer use? What words provide the connection?

_____

_____

3. How does the writer develop the topic sentence in paragraph 4? What specific details are included that make that evidence convincing?

_____

_____

_____

_____

_____

4. In the conclusion, the writer summarizes the lesson learned. What key words from the introductory paragraph does the writer include in the lesson?

_____

_____

Guidelines for Revising Essays

In addition to the Author's Chair, which appears on the inside back cover of this book, the following questions will help you make sure your essay has unity, coherence, and adequate support.

Guidelines for Revising Essays

Read your thesis statement.

1. Does it state clearly what your essay will be about?

2. Does your thesis match the body? Specifically, does every point support your thesis? Have you covered everything you promised to cover?

Read the first sentence of each paragraph.

1. Is the first sentence of each paragraph a topic sentence? In other words, does it tell readers what that paragraph is about?

2. Do your topic sentences connect to one another or to the thesis?

3. Read the topic sentences one right after the other. Do they summarize your major points? Do they take readers where your thesis statement promised to take them?

Read the whole essay.

1. Have you included enough specific evidence to make your thesis convincing?

2. Have you left any gaps where readers will not understand how one idea leads to the next? Would a transition word or transition sentence that refers to a previous point clarify how your ideas are connected?

3. Do the details in each paragraph support the topic sentence? Did you take any unannounced side trips?

4. Have you included enough specific details to make your point clear and vivid?

Read the conclusion.

1. Does the conclusion flow from the essay?

2. Does your conclusion refer to your introduction, giving readers a sense of completeness?

Review: Writing a More Developed Paper: The Essay

- Give the main idea of the essay in the thesis statement.

- Develop your thesis in the supporting paragraphs, beginning each paragraph with a topic sentence.

- Connect the paragraphs to one another or to the thesis.

- Connect the ideas within each paragraph.

- Write a conclusion.

- Use the *Guidelines for Revising Essays* on page 86 and this page.

- Use the *Guidelines for Editing* on page 67.

- Proofread your essay, giving it one final reading. Read it aloud slowly, checking for words left out and for handwriting or typing errors.

 REVIEW PRACTICE Individually or in groups, read the following essay and discuss your answers to the questions that follow.

I'm Done Complaining

1   Don't find fault. Find a remedy. These words of Henry Ford fit me perfectly. I was always finding fault, always complaining about something, and I never tried to fix it. Last spring, my mother had a long talk with me. Surprisingly, I listened and realized that complaining all the time fixes nothing. If I want to solve a problem, I have to put in the effort to solve it. There are three areas of my life where I once found fault but am now finding remedies.

2   I once found fault with alcoholism. A person who is close to me is an alcoholic. I always turned on him in anger. When he was drunk, he said unkind things. I would respond by egging him on, making him even angrier. Even when he was sober, I was angry, always blaming him for spending too much money on alcohol. I repeatedly called him a loser, never thinking about what he was feeling or wondering why he was drinking so much. Now, instead of complaining, I am finding a remedy. I am going to Al-Anon.*

---

*Al-Anon is a support group for friends and family members of an alcoholic.

3   I used to continually complain about being broke. This past year, I did not realize how much money I was spending. I opened the bills, put them in a pile, and ignored them. I blamed my money problems on my parents, my friends, the economy, and myself. I have now found a remedy. I decided that I am too young to be in debt, and I have begun a second job.

4   I also used to find fault with school. I griped about my boring classes and criticized my demanding teachers. Graduating from high school was a relief. But after working a series of part-time jobs, I saw that I was going nowhere. I realized that my attitude about school was the real problem, and the remedy was changing my attitude. I am now a first-semester community college student and see school as more than boring and demanding. It is my passport to the future. I am determined to succeed and make something of my life.

5   Don't find fault. Find a remedy. Those are my borrowed words of wisdom. When problems in my life look as if they will never be fixed, I do something about them. With a little effort, things can be changed. Solving problems instead of complaining about them is making me a better person.

—Student Writer

1. In the introductory paragraph, the writer includes the words of Henry Ford, explains how those words apply to the writer's life, and then includes a forecast of how this essay will be developed. What sentence gives us that forecast?

   _____

   _____

2. The writer found fault in three areas of life. What are those three areas?

   _____

3. The writer states in the thesis that for each fault, there is now a remedy. What is the remedy for each fault?

   _____

   _____

   _____

4. How does the writer's conclusion give readers the sense that the essay has come full circle?

   _____

   _____

   _____

   _____

Essay-Writing Ideas

Additional ideas for essays are listed in Chapter 25.

Writing Idea 1

Write about one of your strengths—one of the qualities that has helped you survive or succeed. This assignment is related to what Career Directions, a career counseling company, does for its clients. A consultant at Career Directions asks the client to write about accomplishments to date. The consultant and the client then sit down together, read the accomplishments, and determine what strengths or qualities have made them possible. Knowing your strengths is important before going into an interview because companies often ask job seekers what they can offer the company.

Begin by freewriting about something you have accomplished. You could choose, for instance, an accomplishment in school, in a previous job (paid or unpaid), in sports, or in a relationship. Consider such things as getting along with someone difficult, solving a problem, or working your way through a difficult situation. Then share your ideas in small groups and discuss what qualities helped you succeed.

Option for organizing ideas: Choose one quality as your thesis. For example, your thesis might be *I am determined, I am responsible,* or *I am a team worker.* Begin your essay by stating the thesis. In the body of the essay, support the thesis by describing one or more accomplishments, explaining how these achievements reveal your quality.

Writing Idea 2

Choose a current controversial issue at college, at work, or in your community. Use the Discovery Activities to explore people's various positions on this issue. In your thesis statement, name the issue and your position on it. Here are some possible topics:

a. Should the tradition of giving grades in college be abolished?

b. Should community service be a requirement for high school graduation?

c. Should parents be held legally and financially responsible for their children's actions?

d. Who should be responsible for teaching morals and values: families, schools, religious institutions, communities?

Option for organizing ideas: In the first section of your essay, write about one or more opposing positions, to make readers aware that you recognize other views. Then explain your own position, using topic sentences to state your reasons. Make sure you use specific details to support your argument.

Writing Idea 3

Write about an experience that has affected your life. You could choose, for example, marriage, divorce, becoming a parent, going to college, getting or losing a job, finding or losing a friend, the death of a friend or relative, an injury, or an accomplishment.

Option for organizing ideas: In your thesis statement, name the experience and what you learned from it. For example, you might write, *Going to college has taught me the importance of being organized.* In the first section of your essay, describe the experience so it is real for readers. To do this, imagine the situation: what do you see and hear? Readers need to understand what happened in order to appreciate its effects on you. In the second section, explain how the experience affected you, including what it taught you.

Writing Idea 4

People throughout time have needed community, a group of supportive people. Look at some part of American culture (families, neighborhoods, groups) and decide where community either exists or is lacking. In your essay, discuss the importance of community and how it affects people.

Option for organizing ideas: You could take either a positive or a negative approach. If you take a positive one, state in your thesis where the experience of community is found. If you take a negative approach, state in your thesis that our culture lacks places where people can experience a sense of community. Whatever approach you take, develop the first section of your essay by describing the situation. Develop the second section by explaining how people are affected.

Writing Idea 5

Who has made a difference in your life? Most of us are not immediately affected by public figures highlighted in the media. Instead, we gain valuable insights from everyday people in our lives. Write about someone who made or is making a difference in your life. Describe that person and give enough background information to help readers understand the time, the situation, and the reason why this person was or is important to you. In your thesis statement, name the person and state the difference that he or she has made in your life.

Option for organizing ideas: In the first section of your essay, describe *how* that person has been important. Give specific details, so readers can see and hear what took place. In the second section, explain *why* this person has been important, and what you have learned about yourself, others, or life in general.

Part 2

Writing Sentences

Chapter 6

Writing Core Sentences

- ◆ Subjects and Verbs
- ◆ Core Sentences
- ◆ *Focus on Fragments*

Subjects and Verbs

Talking consists of stringing ideas together. Writing involves putting ideas into different structures, called sentences. Every sentence has two essential parts: a subject and a verb. When we talk, we have a subject and a verb in mind, but we don't always state them. We might say, "Down the street," and the person we are talking with would know exactly what we mean. When we write, we need to state who is down the street or what is happening down the street. The subject and the verb connect to explain *who is doing what* or *what is happening*.

Subjects

The subjects of sentences can be either nouns or pronouns. Pronouns are words used in place of nouns, words such as *he, she, it, we, you,* and *they.* Nouns are words that name people, places, and things. An easy way to discover nouns is by saying the word *the* first. Any word that makes sense after *the* can be used as a noun.

Nouns		
class	movie	truth
reward	agreement	crowd
child	opportunity	astronomers
performance	jeans	cafeteria
computer	friend	shoes
music	college	decision

PRACTICE 1   Think of words that make sense after the word *the*. Add five nouns to the preceding table of nouns.

Verbs

A verb makes a point about the subject of a sentence, often explaining what that subject is doing, was doing, or will be doing.

David *thinks*.	Scientists *are investigating*.
She *will celebrate*.	We *were wondering*.
Musicians *practice*.	The visitor *stayed*.

Here is one quick way to discover verbs. Say, "I like to. . . ." A word that fills the slot will be a verb.

Verbs					
listen	bring	inspire	ask	tell	understand
see	spend	try	collect	go	wander
eat	protect	decide	wear	ignore	sing

PRACTICE 2   Say to yourself, "I like to. . ." and fill in the blank. That word will be a verb. Add five verbs to the preceding table.

Verbs are flexible words: they change form to show time. Take a thought and put *yesterday* or *tomorrow* in front of it. The word that has to change will be the verb.

Janice <u>washes</u> the car.
Yesterday Janice <u>washed</u> the car.
Tomorrow Janice <u>will wash</u> the car.

PRACTICE 3   The following sentences are written in the present tense (to show present time). Place *tomorrow* in front of each one and change the verb that needs to be changed. The first one has been done for you; the helping verb *will* has been added.

EXAMPLE: Patrick appreciates our kindness.

Tomorrow Patrick will appreciate our kindness.

1. The students memorize formulas for the algebra test.

2. That station plays my favorite music.

3. We rent videos for inexpensive entertainment.

_____

_____

PRACTICE 4　Place *yesterday* in front of each sentence and change the word that needs to be changed. That word will be a verb. The first one has been done for you; a *-d* or *-ed* ending has been added.

EXAMPLE:　Patrick appreciates our kindness.

Yesterday Patrick appreciated our kindness. _____

1. The students memorize formulas for the algebra test.

_____

_____

2. That station plays my favorite music.

_____

_____

3. We rent videos for inexpensive entertainment.

_____

_____

When you added *tomorrow*, you changed the time from present tense to future tense by adding *will*. When you added *yesterday*, you changed the time from present tense to past tense by adding *-d* or *-ed* to the end of the verb. Tense, as we have noted, shows time.

Core Sentences

Subjects and verbs connect to form core sentences. Sometimes our sentences are just bare bones in a skeleton.

Skeleton: <u>Children</u> <u>play</u>.

Most of the time our ideas are more descriptive, and we include additional details (modifying words) around the subject and the verb.

Skeleton with detail: The neighborhood <u>children</u> <u>play</u> basketball at the community center.

- In the two previous sentences, as in future examples, the subject is underlined once, and the verb is underlined twice.

- Notice that in both sentences, the subject is *children* and the verb is *play*.

The modifying words do not change the skeleton of a core sentence. Every sentence has a skeleton consisting of a subject and a verb.

> People gathered.
>
> People from all walks of life gathered in Washington, D.C. for the celebration.

Sentences often have more than one subject and verb.

More than one subject

> Video surveillance and security cameras record the bank's transactions.

More than one verb

> The photographer looked beyond physical appearances and revealed the spirit of the land and people.

More than one subject and more than one verb

> The pediatrician and the intern diagnosed the illness and prescribed antibiotics.

Three Structures

Subjects and verbs can connect in any of three different structures. These three structures form the skeleton of all core sentences.

1) Subject "is" something. In this structure, the verb links the subject to words that describe the subject. An important linking verb is the verb *be* with its most common forms: *am, is, are, was, were, has been*, and *have been*.

> Celina was happy.
>
> Computers are efficient.

2) Subject does the action. In this structure, the verb expresses what action the subject performs.

> Tiffany smiles.
>
> The telephone rang.

3) Subject receives the action. In this structure, the subject is receiving, not doing the action. Because the subject is passive, this pattern is called the passive voice.

> Greg has been accepted.
>
> The engines were tuned.

PRACTICE 5   In the following sentences, underline the subject once and the verb twice.

Subject "is" something

1. Maps are available at the ecology center.

2. Yellowstone National Park is one of America's most valuable natural resources.

3. Three companies were leaders in science and technology.

4. Walter has been a loyal friend since grade school.

Subject does the action

5. Sunglasses protect eyes from ultraviolet radiation.

6. The truck is pulling the stranded semi out of the ditch.

7. We will listen to the weather channel for today's forecast.

8. The report predicted the consequences of greenhouse gases on global warming.

Subject receives the action

9. The concert has been rescheduled for next weekend.

10. Commercial planes are flown by experienced pilots.

11. The speech and the discussion were televised on national news.

12. Two bills were passed by slight margins.

Complete Subjects and Predicates

In the preceding sentences, we concentrated on the skeleton of a sentence. It is also important to look at the words surrounding (modifying) the subject and verb. The subject and its modifying words are called the *complete subject*. The verb and its modifying words are called the *complete predicate*.

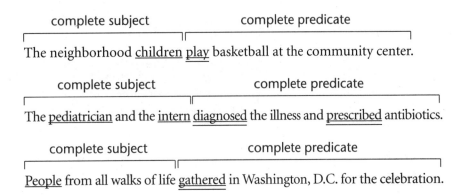

Complete subjects and predicates connect to explain *who is doing what* or *what is happening*. As you edit your writing, make sure each sentence has these two parts.

PRACTICE 6   Draw a line between the complete subject and the complete predicate. The first two have been done for you.

EXAMPLE: Adults and children | visited the art gallery.

The jet engine | was inspected for faulty wiring.

1. Free summer concerts contribute to the cultural life of the city.

2. The institute offers classes in early childhood development and education.

3. Their salaries are determined by job performance.

4. Safety and efficiency are top priorities for airlines.

5. Community residents recognize both the problem and the solution.

6. The tornado peeled up more than 130 feet of asphalt highway and dropped it 650 feet away.
7. Car-pooling and public transportation will relieve traffic congestion and reduce air pollution.
8. Our new manager has been sympathetic.
9. The State Department restricted the export of satellites for two years.
10. The finance committee for the Board of Education met for five hours and planned next year's budget.

Connecting Subjects and Predicates

Complete subjects and complete predicates connect directly. Do not separate them with a comma. When we talk, we often pause after the subject. When writing, do not separate subjects and predicates with a comma.

Correct:	*His determination has carried him through many tough situations.*
Incorrect:	His determination, has carried him through many tough situations.

Correct:	*Carlos and his family showed me that honor is more important than winning.*
Incorrect:	Carlos and his family, showed me that honor is more important than winning.

Focus on Fragments

A sentence needs both a subject and a predicate. If one of these parts is missing, you will have only part of a sentence, known as a sentence fragment. Here are examples of three common types of sentence fragments.

1. Fragments that contain no subject

   Fragment: Listened to their children's concerns and answered their questions.

   Sentence: <u>Parents</u> listened to their children's concerns and answered their questions.

2. Fragments that contain no verb

   Fragment: The most difficult decisions now behind us.

   Sentence: The most difficult decisions <u>are</u> now behind us.

3. Fragments that contain neither a subject nor verb

   Fragment: How to balance responsibilities at work, at home, and at school.

   Sentence: <u>We</u> <u>learned</u> how to balance responsibilities at work, at home, and at school.

If fragments have been a problem for you in the past:

Look for the subject and the predicate. Read each of your sentences to make sure it answers the question *Who is doing what?* or *What is happening?*

Begin at the end of your paper and read it sentence by sentence. When you read your written ideas in reverse order, you can see more clearly groups of words that do not state a complete thought because they lack either a subject or a predicate.

PRACTICE 7 Individually or in groups, rewrite the following fragments so they are sentences.

1. People with a positive attitude.

_____

_____

_____

2. Activities such as after-school sports.

_____

_____

_____

3. At the intersection of Main Street and Lincoln Avenue.

_____

_____

_____

4. Appreciated our comments and suggestions.

_____

_____

_____

5. Not only physically but emotionally.

_____

_____

_____

Review: Writing Core Sentences

- Check your sentences to make sure they have two parts. You can look for the skeletal structure and identify the subject and verb, or you can look for the complete subject and predicate. Use whichever method is easier for you.

- Do not separate complete subjects from predicates; do not insert a comma.

REVIEW PRACTICE 1   Create five sentences by connecting a complete subject with an appropriate complete predicate from the list that follows. Then write those sentences. (Make sure there is no comma between the subject and predicate.)

Complete Subject	Complete Predicate
1. Volunteers in the city and suburbs	a. shared the joy of Andrea's graduation.
2. An explosion and a fire	b. ran out of fuel 300 feet from the finish line.
3. Democrats and Republicans	c. will search for a new record producer.
4. One of the race car drivers	d. have raised $2.1 million for a medical center.
5. The producer and songwriter	e. debated regulations for managed-care organizations.
6. Friends and family	f. ripped through the single-story wood-frame home.

REVIEW PRACTICE 2   The following paragraph is an advertisement for the American Diabetes Association. Like many advertisements, it includes fragments to give it a conversational tone. As an advertisement, it is effective; as formal writing, it would be ineffective. Circle the fragments.

Augusta and Sam Hopkins have lived through 43 years of marriage. And lots of physical changes. But lately, Augusta has been showing signs of blurred vision. Chronic fatigue. Numbness in her fingers and toes. She thinks she's just getting on in years. The truth is that Augusta has diabetes. The problem is that she doesn't know it. Just like 8 million other Americans. You could be one of them. If you're over 45, underactive, overweight and have a family history of diabetes, you could have it and not know it. If you suffer from extreme thirst, frequent urination, intense hunger, sores that heal slowly, or any of Augusta's symptoms, you could have diabetes and should see your doctor. Immediately. You need to know more. Early detection could save your life.

—Adapted from *Time*

EXTRA CHALLENGE Draw a line between the complete subjects and complete predicates in the following excerpt from *U.S. News and World Report:*

A newborn baby's brain develops with phenomenal speed. Billions of nerve cells grow rapidly and form connections. These brain cell connections approach the level of an adult brain by the time the baby is two years old. One quadrillion brain cell connections have been formed by the time the child is three. The three year old child's brain connections are the keys to creativity and intelligence in later life.

—Adapted from Mortimer Zuckerman,
"Attention Must Be Paid"

Chapter 7

Writing with Verbs

- ◆ Verb Overview
- ◆ Present Tense
- ◆ Past Tense
- ◆ Helping Verbs
- ◆ Particular Verbs
- ◆ *Focus on Apostrophes*
- ◆ *Focus on Fragments*

Verb Overview

At first, on that November night in 1966, Victoria Drowns thought she was going insane. She *pressed* her face against the window of the train and again *stared* upward as the Texas landscape *flashed* by. No, it was real. The sky *was exploding*. There seemed to be no other conclusion: it was the end of the world. Looking around the compartment, she saw that everyone was asleep. She *hesitated*. What's the correct protocol for the end of the world? Do you wake people up or let them sleep through it? Just then the conductor came by, and together they watched the bewildering exhibition until dawn *erased* the show. They had witnessed one of the most amazing celestial events of all—a meteor storm, a spectacle surpassing any other. (Italics added.)

—Bob Berman, "Meteor Storm"

Vivid verbs, verbs such as *pressed, stared, flashed, was exploding, hesitated,* and *erased,* add valuable description to writing. Verbs carry power, and it is important to use them correctly.

We have seen that verbs have different tenses (pages 94–95), such as present, past, and future, to indicate different time situations. We change tense by using the appropriate form of a verb. Except for the verb *be,* all English verbs have five forms.

REGULAR VERB FORMS

1st form Base Form	2nd form Past Tense	3rd form Past Participle	4th form Present Participle	5th form -s Form
talk	talked	talked	talking	talks
listen	listened	listened	listening	listens

A verb is *regular* when its past tense and past participle are formed by adding *-d* or *-ed* to the base form. (The verbs *talk* and *listen* are regular verbs.) A verb is *irregular* when its past tense and past participle are not formed by adding *-d* or *-ed.* (The verbs *eat* and *sing* are irregular verbs.) We focus on irregular verbs in Chapter 8.

IRREGULAR VERB FORMS

1st form Base Form	2nd form Past Tense	3rd form Past Participle	4th form Present Participle	5th form -s Form
eat	ate	eaten	eating	eats
sing	sang	sung	singing	sings

Present Tense

The present tense refers to events that are happening right now or to actions that occur often. The present tense uses the base form and the *-s* form. Using the correct form of the verb with each subject is called *subject-verb agreement.*

PRESENT TENSE VERB CHART

	Singular	Plural
1st person	I work. Michael and I work.	We work.
2nd person	You work.	You work.
3rd person	He, she, it works. Robert works. Marie works.	They work. Robert and Marie work.
	The student works.	Students work.
	The computer works.	Computers work.

Whenever the subject of a present tense verb is *he, she,* or *it,* the verb ends in *-s.* This means not only the pronoun *he,* but any male's name; not only *she,* but any female's name; not only *it,* but anything that is an it. In other words,

When the subject is a singular noun (one), the present tense verb ends in *-s.*

When the subject is a plural noun (more than one), the verb does *not* end in *-s.*

PRACTICE 1   Write the correct present tense form of the verb in the blank. The first one has been done for you.

EXAMPLE: Jason agrees with us.   Jason and Valerie _agree_ with us.

1. This diagram reveals.   Those diagrams _____.

2. I understand people.   Albert and I _____ people.

3. Programs offer guidelines.   One program _____ guidelines.

4. Memories remain.   A single memory _____.

5. Debra asks questions.   Debra and Greg _____ questions.

PRACTICE 2   Write the correct present tense form of each verb in the blank. The first one has been done for you.

EXAMPLE:

save: I _save_ money because it helps me feel secure. My aunt _saves_

because she wants to invest in real estate. Alfred and Alice _save_

because they want to take a vacation.

1. live: I _____ across the street from a factory. He _____ on a farm, far

from the city noise. We both _____ in neighborhoods where people care

about one another.

2. see: People often _____ only what they are looking for. Yet we all have

the ability to _____ beneath the surface and understand other human

beings. For example, my sister _____ beneath her friend's negative atti-

tude and recognizes a caring, sensitive person.

3. give: The nurse in the intensive care unit _____ full attention to the

patients. The heart monitor and electrocardiogram _____ continuous

reports on patients' vital signs. This attention _____ the patients'

families peace of mind.

4. look: Frank _____ toward the future, but Nicole _____ back to the past. As they work on their relationship, they both _____ for ways to enjoy the present.

5. stand: During the week, the last-minute shopper _____ in the grocery store checkout lane and then _____ in line at the gas pump before heading home. On weekends, moviegoers _____ in lines for tickets and popcorn. For both the daily necessities and weekend entertainment, we all need patience as we _____ in line.

Past Tense

The past tense refers to events that have already happened. Writing in the past tense involves adding *-d* or *-ed* to the base form of regular verbs: *dreamed, lived, sneezed.* When we talk, we may not always pronounce these endings. When writing, it is important to spell past tense verbs correctly by including the *-d* or *-ed* ending.

PRACTICE 3 Add a *-d* or *-ed* verb ending to each verb in parentheses. Write the correct past tense form in the blank.

My high school goal was to meet the track sectional qualifications and participate in the state track meet. As a high school sophomore and junior, I ran the sectionals, but I always _____ (choke) and failed to make the time qualifications. I never made it to state. But my senior year was different. When my race was _____ (announce), I _____ (proceed) to the line. The starter _____ (yell) his commands, _____ (fire) his gun, and _____ (ignite) the team on a race against time. Suddenly I _____ (blank) out. No thoughts were in my head. I just ran. I was numb until I _____ (reach) the finish line. I thought I had cracked under pressure again because I saw others finish before me. But then I _____ (realize) my running time. I was in total awe. In order to qualify for the state meet, I had to clock a time of 10.8 or better. I had done just that. I was going to state.

—Student Writer

Helping Verbs

Helping verbs include the various forms of *be*, *do*, and *have*, and the words *may, might, must, can, could, will, would, shall,* and *should.* As we look at writing with these helping verbs, let's review the five forms of a verb.

Base Form	Past Tense	Past Participle	Present Participle	-s Form
dance	danced	danced	dancing	dances

Helping verbs can be added to the *base form*, the *past participle*, and the *present participle.* Here are the most common helping verb and verb form combinations:

1. *Base form:* dance

   When helping verbs are combined with the base form, the base form does not change.

may dance	do dance	can dance	will dance	shall dance
might dance	does dance	could dance	would dance	should dance
must dance	did dance			

2. *Past participle:* danced

has danced	could have danced
have danced	should have danced
had danced	would have danced

3. *Present participle:* dancing

is dancing	has been dancing	could have been dancing
are dancing	have been dancing	should have been dancing
was dancing	had been dancing	would have been dancing
were dancing		

Particular Verbs

We have reviewed the five forms of the verb and how those forms combine with helping verbs to produce a variety of tenses. Now we will focus on writing with particular verbs that can be trouble spots for writers.

The Verb Be

The verb *be* is perhaps the most challenging verb in English because it has so many irregular forms. The verb *be* can stand alone as the main verb in a sentence, or it can be used as a helping verb.

Present Tense

THE VERB *BE*: PRESENT TENSE		
	Singular	**Plural**
1st person	I am	we are
2nd person	you are	you are
3rd person	he, she, it (person or thing) is	they (people or things) are

PRACTICE 4   Add present tense forms of the verb *be* to the following paragraph. Refer to the chart to make sure the verb you use agrees with the subject. The first answer has been supplied for you.

Our college now has an advisory council for campus concerns. I __*am*__

a student representative on this committee. Student representatives

_____ essential to the decision-making process because we understand

the needs of the student body. Our immediate concern _____ the need

for efficient registration. Our other concerns _____ the overcrowded

parking lot, expensive cafeteria food, and bookstore hours and prices.

—Student Writer

Past Tense

THE VERB *BE*: PAST TENSE		
	Singular	**Plural**
1st person	I was	we were
2nd person	you were	you were
3rd person	he, she, it (person or thing) was	they (people or things) were

PRACTICE 5   Change the verbs you added in the previous exercise to past tense by using past tense forms for the verb *be*. The first answer has been supplied for you.

Last year our college had an advisory council for campus concerns. I

__*was*__ a student representative on this committee. Student representatives

_____ essential to the decision-making process because we understood

the needs of the student body. Our immediate concern _____ the need

for efficient registration. Our other concerns _____ the overcrowded

parking lot, expensive cafeteria food, and bookstore hours and prices.

—Student Writer

The Verb *Be* as a Helping Verb

The verb *be* can also be used as a helping verb. As a helping verb, it has the same forms you saw listed in the boxes for "present tense" and "past tense."

The verb *be* as a helping verb: present tense form
> I *am thinking*.
> Jerome *is considering* a career change.
> We *are installing* new software on the computer.

The verb *be* as a helping verb: past tense form
> The engine *was running* smoothly.
> Charles *was reviewing* his speech when his name was called.
> The drivers *were waiting* for the traffic to clear.

PRACTICE 6   Fill in the correct present tense form of *be*: *am, is,* or *are*. The first one has been done for you.

EXAMPLE: The finalist __is__ concentrating on winning.

1. You _____ running ahead of schedule.

2. Jazz _____ attracting people of all ages to the concert hall.

3. Chris _____ thinking about the work he needs to finish.

4. Many companies _____ placing more emphasis on balancing work and family life.

5. The Secretary of State _____ calling the encounter a turning point in the negotiations.

PRACTICE 7   Fill in the correct past tense form: *was* or *were*. The first one has been done for you.

EXAMPLE: American economic growth __was__ predicted to continue.

1. The neighbors _____ trying to control the fire when the fire department arrived.

2. I understand why you _____ hurrying this morning.

3. The qualifying race _____ canceled because of the rain.

4. The company president _____ offering opportunities for employees to broaden their skills.

5. American and European investors _____ looking for potential profits in foreign investments.

PRACTICE 8   The following paragraph contains one error in using *be* as a helping verb. Correct that error.

> "Are you responsible?" was the first question that my boss asked when
> he interviewed me. At first I was surprised by his abrupt question, but
> then I realized that he were giving me a message. He demanded nothing
> but the best from his employees. I was not intimidated because I was up
> to the task. I, too, wanted to give him a message. "Yes," I said. "I am where
> I am today because I am determined, trustworthy, and responsible."
>
> —Student Writer

The Verb Have

The verb *have* can stand alone as the main verb in a sentence, or it can be used as a helping verb. Notice the irregular spelling of the third person singular form, *has*.

THE VERB *HAVE*: PRESENT TENSE

	Singular	Plural
1st person	I have	we have
2nd person	you have	you have
3rd person	he, she, it (person or thing) has	they (people or things) have

The verb *have* can stand alone as the verb in a sentence.

> Charles *has* a positive attitude.
> Charlene and Scott *have* tickets for the game.

The verb *have* can also be used as a helping verb.

> Louis *has lived* here for a long time.
> They *have walked* with me.

Often the word *not* or the contraction of *not* (*n't*) is included with a form of *have*.

> Shandra *has not* (*hasn't*) ignored our advice.
> Our hopes for the future *have not* (*haven't*) changed.

PRACTICE 9   In the following sentences, underline the correct verbs. The first one has been done for you.

EXAMPLE: Effective advertising (<u>has,</u> have) attracted first-time customers to the outlet.

1. Javier and his brother (has, have) plans to start a business in July.

2. We (has, have) two weeks to register for the summer term.

3. The car (has, have) not been vacuumed since last summer.

4. We (has, have) struggled, but we (has, have) accomplished our goals.

5. His strong moral conscience (has, have) inspired all of us to be honest.

The Verb Do

The verb *do* can stand alone as the main verb of a sentence, or it can be used as a helping verb. Notice the irregular spelling of the third person singular form, *does*.

THE VERB *DO*: PRESENT TENSE		
	Singular	**Plural**
1st person	I do	we do
2nd person	you do	you do
3rd person	he, she, it (person or thing) does	they (people or things) do

The verb *do* can stand alone as the verb in a sentence.

Terry *does* his homework early in the morning.
Ed and Tina *do* their homework late at night.

The verb *do* can also be used as a helping verb.

Jerald *does think* about us often.
We *do wonder* what tomorrow will bring.

When writing in the past tense, change the helping verb *do* to *did,* but do not change the base form of the verb.

The mechanic *did overcharge* us, but he apologized and reimbursed us.
We *did see* the sign; we just could not read it.

Often the word *not* or the contraction of *not (n't)* is included with a form of *do.*

Sheila *does not (doesn't)* like lima beans.
State senators *did not (didn't)* vote on the bill presented in February.

PRACTICE 10   In the following sentences, underline the correct verb. The first one has been done for you.

EXAMPLE: My sister (don't, <u>doesn't</u>) like to be awakened by an alarm clock.

1. They (do, does) their homework with the TV blaring.

2. On weekends, our friends (do, does) volunteer work for nonprofit organizations.

3. It (do, does) not matter what gets in the way; I will succeed.

4. The musicians (don't, doesn't) expect their contract demands to be disputed.

5. Although she may be late for the ceremony, she (do, does) plan to attend.

Fixed-Form Helping Verbs

The following helping verbs are called fixed-form because they do not change form. Whether the subject is singular or plural, the verb stays the same. Therefore, do not add *-s*.

THE FIXED-FORM HELPING VERBS	
3 *m's*	**3 pairs**
may	can, could
might	will, would
must	shall, should

One friend *may stay*; many friends *may stay*.

One musician *might play*; many musicians *might play*.

One employee *will transfer*; many employees *will transfer*.

- Notice how the fixed-form helping verbs are the same for both singular and plural subjects.

- Notice that neither the fixed-form helping verb nor the base form ends in *-s*.

PRACTICE 11   Edit the following sentences by correcting any fixed-form verb errors. Not every sentence has errors. The first one has been done for you.

EXAMPLE: We can ~~schedules~~ *schedule* our appointment for Wednesday or Thursday.

1. Opportunities may arrive when we least expect them.

2. Randall can understands almost anything when he concentrates.

3. The company may distributes bonuses if productivity rises.

4. The executive musts take the 6:30 morning flight to arrive in time for the meeting.

5. As soon as the treasurer completes the necessary calculations, she will presents the annual budget.

Can and Could

Use *could* as the past tense of *can.*

> Today we *can see* the sun.
> Yesterday we *could see* only clouds.

- In the first sentence, *can* shows that the action is in the present.
- In the second sentence, *could* shows that the action is in the past.
- Notice that *could* carries the past tense information. The correct verb in this sentence is *could see,* not *could saw.*

Will and Would

Use *would* as the past tense of *will.*

> The lawyer *hopes* that she *will convince* the jury.
> The lawyer *hoped* that she *would convince* the jury.

- In the first sentence, *will* shows that the action will happen in the future.
- In the second sentence, *would* shows that the action happened in the past.
- Notice that *would* carries the past tense information. The correct verb in this sentence is *would convince,* not *would convinced.*

PRACTICE 12   Fill in the blanks with the correct form of the verb in parentheses.

1. (can, could) Denise works weekends, and she _____ select the time slots she wants.

2. (can, could) Last year, Denise worked weekends, and she _____ select the time slots she wanted.

3. (can, could) As I watched the movie, I _____ understand why it received rave reviews.

4. (will, would) The surgeon predicts that the broken bone _____ heal quickly.

5. (will, would) The surgeon predicted that the broken bone _____ heal quickly.

Focus on Apostrophes

Sometimes people mistakenly add apostrophes to present tense verbs. Do not use an apostrophe when adding -*s* to a verb.

> Incorrect: Frank concentrate's on today as he prepare's for tomorrow.
>
> Correct: Frank *concentrates* on today as he *prepares* for tomorrow.

Use an apostrophe to form a contraction or to show possession (ownership).

> Contraction: We *don't* worry about situations we *can't* change.
>
> Possession: *Jackie's* interview is scheduled for Thursday.

(Contraction and possession are explained in Chapter 22.)

Focus on Fragments

The -*ing* verb form cannot stand alone as the main verb in a sentence. It needs a helping verb.

> Fragment: Karen running to catch the train
>
> Sentence: Karen *is running* to catch the train.
>
> Fragment: Our neighbors saving their money for a down payment.
>
> Sentence: Our neighbors *are saving* their money for a down payment.
>
> Fragment: Children skateboarding down State Street
>
> Sentence: Children *were skateboarding* down State Street.

As you edit your writing, check for verbs that end in -*ing*. If you want this verb to be the main verb in the sentence, be sure to include a helping verb.

is thinking	*has been* thinking	*could have been* thinking
are thinking	*have been* thinking	*should have been* thinking
was thinking	*had been* thinking	*would have been* thinking
were thinking		

PRACTICE 13   The following groups of words are not sentences. Add helping verbs to make them sentences.

1. Currently, employees participating in the annual blood drive.

   _____

   _____

2. While the weather channel predicting sunshine, it started to rain.

   _____

   _____

3. Last month, movie theaters promoting the Oscar winners.

   _____

   _____

4. Local citizens supporting neighborhood watch groups.

   _____

   _____

5. The conference members debating sensitive issues that include domestic violence and unemployment.

   _____

   _____

Review: Writing with Verbs

- When writing with the present tense, add -s when the subject is *he, she, it,* or a singular noun.

  Adding -s to the end of a verb can be confusing because we use -s to make nouns plural. We say *one joke, many jokes; one dream, two dreams.* However, the -s ending is also used for another, entirely different purpose. It goes at the end of present tense verbs that have *he, she, it,* or a singular noun as a subject.

- Add -d or -ed to form the past tense of all regular verbs.

- If you want an -*ing* verb form to be the main verb of a sentence, use it with a helping verb such as *is, are, was, were, has been,* or *have been.*

- The more specific the verb, the more powerful your writing will be. *He walked to the corner* gives us general information. *He swaggered, staggered, charged, tiptoed, crawled, limped,* or *sprinted to the corner* will create a more vivid picture in readers' minds.

REVIEW PRACTICE Individually or in groups, read the following paragraph and correct the helping verb errors.

In the pioneer days, people realized that they could not survived the battle of life alone. They needed a group of faithful people, a community, to beat the obstacles of life. But today, communities does not act as support groups. People does not feel they owe anyone anything. We do not look out for other people because they may gets in our way to the top. If we step on others as we climb the ladder, we are called successful, not immoral. Our battle today is to get to the top. So we live by the rules of greed and self-centeredness. We live for ourselves, not the community. Many people will get to the top of the ladder, but when they get there, they may sees that no one is holding up the ladder.

—Student Writer

EXTRA CHALLENGE Individually or in groups, edit the following paragraph by correcting the past tense errors.

When I was in grade school, I was angry with my parents for their rigid rules. I thought they were forcing me to live up to their expectations and trying to mold me into someone I was not. Because I was not allow to be my own person, I rebel at school. I did anything for attention, anything to prove that I was not going to follow anyone else's rules. When I was a sophomore in high school, I finally realize that my parents had been preparing me to cope in a world where few people cared what happen to me. In my freshman classes, teachers did not push me to study or to listen in class. Friends did not care if I fail because they enjoyed seeing me as the clown. After nearly flunking out, I realize my parents had been equipping me to handle these challenges. What I once interpreted as punishment, I now see as a gift. I did not learn easily,

but I learned. I recognize now that the key to my future success in

college and in the working world is that simple but difficult lesson

my parents taught me: be responsible.

—Student Writer

- Do not add *-d* or *-ed* to the two-word verb forms: *to live, to mold, to be, to prove, to follow, to cope, to study, to listen,* and *to handle.* The word *to* plus a verb is called an *infinitive,* which we will study in Chapter 9. The infinitive never changes form. It stays the same regardless of what tense you are using.

Chapter 8

Writing with Irregular Verbs

- ◆ Irregular Verbs
- ◆ A List of Irregular Verbs

Irregular Verbs

We ate too much last night.

The past tense of *eat* is *ate*. We don't say, "We eated too much last night." *Eat* is an irregular verb.

Irregular Verb Forms

Irregular verbs have irregular forms for the past tense and the past participle.

SOME COMMON IRREGULAR VERBS				
1st form Base Form	2nd form Past Tense	3rd form Past Participle	4th form Present Participle	5th form *-s* Form
go	went	gone	going	goes
see	saw	seen	seeing	sees
write	wrote	written	writing	writes

The forms of irregular verbs are unpredictable; they must simply be memorized. It is equally important to understand how they are used as verbs in a sentence.

The second form, the past tense, always stands alone. It never takes a helping verb.

> She *went* to North Carolina to visit her parents.
> We *saw* a great film last weekend.
> He *wrote* five essays last semester.

The third form, the past participle, never stands alone. It always needs a helping verb.

> She *has gone* to North Carolina many times to visit her parents.
> We *have seen* many great films.
> He *has written* five essays.

Let's focus on the verb *see*. The second form, *saw,* is always used alone. Therefore, do not add a helping verb to *saw*.

Incorrect	We ~~have~~ saw the advertisement in the newspaper.
Correct	We *saw* the advertisement in the newspaper.

The third form, *seen,* cannot stand alone as a main verb in a sentence. It must be used with a helping verb. Therefore, do not use *seen* alone.

Incorrect	We ~~seen~~ the advertisement in the newspaper.
Correct	We *have seen* the advertisement in the newspaper.

A List of Irregular Verbs

Although some irregular verbs are well known and seldom cause problems, others are often used incorrectly. Read the following list of irregular verb forms, keeping in mind how they are used as verbs in a sentence. The second form (the past tense) always *stands alone*. The third form (the past participle) *always needs a helping verb*. Put a check mark beside any verb form that you are not using correctly and review these checked verbs in the future.

1st form Base Form (Today I . . .)	2nd form Past Tense (used alone) (Yesterday I . . .)	3rd form Past Participle (needs a helping verb) (Often I have . . .)
beat	beat	beaten
become	became	become
begin	began	begun
bend	bent	bent
bite	bit	bitten
bleed	bled	bled
blow	blew	blown
break	broke	broken
bring	brought	brought
build	built	built
buy	bought	bought

1st form **Base Form** (Today I . . .)	2nd form **Past Tense** (used alone) (Yesterday I . . .)	3rd form **Past Participle** (needs a helping verb) (Often I have . . .)
catch	caught	caught
choose	chose	chosen
come	came	come
cut	cut	cut
dig	dug	dug
do	did	done
draw	drew	drawn
drink	drank	drunk
drive	drove	driven
eat	ate	eaten
fall	fell	fallen
feed	fed	fed
feel	felt	felt
fight	fought	fought
find	found	found
fly	flew	flown
forget	forgot	forgotten
forgive	forgave	forgiven
freeze	froze	frozen
get	got	gotten
give	gave	given
go	went	gone
grow	grew	grown
have	had	had
hear	heard	heard
hide	hid	hidden
hit	hit	hit
hold	held	held
hurt	hurt	hurt
keep	kept	kept
know	knew	known
lay (put)	laid	laid
lead	led	led
leave	left	left
lend	lent	lent
let	let	let
lie (recline)	lay	lain
lose	lost	lost
make	made	made
meet	met	met
put	put	put
quit	quit	quit

1st form Base Form (Today I . . .)	2nd form Past Tense (used alone) (Yesterday I . . .)	3rd form Past Participle (needs a helping verb) (Often I have . . .)
read	read	read
ride	rode	ridden
ring	rang	rung
rise	rose	risen
run	ran	run
say	said	said
see	saw	seen
sell	sold	sold
send	sent	sent
set (put)	set	set
shake	shook	shaken
shut	shut	shut
sing	sang	sung
sink	sank	sunk
sit (rest)	sat	sat
sleep	slept	slept
speak	spoke	spoken
spend	spent	spent
stand	stood	stood
steal	stole	stolen
stick	stuck	stuck
sting	stung	stung
swear	swore	sworn
sweep	swept	swept
swim	swam	swum
swing	swung	swung
take	took	taken
teach	taught	taught
tear	tore	torn
tell	told	told
think	thought	thought
throw	threw	thrown
try	tried	tried
understand	understood	understood
wear	wore	worn
win	won	won
write	wrote	written

PRACTICE 1   Fill in each blank with the correct verb form. The first two sentences have been done for you.

EXAMPLE: grow: Stephen and Diane _grew_ three inches last year.

They have _grown_ out of all their clothes.

1. know: When the scores were posted, we _____ she would get the medal.

   If we had checked the weather report, we would have _____ about the icy roads.

2. find: Last night, they _____ their keys in the parking lot.

   We have _____ valuable web sites on the Internet that help students write papers.

3. throw: When we were painting my room, we _____ away the old, torn posters.

   I can't find the receipt; I must have _____ it away.

4. come: When the rain began, the children _____ inside.

   We have _____ too far to turn back now.

5. do: We have _____ our best to succeed in this class.

   He _____ the paperwork and then submitted the proposal.

6. break: When she had the measles, she _____ out in a rash.

   My neighbor has _____ too many promises.

7. bring: Have you _____ your lunch?

   Last weekend we _____ our favorite dessert to the picnic.

8. go: Yesterday, we _____ shopping for a new dishwasher.

   We should have _____ shopping last week when they were on sale.

9. drive: We have _____ along that road often.

   She _____ until midnight, then I took over.

10. see: Have you _____ today's headlines?

    When we _____ Jean and John together, we knew something had changed.

11. eat: They _____ all the food and then left.

    We have _____ there too often; let's go somewhere else.

12. write: We _____ down the telephone numbers and addresses

    before leaving.

    Deena has _____ all the cousins and invited them for Thanksgiving

    dinner.

13. choose: They _____ the wrong exit and got lost.

    I would have _____ that job if I had been thinking clearly.

14. become: She has _____ more patient in the past year.

    As the hurricane gained force, we _____ more concerned about

    our safety.

15. ring: Ever since he moved in, the phone has _____ constantly.

    Yesterday, the telephone _____ all afternoon.

16. see: We _____ the best movie last night!

    You should have _____ Judy's face when we surprised her with a

    birthday party.

17. fight: Yesterday, two-year-old Marvin and three-year-old Kathy _____

    all afternoon.

    They have _____ too much, and the family is exhausted.

18. speak: Yesterday, the Ecuadorian woman on the phone _____

    Spanish.

    Sandra has _____ Spanish since she was a child.

19. run: We have _____ this race too often.

    Last week, electricians _____ wires through the drywall.

20. begin: We _____ to worry when no one answered the door or the

    phone.

    We could have _____ the trip on Saturday, but I had to work

    overtime.

PRACTICE 2   Correct any verb errors in the following sentences.

1. They should have went with her.

2. I seen your e-mail and was anxious to read it.

3. Al and I have did so many things together.

4. In the below-zero weather, the pipes in our kitchen freezed.

5. If caller ID had been working, the telephone numbers would have came up on the screen.

Review: Writing with Irregular Verbs

• The second verb form (past tense) always stands alone. The third form (past participle) never stands alone as a main verb in a sentence; it always needs a helping verb. Here is a quick review of how to use some troublesome irregular verbs correctly:

(see, saw, have seen)
We saw Tiffany yesterday.
We have seen her often.

(go, went, have gone)
We went out for dinner last night.
We have gone out for dinner three weekends in a row.

(come, came, have come)
The children came inside when the thunder began.
They should have come in earlier.

(do, did, have done)
James does well under pressure.
James has done well on all his exams.

(eat, ate, have eaten)
Our guests ate the food and complimented the hostess.
They have eaten everything on the buffet table.

 REVIEW PRACTICE   Edit the following paragraph by correcting the irregular verb errors.

High school was a game to me, a game of hide-and-go-seek. The

only way I would enter a classroom was if someone found me first.

I runned, I played, and I skipped class. Being with the in-crowd

was more important than learning how to read and write. I did

not need those skills because I had it all together. I was part of the in-crowd, and having fun was more important than boring books, rules, and teachers. School was not part of my life; it was not in my plans. But one day a caring teacher found me when I didn't want to be found. She was a tough individual who seen potential in me. She teached me, encouraged me, and supported me. I realized then that school is for those who hunger for more knowledge, for those who desire to live a successful life. I realized that my little game of hide-and-go-seek was a game for children. I choosed instead to play the game of the real world.

—Student Writer

 EXTRA CHALLENGE Individually or in groups, rewrite the following paragraph, changing the underlined verbs to past tense form.

My father <u>rides</u> the subway home from work in Manhattan to the Cortelyou Road station in Brooklyn, then <u>walks</u> the twenty minutes from the station to our house. On the lucky days when he <u>comes</u> home while it <u>is</u> still light, Mimi and I <u>wait</u> for him to appear at the end of the street. When we <u>see</u> his tall thin shape taking form, we <u>run</u> to him. He <u>lifts</u> us up, one by one, and <u>holds</u> us in his arms, then <u>sets</u> us down and <u>walks</u> the last half block with us— a little girl fastened to the end of each arm.

—Deborah Tannen, "Daddy Young and Old"

Maintaining Agreement and Consistency

◆ Subject-Verb Agreement

◆ *Focus on* There

◆ Consistent Time

Subject-Verb Agreement

Because subjects and verbs form the skeleton of a sentence, they must agree, or in simpler words, they must match. We began looking at subject-verb agreement in Chapter 7 when we wrote with present tense verbs. In this section, we will review the present tense and then note how other particular types of words agree with verbs.

Present Tense Review

Add *-s* or *-es* to a present tense verb when the subject is *he, she, it,* or a singular noun. If the subject is *we, they,* or a plural noun, do not add *-s* or *-es.*

She works on weekends.

Ron (singular) works the midnight shift.

Shawn and I (plural) work during summer vacation.

PRACTICE 1   Edit the following paragraph for present tense verb endings by adding -*s* where necessary.

> My mother nurtures, love, and even spoils my children. When I am irritable and need some space, she come over and patiently listen to them. When I have no time, she take them food shopping and lets them pick out their favorite candy. She give without needing or demanding anything in return. Sometimes she even show up unexpectedly and announces, "Get ready, we are going out for lunch today." My mom never wait for birthdays. She see a regular Saturday as a day for celebration. She give just because she wants to give. It all seems so simple for my mom.
>
> —Student Writer

Groups as Singular

When a group acts as one unit, it is treated as singular. For example, a committee consists of more than one person, but because it acts as a unit, *committee* is considered singular.

Groups that are usually treated as singular	
family	crowd
team	committee
class	jury
Board of Education	public
choir	audience

When the group acts as a unit, think of it as one. Translating, in your mind, the group word to *it* will help you remember to treat a group word as singular.

> The team (it) is practicing on Saturdays.
> The public (it) sees beneath many political promises.
> The group (it) knows its way around campus.
> The choir (it) is rehearsing for the concert.

Amounts as Singular

Usually quantities of time, money, weight, and length are singular because they refer to one unit. Therefore, think of them as an *it*.

Ten years (it) is a long time to wait.
One hundred dollars (it) is a significant amount of money for almost
    everyone.
Eleven pounds (it) is too much weight to lose in a month.
Two hundred yards (it) is a long sprint.

There Is/There Are *and* Here Is/Here Are

There is, there are, here is, and *here are* act as arrows pointing to the subject of a sentence. *There* and *here* are not the subjects themselves. Whenever you begin a sentence with *there* or *here,* look past this first word and find the subject it points to.

There is a car in her driveway.

- *There* points to *car,* the subject. Because *car* is singular, the verb is singular: *is.*

There are six cars in her driveway.

- *There* points to *cars,* which is plural. Therefore the verb is plural: *are.*

Here is my checkbook.

- *Here* points to *checkbook,* which is singular. Therefore the verb is singular: *is.*

Here are my bills.

- *Here* points to *bills,* which is plural. The verb is therefore plural: *are.*

PRACTICE 2   In the following sentences, underline the subject once and the correct verb twice. The first one has been done for you. As you select the correct verb, this verb summary may be helpful:

Singular	**Plural**
One person or thing *is*	People or things *are*
One person or thing *was*	People or things *were*

EXAMPLE: Here (is, <u>are</u>) the <u>forms</u> that need to be filled out by Friday.

1. Here (is, are) the disk you will need for the computer class.

2. Here (is, are) three important proposals to consider.

3. There (was, were) countless opportunities for community service.

4. There (was, were) too many people in line, so we went home.

5. There (is, are) a piece missing from the puzzle.

> ### *Focus on* There
>
> Starting a sentence with *there* often weakens your point. As you edit your writing, see if omitting *there* will make your sentence more direct. Notice how the last two sentences from the previous exercise can be written more directly by omitting *there*:
>
>> Too many people were in line, so we went home.
>>
>> A piece is missing from the puzzle.

Commands

Commands are sentences that omit the subject. The subject of a command is taken for granted; it is understood to be *you*.

(You) Stop.   (You) Go.   (You) Leave.   (You) Stay.

PRACTICE 3   Each of the following quotations includes at least one command. Find each command and write *(You)* above the verb.

1. Be kind. Everyone you meet is fighting a hard battle.

   —John Watson

2. Develop success from failures. Discouragement and failure are two of the

   surest stepping stones to success.

   —Dale Carnegie

3. Remember that everyone you meet is afraid of something, loves

   something, has lost something.

   —H. Jackson Brown

4. Don't find fault. Find a remedy.

   —Henry Ford

5. Hold fast to dreams, for if dreams die, life is a broken winged bird that

   cannot fly.

   —Langston Hughes

Consistent Time

In this section, we look at two possible trouble spots. The first involves recognizing that infinitives do not show a change in time. The second involves editing to make sure you do not switch the time unexpectedly and confuse readers.

Infinitives

An infinitive is made up of the word *to* and the base form of a verb: *to walk, to explain, to drive, to enjoy*. The infinitive is never the main verb of a sentence and therefore does not change tense. The main verb in the sentence carries the time change.

The verbs in the following sentences are in italics. Notice that *want* shows the change in time: *wants, wanted, will want, would have wanted*. The infinitive *to leave* does not change form.

My cousin *wants* to leave for vacation on Saturday morning.

My cousin *wanted* to leave for vacation on Saturday morning.

My cousin *will want* to leave for vacation on Saturday morning.

My cousin *would have wanted* to leave for vacation on Saturday morning.

When you are writing about past events, do not add *-d* or *-ed* to the infinitive. For example, "We decided to solved the problem" is incorrect. The correct way of writing that sentence is *We decided to solve the problem.*

PRACTICE 4 Some of the following sentences use infinitives correctly; others contain errors. Correct the errors.

1. It took energy and discipline to changed my life around.

2. After graduating from college, Mary decided to enrolled in a pharmacy program.

3. Gary's friend offered to give us a ride.

4. We began to realized that the game was over.

5. They hope to analyze, discuss, and take action on the important issues facing their community.

Consistent Tense

Verb tenses show time differences. For example, we could write, *Yesterday he felt sick. Today he feels better. Tomorrow he will feel fine.* The verbs in these sentences change tense because the writer wants to show the difference between yesterday, today, and tomorrow. Change the tense of your verbs when you want to indicate a specific change in time.

Be careful that you don't unexpectedly switch to the present tense of talking style. We often talk about something that happened in the past by using the present tense, as in "She *says* this . . . , he *says* that. . . ." When you are writing in the past tense, make sure that you don't unexpectedly switch to the present tense.

INCORRECT:

> Jeff *decided* to go upstairs to check on our daughter. He *comes* back down to the kitchen table, where I *am sitting*. He *had* this strange look on his face, a look of hurt and disappointment.

—Student Writer

This writer switches from past tense *decided* to present tense *comes* and *am sitting*, then back to past tense *had*. Keep the tense consistent unless you are indicating a time change in the events you are describing. Choose either past or present and stay with it. Here is the same paragraph, rewritten with consistent tense:

CORRECT:

> Jeff *decided* to go upstairs to check on our daughter. He *came* back down to the kitchen table, where I *was sitting*. He *had* this strange look on his face, a look of hurt and disappointment.

—Student Writer

PRACTICE 5   In the following section of a paragraph, the writer begins with past tense but then switches to the talking style of present tense. Underline the verbs that are in the wrong tense and change them to past tense.

> My job included assisting the mentally ill and the mentally retarded.
>
> One day, a female patient flew into a fit of anger. She called the staff
>
> disrespectful names and screamed obscenities. A few minutes later,
>
> the supervisor comes and says the patient had to be restrained. As I am
>
> restraining her, the patient throws her fists in my face because I am trying
>
> to hold her down.

—Student Writer

Review: Maintaining Agreement and Consistency

As you edit your writing for subject-verb agreement and consistent tense, keep the following facts in mind.

- Present tense verbs end in *-s* or *-es* when the subject is *he, she, it,* or a singular noun.

    The restaurant stays open until midnight.

- Groups and amounts are often singular in meaning.

    The team practices every Saturday.

    Two thousand dollars is a lot of money.

- *There is/there are* and *here is/here are* point to subjects. *There* and *here* cannot be subjects.

    There are three important steps we need to take.

    Here is one person we can trust.

- Commands are sentences that omit the subject, which is understood to be *you.*

    Please stay.

- Infinitives (*to* plus a verb) never change tense.

    We decided to ask for directions.

- Keep the same tense unless the time in a piece of writing changes. Be careful not to switch to the talking style of present tense.

    We saw the light turn red, but the truck ~~does~~ *did* not stop.

 REVIEW PRACTICE Individually or in groups, edit the following paragraph for subject-verb agreement errors.

There is many superficial people in our society. They stand behind barriers and keeps others at a distance as they protects their pride and ego. Leon Collins is different. He move beyond pride and ego because he has a higher purpose. Leon is a loyal friend who believes in giving himself to others. He is a member of a group that help young boys become men. The group meet every week, and Leon never misses a meeting. He listens to the boys' stories without judgment, answers their questions with honest words, and give them clear direction. Because he has nothing to lose, he has nothing to fear. He need no walls to hide behind.

—Student Writer

EXTRA CHALLENGE Applying for a job includes submitting a résumé, which is an outline of your qualifications for the job, including your education, work experience, and accomplishments. In small groups, practice writing the work-experience section of a résumé. Consider any job you have performed. Full-time and part-time jobs, a summer job, or volunteer work are all good to include because they show that you have job-worthy strengths. First, list the job or position you held, beginning with the most recent. Under the job title, select verbs that highlight your responsibilities and use those verbs to begin short, descriptive phrases. The verbs in the list should be in the same tense. For example:

Baldwin High School, Student Office Assistant
- Greeted visitors and assisted secretaries with filing
- Prepared daily announcements on a word processor
- Stocked and shelved office supplies

St. James Hospital, Volunteer
- Distributed mail to patients on a daily basis
- Improved patient morale by reading them magazine articles
- Transported patients from emergency room to admitting office

Snack Shack, Employee
- Worked the cashier station and drive-through window
- Improved methods of completing customer orders
- Checked accuracy of cash reports
- Supervised new employees

Baldwin Community Center, Child Care Provider
- Provided child care during adult education classes
- Initiated new child-development activities
- Established rapport with parents

Footgear, Sales Clerk
- Assisted customers with style and size selection
- Managed and organized purchase invoices for weekly deliveries
- Coordinated seasonal displays
- Maintained income and expense ledgers

Verbs that are commonly used in résumés are listed below. Consult this list not only for this assignment, but for future résumés.

accomplished	calculated	decided
achieved	changed	defined
acquired	circulated	demonstrated
addressed	consolidated	designated
appointed	constructed	designed
arranged	consulted	determined
assembled	contributed	developed
assessed	coordinated	devised
assisted	counseled	directed
broadened	created	distributed

documented	installed	reinforced
doubled	instituted	represented
eliminated	involved	requested
encouraged	maintained	researched
enforced	managed	reviewed
established	maximized	scheduled
estimated	measured	secured
evaluated	modified	selected
executed	monitored	served
expanded	motivated	simplified
facilitated	multiplied	stabilized
guided	organized	strengthened
hired	performed	supervised
identified	persuaded	supported
implemented	presented	surpassed
improved	processed	targeted
influenced	produced	taught
informed	purchased	trained
initiated	recommended	
inspired	recorded	

Punctuating Sentences and Using Coordinating Conjunctions

◆ Sentence Signs

◆ Periods

◆ Semicolons

◆ Commas: An Overview

Sentence Signs

When we talk, we communicate with more than words. The way we say those words adds to the meaning. A speaker's voice changes in tone, volume, and pitch; it pauses and stops. Writing, though, is just a series of words arranged on paper or a computer screen. Therefore, writers use punctuation marks to signal readers how to read the writers' thoughts.

Think of the different signs and signals you see on the road: stop signs, merge signs, yield signs, railroad signs, and traffic lights. These signs give a variety of messages, and each is positioned carefully. Writing uses punctuation marks in the same way.

SIGNS

. Red light: full stop

; Flashing red light: quick stop

, Yellow light: pause

The period is a strong sign.

A period holds two sentences apart.

The semicolon is a sign of medium strength.

Notice that the semicolon is made up of a period on top of a comma. It has qualities of both: it is stronger than a comma but weaker than a period. A semicolon is strong enough to keep two related sentences apart.

A comma is a weak sign.

A comma is not strong enough to hold two sentences apart. Therefore, do not use a comma to separate two sentences.

Periods

Periods are essential to writing. The period tells readers to stop and take a breath before moving on to the next sentence. If you do not put a period at the end of a sentence, readers will continue to read and become confused. Your sentence becomes a *run-on* as it *runs on* into the next sentence.

Pay special attention to pronouns, words such as *he, she, it, they, I,* and *we*. Pronouns are often used as subjects that begin a new sentence.

Incorrect: Successful <u>people</u> <u>have learned</u> how to face challenges they <u>realize</u> that challenges can be opportunities to gain insight and strength.

Correct: Successful <u>people</u> <u>have learned</u> how to face challenges. <u>They</u> <u>realize</u> that challenges can be opportunities to gain insight and strength.

Run-ons are caused by failing to mark the end of a sentence with a period. There are two kinds of run-ons: *fused sentences* and *comma splices*.

  1. A fused sentence is two sentences joined together without any punctuation.

Incorrect: The assignment was easy it took me only half an hour to complete.

Correct: The assignment was easy. It took me only half an hour to complete.

  2. A comma splice is two sentences joined together with only a comma.

Incorrect: The people I work with are more than co-workers, they are family.

Correct: The people I work with are more than co-workers. They are family.

If fused sentences and comma splices have been a problem for you in the past, follow these suggestions:

1. *Read your writing aloud*. Notice when your voice falls in pitch and stops; these two changes usually signal the end of a sentence. Then check whether the words you just read contain a subject and a verb and communicate a complete thought. If they do, you have written a sentence and need to mark its end with a period. Make sure you read aloud; reading silently does not work.

2. *Study the sentence patterns on the inside front cover of this book*. Glancing at them will help you identify what pattern you are using and remind you of your options.

3. *Change from talking style to writing style, as necessary*. Check to see if you have strung ideas together with unnecessary *and*'s and *so*'s. Omit these words and end the sentences with a period.

PRACTICE 1   Correct the following run-ons by separating the sentences with a period.

1. I must learn to be patient, it will take me two years to complete the required courses.

2. We ignored the consequences of our words and actions we just lived for the moment.

3. The training program was more than an opportunity it was a dream come true.

4. I felt insecure about my age, I felt younger students would look down on me.

5. Elderly people should be respected and appreciated, they have wisdom to share with younger generations.

Semicolons

The semicolon tells readers to stop briefly. Semicolons are used to separate two sentences that are closely related in meaning.

Because the following two sentences are closely related in meaning, they can be separated by either a period or a semicolon.

My <u>sister</u> <u>likes</u> cable television. My <u>brother</u> <u>prefers</u> reading a book.

My <u>sister</u> <u>likes</u> cable television; my <u>brother</u> <u>prefers</u> reading a book.

> ### SENTENCE PATTERNS
>
> Sentence . Sentence .
>
> Sentence ; sentence .

Ordinarily, there is no need to use a semicolon. A period works just as well.

PRACTICE 2   Fix the following run-ons in two ways. Correct the first run-on in each set by using a period. Correct the next run-on in that set by using a semicolon. When you use a period, the second sentence should begin with a capital letter. When you use a semicolon, do not capitalize the first word in the next sentence. The first set has been done for you.

                                   . You

EXAMPLE: I will take care of the children ~~you~~ take care of the adults.

                                    ;

           I will take care of the children ⌄you take care of the adults.

1. You will probably get the job your interview went well.

    You will probably get the job your interview went well.

2. My aunt voted Republican my uncle voted Democrat.

    My aunt voted Republican my uncle voted Democrat.

3. Teresa is a careless driver she has had three tickets in the past two months.

    Teresa is a careless driver she has had three tickets in the past two months.

4. Last semester Robert had three night classes this semester he has none.

    Last semester Robert had three night classes this semester he has none.

5. The union favored striking the company opposed it.

    The union favored striking the company opposed it.

Commas: An Overview

Commas are used in only four situations. We focus on the first and second uses in this chapter. In later chapters, we concentrate on the third and fourth uses as we add additions to the core sentence.

Summary of Commas

Commas have the following functions.

1. Separate items in a series
   - *Please bring my coffee pot, car keys, battery charger, and sleeping bag.*

2. Connect two sentences with a coordinating conjunction *(and, but, or, so, yet, for, nor)*
   - *The rain pounded for three straight days, and every basement on our block was flooded.*

3. Set off introductory words
   - *An experienced long-distance runner, Daryl ran the marathon.*

4. Set off words interrupting the flow of thought

   Words in the middle of a sentence
   - *Daryl, giving it the best he had, ran the marathon.*

   Words at the end of a sentence
   - *Daryl ran the marathon, a physically demanding accomplishment.*

Separating Items in a Series

When you are writing three or more items in a series, use commas to separate the items so that readers can tell how many items there are. The items may be either single words or groups of words.

> Honesty, integrity, and sensitivity can be neither bought nor sold.
>
> We need to decide if we should call a taxi, take the bus, wait for the train, or walk.

Do not place the comma before the first item in a series or after the last.

> item , item , item , and item

The new car features road-hugging suspension, speed-sensitive steering, traction control, and antilock brakes.

- Notice that there is no comma before the first item *(road-hugging suspension).*

Moderate exercise, a balanced diet, and supportive friends contribute to good health.

- Notice that there is no comma after the last item *(supportive friends).*

PRACTICE 3   In the following sentences, use commas to separate the items in each series. The first one has been done for you.

EXAMPLE: Major television stations are trying to win back audiences who have turned to cable, the Internet, or plain solitude.

1. People can use the Internet to purchase products make plane reservations or conduct research.

2. The house for sale has a new roof storm windows a nicely maintained yard a two-car garage and a ridiculously high price.

3. Fresh produce cut flowers and homemade bread are on sale at the Farmers' Market.

4. Basketball football and wrestling require strength and endurance.

5. We threw our boots a backpack a spare tire a five-gallon gas can and a six-gallon water jug into the back of the truck.

PRACTICE 4   The commas separating the items in a series have been removed from the following paragraph. Replace them so the items do not run together.

> I wasn't aware of not hearing until I began to wear a hearing aid at the age of thirty. It shattered my peace. I could hear shoes creaking papers crackling pencils tapping phones ringing and refrigerators humming. Cars bikes dogs cats and kids seemed to appear from nowhere and fly right at me.
>
> —Adapted from Nicolette Toussaint,
> "Hearing the Sweetest Songs"

Avoiding Fragments with Items in a Series

A series of items is not a sentence when it does not have a subject and a verb. The items need to be connected to a sentence. A common writing error is treating a series of items as if it were a sentence. This error can be avoided in either of two ways. First, you can connect the series to a sentence by using a comma and the words *such as* or *like*. Second, you can omit words and include the series directly in the sentence.

First Solution

Connect the series to a sentence by using a comma and the words *such as* or *like*.

EXAMPLE 1

Problem: Her favorite colors are earth tones. Like beige, rust, and green.

• *Like beige, rust, and green* is not a sentence. There is neither a subject nor a verb.

Solution: Her favorite colors are earth tones, like beige, rust, and green.

• The series is now connected to a sentence with the word *like*.

EXAMPLE 2

Problem: I worked with several contractors and learned how to work in other trades. For example plumbing, heating, and carpentry.

• *For example plumbing, heating, and carpentry* is not a sentence. There is neither a subject nor a verb.

Solution: I worked with several contractors and learned how to work in other trades, such as plumbing, heating, and carpentry.

• The series is now connected to a sentence with the words *such as*.

Second Solution

Omit words and include the series directly in a sentence.

EXAMPLE 1

Problem: This year I am working on three goals. Being honest with myself, putting the past behind me, and concentrating on new opportunities.

• The three items in the series are not sentences because they lack a subject and a complete verb.

Solution: This year I am working on being honest with myself, putting the past behind me, and concentrating on new opportunities.

• The items in the series have been included directly in the sentence.

EXAMPLE 2

Problem: My recent job taught me important skills. How to keep an inventory sheet. How to balance deposits. And how to make up schedules.

• The three "how to" ideas are not sentences because they lack a subject and a verb.

Solution: My recent job taught me how to keep an inventory sheet, balance deposits, and make up schedules.

• The items in the series have been included directly in the sentence.

PRACTICE 5 Correct the following fragments where writers separated the series of items from the preceding sentence. Correct the fragments in two ways. First, write a sentence where you attach the series to the sentence with a comma and the words *such as* or *like*. Then write a sentence where you omit words, change the verb form in the fragment if necessary, and include the series directly in the sentence. The first one has been done for you.

EXAMPLE: I have learned valuable lessons. For example, appreciating the moment, controlling my tensions, and trusting the process.

I have learned valuable lessons, such as appreciating the moment, controlling my tensions, and trusting the process.

or

I have learned to appreciate the moment, control my tensions, and trust the process.

1. They want to live in an apartment to avoid the typical homeowners' headaches. Like flooded basements, leaking roofs, and rusted appliances.

_____

_____

_____

or

_____

_____

2. The company provides all employees with benefits. For example medical insurance, dental insurance, and a pension.

_____

_____

or

_____

_____

3. We want to travel to many places. Such as the Caribbean, Belize, and Hawaii.

_____

_____

or

_____

4. Employers have basic expectations of employees. For example, arriving on time, being prepared, and working efficiently.

_____

_____

_____

or

_____

_____

5. The weekend conference offers a variety of activities. For instance, indoor and outdoor sports, stimulating speakers, small discussion groups, and evening entertainment.

_____

_____

_____

_____

or

_____

_____

_____

Connecting Two Sentences: Coordinating Conjunctions

A comma by itself is not strong enough to separate two sentences. However, if a comma has the right "help," it can connect two sentences. That help is provided by any of these seven coordinating conjunctions: *and, but, or, so, yet, for, nor*. You can connect two sentences by using a comma and a coordinating conjunction.

A lie has speed, but truth has endurance.

—Edgar Mohn

A lie has speed is a sentence. *Truth has endurance* is a sentence. A comma and the word *but* connect these two sentences. Notice that the comma comes *before* the word *but*. One way to remember this point is by saying the word *comma* aloud, referring to these conjunctions as "comma *and*," "comma *but*," "comma *or*," "comma *so*," "comma *yet*," "comma *for*," and "comma *nor*."

Sentence Patterns

Sentence. Sentence.	Sentence, **so** sentence.
Sentence; sentence.	Sentence, **yet** sentence.
Sentence, **and** sentence.	Sentence, **nor** sentence.
Sentence, **but** sentence.	Sentence, **for** sentence.
Sentence, **or** sentence.	(Here, **for** means *because*.)

When you use a coordinating conjunction, make sure you have a sentence on both sides.

1. We submitted a bid on the car, **and** we are waiting for the seller's response.

2. We submitted a bid on the car, **but** we don't know if it will be accepted.

3. We submitted a bid on the car, **yet** that doesn't mean we bought it.

PRACTICE 6   The commas that belong with coordinating conjunctions have been omitted from the following sentences. Read each sentence, notice the underlined subjects and verbs, and correct the punctuation by inserting a comma. The first one has been done for you.

EXAMPLE:

Pale <u>light</u> <u>was pouring</u> through the windows, and the <u>trees</u> <u>thrashed</u> in

the wind.

—Erla Zwingle, "Catherine the Great"

1. The <u>river</u> <u>tasted</u> good and <u>I</u> <u>sat</u> in the shade under a cluster of

silvery willows.

—Leslie Marmon Silko, "Yellow Woman"

2. <u>Money</u> <u>has</u> an attraction for some people but <u>nobody</u> <u>can wear</u> two

pairs of shoes at one time.

—Charles F. Feeney, *Time*

3. My <u>father</u> <u>could</u> no longer <u>go</u> off to work so <u>he</u> <u>built</u> furniture in

his shop.

—Jamaica Kincaid, *Annie John*

4. The <u>house</u> <u>is</u> dark but through the slats of the front windows a frail gray <u>light</u> <u>seeps</u> in like the mist.

—Esmeralda Santiago, *América's Dream*

5. He <u>was</u> tall and slender and his thin <u>shoulders</u> <u>stooped</u>.

—Willa Cather, *My Antonia*

Using the Word And

Use a comma when *and* connects two sentences. If there really are two sentences, there will be a subject and a verb on both sides of the *and*. Most of the time, the word *and* connects two words or two phrases (groups of words), not two sentences. Do not use a comma when *and* connects two items that are not sentences.

I talked patiently to Richard and Dan.

	Richard
I <u>talked</u> patiently to	**and**
	Dan.

We worked until noon and partied until midnight.

	<u>worked</u> until noon
<u>We</u>	**and**
	<u>partied</u> until midnight.

• In the first sentence, *and* connects *Richard* and *Dan*—two nouns. In the second sentence, *and* connects *worked* and *partied*—two verbs. Neither *and* connects two sentences. Therefore, there are no commas.

I talked patiently to Richard and Dan, and they agreed to help with the project.

I <u>talked</u> patiently to Richard and Dan

and

<u>they</u> <u>agreed</u> to help with the project.

We worked until noon, and we partied until midnight.

<u>We</u> <u>worked</u> until noon

and

<u>we</u> <u>partied</u> until midnight.

- A comma is used because *and* connects two sentences. There is a subject and verb on both sides of the *and*.

Use a comma with *and* only when the *and* connects two sentences. Remembering this rule will solve a lot of comma confusion. You won't need to wonder whether to use a comma whenever you write the word *and.*

A helpful way of deciding whether you have written two sentences is to use the pencil test. Place your pencil on the word *and*. Read the words to the left and ask yourself, "Is that a sentence with both a subject and a verb?" Then read the words to the right, asking again, "Is that a sentence with both a subject and a verb?" If there is a sentence on each side, add a comma.

PRACTICE 7   In the following sentences, add a comma where necessary. Use the pencil test for help.

1. Navigation and radar systems help keep planes on schedule.

2. Antonio grabbed a handful of potato chips and bolted out the door.

3. Joe plays basketball every night and his children join him.

4. Adults and teens at the retreat shared stories and developed lasting friendships.

5. You will need a driver's license and a major credit card to cash a check.

6. The electronic equipment was hit by lightning and the voltage burned out the circuits.

7. Both lawyers and doctors claim that lawsuits cause higher health care costs.

8. The fire hydrant sprayed water onto the burning-hot street and children splashed in delight.

9. Our eyes act like a camera and capture an image.

10. We signed the mortgage on June 23 and on June 24 we moved in.

PRACTICE 8

SENTENCE COMBINING When we talk, we string ideas together as they come to mind. As we work those ideas into writing, we need to condense them into compact sentences. Sentence-combining exercises will give you practice. Combine each pair of sentences into one sentence by using one of the coordinating conjunctions: *and, but, or, so, yet, for*. The first one has been done for you.

EXAMPLE: Everyone in my family caught the flu. I didn't.

Everyone in my family caught the flu, but I didn't.

1. Prices went up. Demand went down.

_____

2. We can leave at 7:00 and drive to the airport. We can leave at 5:45 and catch the bus.

_____

_____

3. His job is a high-wire act. He appears to handle it with ease and energy.

_____

_____

4. The summer heat reached 134 degrees. The asphalt melted.

_____

_____

5. Automobile sales have decreased. The production schedules have been trimmed.

_____

_____

6. I am never bored when I'm with Natalie. She always comes up with unusual things to do.

_____

_____

7. Heat stroke can cause brain damage and death. Immediate treatment quickly reverses the potential damage.

_____

_____

8. We can save time and skip lunch. We can take a break and eat lunch in the cafeteria.

_____

_____

9. The sun had gone down. The snow beneath the streetlights cast light around us.

_____

_____

10. Customers can purchase a wide variety of over-the-counter drugs. They need to read the labels and consult the pharmacist to avoid adverse drug reactions.

_____

_____

_____

Review: Punctuating Sentences and Using Coordinating Conjunctions

- End your sentences with a period. If two sentences are closely connected in meaning, you can use a semicolon between them.

- Use commas in a core sentence only if you are writing a series of items or if you are connecting two sentences with *and, but, or, so, yet, for,* or *nor.*

- When you edit your writing, look for the word *and.* Use the pencil test to decide if there is a sentence on both sides. If not, do not use a comma. Most of the time, you will not need a comma.

 REVIEW PRACTICE Individually or in groups, edit the following paragraph by correcting comma errors.

My goal is to become an independent person. I have spent half my life depending on my parents and, it is now time to live independently. I want my own freedom, space, and privacy. One of the biggest challenges in becoming independent is money. Monthly payments for rent, utilities my car and insurance will be due. I also foresee another problem. I will no longer have others to blame when things go wrong. I will

need confidence, and inner strength to take care of myself
physically, and emotionally. I will need to grow up. Becoming
an adult has its positive, and negative sides but it is an essential
step to independence.

—Student Writer

 EXTRA CHALLENGE Individually or in groups, read the following paragraphs
and underline the sentences that are connected with the coordinating conjunctions *and*, *but*, or *for*.

I returned to Rainy Mountain in July. My grandmother had died
in the spring, and I wanted to be at her grave. She had lived to be
very old and at last infirm. Her only living daughter was with her
when she died, and I was told that in death her face was that of a
child.

—N. Scott Momaday, *The Way to Rainy Mountain*

In our isolated Greek village, my mother had bribed a cousin
to teach her to read, for girls were not supposed to attend school
beyond a certain age. She had always dreamed of her children
receiving an education. She couldn't be there when I graduated
from Boston University, but the person who came with my father
and shared our joy was my former teacher, Marjorie Hurd.

—Nicholas Gage, "The Teacher
Who Changed My Life"

Part 3

Writing Sentences with Varied Rhythms

Changing the Rhythm of Sentences

Changing the Rhythm of Sentences

In previous chapters, we focused on the core sentence, a sentence consisting of a subject and a predicate without any additional information interrupting the flow of ideas. Most writing consists of core sentences because they are straightforward. Yet reading sentence after sentence written in the core sentence pattern can be monotonous. Readers expect a variation, a change of rhythm.

Writing is like music. Musicians choose notes, arrange those notes to form a melody, and use a pattern of beats and pauses to create the rhythm. Writers choose words, and the way they arrange those words creates the rhythm. When the rhythm changes in music, we hear it. When we change the rhythm in a sentence, we need to let the reader see it. We can do that by using commas.

Summary of Commas

Commas are used to do the following things:

1. Separate items in a series
   - *People can use the Internet to purchase products, make plane reservations, or conduct research.*

2. Connect two sentences with a coordinating conjunction (*and, but, or, so, yet, for, nor*)
   - *The fire hydrant sprayed water onto the burning-hot street, and children splashed in delight.*

3. Set off introductory words
   - *When the mayor addressed the city council, he proposed a new airport.*

4. Set off words interrupting the flow of thought in the middle of a sentence or at the end
   - *The mayor, hoping to create new jobs, proposed a new airport.*
   - *The mayor proposed a new airport, a potential boost to local employment.*

In Chapters 11–18, we practice changing the rhythm of sentences, using commas to set off introductory words and words interrupting the flow of thought. Each chapter begins with spoken words highlighted in bubbles as an example of how we use these words when talking. The chapter then illustrates the varying ways these words and phrases can be presented in writing. Examples of effective sentences are shown. Pay close attention to the examples, rereading them aloud until their patterns stay in your mind. Internalizing the patterns of these sentences will help you write your ideas in similar patterns, which has important benefits:

1. Your writing will be concise and clear.

2. Your sentences will flow smoothly.

3. You will keep readers' interest.

4. You will improve your own reading skills. Understanding how ideas connect in sentences will help you read complicated sentences more easily.

11

Writing with Subordinating Conjunctions

- ◆ Subordinating Conjunctions
- ◆ Subordinate Clauses Take Two Patterns
- ◆ *Focus on Common Errors*

Subordinating Conjunctions

"Why didn't you call me last night?"

"Because I was working"

Because I was working is a subordinate clause.

Subordinate clauses look and sound like this:

> when the music stopped
> if drivers ignore the speed limit
> before we left for vacation
> although Monday is both a national holiday and my birthday
> since we began this course
> whenever we plan a picnic

Subordinate clauses are ideas that begin with a subordinating conjunction. We use subordinate clauses by themselves all the time when we talk. In writing, though, subordinate clauses cannot stand alone. Any idea that begins with one of the following subordinating conjunctions is not a sentence.

Common Subordinating Conjunctions		
after	because	unless
although	before	until
as	even though	when
as if	if	whenever
since	wherever	as soon as
as though	while	whether

Subordinating conjunctions have a lot of power. Put one in front of a sentence, and you will no longer have a sentence.

EXAMPLE 1

She locked the door behind her.

- This group of words is a sentence. Yet, if we add a subordinating conjunction, we set up a questionable situation:

After she locked the door behind her

- What happened after she locked the door? The reader is left wondering. This group of words is a fragment, not a sentence.

EXAMPLE 2

They were watching the football game in the family room.

- This group of words is a sentence. Yet, if we add a subordinating conjunction, we set up a questionable situation:

While they were watching the football game in the family room

- What happened while they were watching the game? This group of words is a fragment, not a sentence.

Whenever you add a subordinating conjunction to a sentence, you no longer have a sentence. As you write with subordinate clauses, keep two facts in mind:

1. A subordinate clause is not a sentence. It cannot stand alone.

2. It needs to be connected to a core sentence, which is usually close by.

Subordinate Clauses Take Two Patterns

Subordinate clauses can be placed either before or after a core sentence.

> PATTERN 1: The subordinate clause before a core sentence:
>
> Subordinate clause , core sentence .
> *After finals are over*, we are going out to celebrate.

> PATTERN 2: The subordinate clause after a core sentence:
>
> Core sentence subordinate clause .
> We are going out to celebrate *after finals are over*.

When you place the subordinate clause *before* a core sentence, mark the end of the subordinate clause with a comma so readers know when that idea ends and the core sentence begins. When you place the subordinate clause *after* a core sentence, a comma is usually not used.

Subordinate Clauses Before a Core Sentence

When a blind man carries a lame man, both go forward.

—Swedish proverb

> Subordinate clause , core sentence .
> *When a blind man carries a lame man*, both go forward.

Notice how the following writers begin their sentences with a subordinate clause, which is in boldface type. Read these sentences aloud and notice how the comma tells you when the subordinate clause is finished and the core sentence begins.

1. **If our goal is to guide our children toward lives of tolerance**, we must first recognize the intolerance that shapes our own lives.

   —Sara Bullard, *Teaching Tolerance*

2. **Although his hair and beard were greying**, he did not look old.

   —John Steinbeck, "The Chrysanthemums"

3. **As she dialed**, she noticed that her fingers were fumbling and damp.

   —Nadine Gordimer, "Happy Events"

4. **After breakfast was done**, they worked constantly.

—Charles Frazier, *Cold Mountain*

5. **Because many of the social structures that once kept our kids secure have broken down**, we have today's appalling data on juvenile crime, gangs, drug abuse, pregnancy, and dropouts.

—Colin Powell, "I Wasn't Left to Myself"

PRACTICE 1   The following sentences are written with the subordinate clause before the core sentence. Because the writers have not marked where the subordinate clause ends, the ideas are confusing. Correct these sentences by placing a comma at the end of the subordinate clause. The first one has been done for you.

EXAMPLE: When people have the tools they need to succeed problems become opportunities.

When people have the tools they need to succeed, problems become opportunities.

1. As soon as the restaurant opened we ordered twenty-ounce chicken burritos with roasted corn-chili salsa.

2. Wherever Mark and Michael travel they seem to find friends.

3. Since Cheryl often swims sixteen laps is an easy workout.

4. While a customer is in the process of disputing charges on a credit card the credit card agency cannot legally charge interest.

5. When the college scheduled its on-campus job fair students met with recruiters to ask them questions about their firms.

PRACTICE 2   Use each of the following subordinate clauses to start a sentence. You will need to add your own core sentences. Remember to mark the end of the subordinate clause with a comma. The first one has been done for you.

EXAMPLE: If we wash the car, *it will rain.*

1. Before we decide to make reservations

_____

_____

2. When the final scores were posted

_____

_____

3. Although no one seemed to notice

_____

_____

4. Whenever I have free time

_____

_____

5. Since the beginning of the year

_____

_____

PRACTICE 3   For each numbered item, create a whole sentence. Complete the subordinate clause, add a comma, and then add a core sentence.

1. _When_ _____

_____

_____

2. _Because_ _____

_____

_____

3. _If_ _____

_____

_____

4. _While_ _____

_____

_____

5. _As soon as_ _____

_____

_____

Subordinate Clauses After a Core Sentence

> He had a habit of telling me jokes whenever he saw me.
>
> —Isaac Asimov, "What Is Intelligence, Anyway?"

Core sentence subordinate clause .
He had a habit of telling me jokes *whenever he saw me.*

Notice how the following writers use subordinate clauses, which are in boldface type. When the subordinate clause comes after the core sentence, a comma is not used.

1. <u>She was looking straight up</u> **as if there were unintelligible handwriting on the ceiling.**

   —Flannery O'Connor, "Revelation"

2. He came **because he is at heart a listener and a searcher for some transcendent realm beyond himself.**

   —Loren Eiseley, "The Hidden Teacher"

3. Each day the land was covered in a haze of mist **as the sun sucked up the last drop of moisture out of the earth.**

   —Bessie Head, "Looking for a Rain God"

4. My relatives murmured with pleasure **when my mother brought out the whole steamed fish.**

   —Amy Tan, "Fish Cheeks"

5. Her victory burned in her **as a flame blackens within a hollow tree.**

   —Nadine Gordimer, *July's People*

PRACTICE 4   In the previous five sentences, underline the core sentence. The first one has been done for you.

PRACTICE 5   In the following exercise, rewrite each sentence so that the subordinate clause comes after the core sentence. The first one has been done for you.

EXAMPLE: If we wash the car, it will rain.

It will rain if we wash the car.

1. Whenever the barometer falls, my grandfather's bones ache.

_____

_____

2. When the car turned the corner, I noticed an alignment problem.

_____

_____

3. After we cleared away half-filled coffee cups and old copies of the newspaper, we sat down to talk.

_____

_____

4. When companies become more efficient, productivity will rise.

_____

_____

5. Until a high-pressure system moves in, we will be stuck with clouds and rain.

_____

_____

6. While the construction crew repaved the parking lot, students had to park on the street.

_____

_____

7. When we wanted to expand our business, we applied for a Small Business Administration loan.

_____

_____

8. Because of pressure from special-interest groups, the president chose not to sign the treaty.

_____

_____

9. As soon as the on-site fitness center opened, employees rushed to reserve time in the gym.

_____

_____

10. After global satellites were installed, the price of communicating by phone and computer decreased.

_____

_____

PRACTICE 6

 SENTENCE COMBINING Subordinating conjunctions will help you avoid writing short, choppy sentences, and they will make the relationships between your ideas clear. In each pair of sentences that follows, make one sentence into a subordinate clause by adding a subordinating conjunction, such as *after, since, as, because, while, when,* and *as soon as.* Then attach the subordinate clause either before or after the remaining sentence. The first one has been done for you.

EXAMPLE: My credit card arrived in the mail. I started to spend money foolishly.

After my credit card arrived in the mail, I started to spend money foolishly.

or

I started to spend money foolishly after my credit card arrived in the mail.

1. The VCR wouldn't record. I returned it to the store.

_____

2. The unexpected news arrived. We stepped back and counted our blessings.

_____

_____

3. Linda slammed on the brakes. She saw the snapped power line lying on the road.

_____

_____

4. Victor scheduled the interview. He learned about the company by visiting its web site on the Internet.

_____

_____

5. Critics gave the new movie national exposure with their positive reviews. Audiences did not share their enthusiasm.

_____

_____

6. The fishing and timber industries declined. The coastal communities began to rely on tourism.

_____

_____

7. The two parties stopped bargaining for power and sought creative approaches for peace. A settlement was reached.

_____

_____

_____

8. New jobs are often created. Companies expand an existing department.

_____

_____

_____

9. The committee members considered policies for political reform. They discussed the differences between illegal contributions and unethical ones.

_____

_____

_____

10. Medical research has made scientific breakthroughs in understanding viruses. Many diseases are being cured.

_____

_____

_____

Focus on Common Errors

Two errors are frequently made with subordinate clauses. The first error is writing a subordinate clause as if it were a sentence. The second error is forgetting to mark the end of the subordinate clause with a comma.

Error 1: Writing a subordinate clause as if it were a sentence

    Incorrect: Whenever their car alarms go off accidentally.

    Correct: Whenever their car alarms go off accidentally, *people are embarrassed*.

Error 2: Forgetting to mark the end of a subordinate clause with a comma

    Incorrect: If our candidate is elected we will have good representation.

    Correct: If our candidate is elected, we will have good representation.

PRACTICE 7 Some of the following sentences are correct. Others contain subordinate clause errors. Individually or in groups, correct where necessary.

1. I remained calm. While everyone else panicked.

2. When he left home at seventeen and joined the Army Reserves he didn't know that his life was taking a new direction.

3. Before we could get out of the parking lot. The truck pulled across the lane and blocked our exit.

4. Health officials are enforcing safety regulations because new kinds of bacteria are entering the food supply.

5. I met the other parents in the neighborhood. Because I was involved in community activities.

6. If we can find the information we need. We will meet the deadline for the project.

7. Families began to gather for the Fourth of July fireworks. As soon as the sun went down.

8. Since the public broadcasting channel gave each political candidate two minutes of free air time. All candidates were able to present their political platforms.

9. After the motivational speaker finished his speech the audience members jumped to their feet and applauded.

10. If sneezing and congestion last longer than a week or recur frequently, an allergic reaction to pollen, dust, or mold should be considered.

Review: Writing with Subordinating Conjunctions

- Make sure you connect a subordinate clause to a core sentence.
  I remained calm. While everyone else panicked.
  I remained calm while everyone else panicked.

- If you begin with a subordinate clause, mark the end of that idea with a comma.
  When the summer heat reached 134 degrees, the asphalt melted.

- If you end with the subordinate clause, a comma is not usually used.
  The asphalt melted when the summer heat reached 134 degrees.

REVIEW PRACTICE Individually or in groups, edit the following paragraph for subordinate clause errors.

I now realize that I have always trusted someone or something. When I was a toddler taking my first steps to walk I trusted my parents to hold me and keep me from falling. When I was six years old and received my first bicycle. I trusted the training wheels to help me maintain balance. As soon as it was time to take the training wheels off I depended on my dad to guide me as I wobbled down the street. I am now older and recognize the importance of trust. Whether it was taking my first steps, learning to keep my balance, or keeping on a straight path I realize that I had to trust someone or something.

—Student Writer

 EXTRA CHALLENGE In the following adaptation of Leo Buscaglia's writing, five commas marking the end of subordinate clauses have been omitted. Individually or in groups, correct the writing by inserting the commas after the subordinate clauses.

It takes courage to love. Although love is often perceived to be effortless anyone who has ever loved knows it takes effort and courage. By its nature, love requires that we risk rejection, overcome barriers of resistance, surmount our weaknesses, and fully utilize our resources. If we are rejected we will need courage to rise up and try again. If we are hurt we must have the confidence that we will heal. If we are desolate we must muster up the human dignity to prevail.

When we have the courage to meet whatever hindrances we may encounter along the way we become more than just re-actors to our lives. We become the actors who determine the courses.

—Leo Buscaglia, *Born for Love*

12

Writing with Adjectives

◆ Adjectives
◆ *-ed* Adjectives
◆ *-ing* Adjectives

Adjectives

"What color car did they buy?"

"Red"

Red is an adjective.

Adjectives look and sound like this:

foolish	important	happy	clumsy
unfamiliar	magical	generous	painful
decent	silent	insensitive	sweaty
sensitive	medical	vicious	sincere
ambitious	comfortable	impatient	honest

An adjective modifies a noun or a pronoun, and it tells *what kind, which one,* or *how many.* Adjectives generally come before the noun or pronoun they modify or after a verb that links them to the subject.

Before a noun:

inquisitive children   *easy* tests

optimistic friend   *damp* basement

After a verb that links the description to the subject:

The children are *inquisitive.*   Those tests were *easy.*

My friend is *optimistic.*   The basement was *damp.*

Notice how adjectives add description, helping us imagine each specific situation. In the following sentences, the adjectives are shown in boldface type.

1. Our shouts echoed in the **silent** streets.

—James Joyce, "Araby"

2. A **faint** wind was prowling about the schoolhouse.

—Albert Camus, "The Guest"

3. The **purple** prunes soften and sweeten.

—John Steinbeck, *The Grapes of Wrath*

4. A **heavy** blanket of **red** dust settled over me.

—Roger Hoffman, "The Dare"

5. The **brief** day drew to a close in a **long, slow** twilight.

—Jack London, "To Build a Fire"

PRACTICE 1 In the five sentences you just read, draw an arrow from each adjective to the noun it describes. The first one has been done for you.

PRACTICE 2 Add specific detail to the following sentences by adding adjectives. You may select adjectives from the previous pages or create your own. The first one has been done for you.

EXAMPLE: The residents helped children with their homework.

The *elderly* residents helped *neighborhood* children with their homework.

1. The driver honked his horn at the intersection.

_____

_____

2. Shoppers swarmed through the aisles.

_____

_____

3. The candidate left the interview.

_____

_____

4. Joggers ran down Elm Street towards the alley.

_____

_____

5. An employee gave us advice.

_____

_____

PRACTICE 3   In the following sentences, circle each adjective and draw an arrow to the noun it describes. The first one has been done for you.

EXAMPLE: A (mild) winter and (wet) spring have produced (near-record) crops in the Midwest.

1. Meditation helps create a peaceful mind and a healthy body.

2. Grandpa had a simple vocabulary and a deep understanding of the human soul.

3. The movie directors are looking for scripts that include character development, emotional insight, and artistic sensibility.

4. The international leaders discussed ways to bring economic growth and political stability to the region.

5. The community wants safe, quiet streets.

Punctuating Adjectives

When two adjectives are next to each other, put a comma between them if the word *and* would make sense between them.

The community wants safe, quiet streets.

> *Safe and quiet streets* makes sense.
>
> Therefore, you can separate the two adjectives with a comma.

She wore new blue jeans.

> *New and blue jeans* does not make sense.
>
> Therefore, do not use a comma.

PRACTICE 4

SENTENCE COMBINING Placing adjectives before nouns will help you write clear and compact sentences. Each of the following pairs of sentences can be combined into one sentence. Take the main information given in the second sentence, use that information as an adjective or as two adjectives, and place the adjective(s) before the appropriate noun(s). The first two have been done for you.

EXAMPLE: We are attending seminars that explain how to start a small business. The seminars are given on the weekend.

> We are attending weekend seminars that explain how to start a small business.

EXAMPLE: The Hubble telescope has given us pictures of galaxies. The pictures are fantastic; the galaxies are distant.

> The Hubble telescope has given us fantastic pictures of distant galaxies.

1. They are looking for a car that gets good gas mileage. The car also has to be safe.

_____

_____

2. The restaurant is featured in our newspaper. The restaurant is new; the newspaper is local.

_____

_____

3. The father sat and held his son until dawn. His son was an infant.

_____

_____

4. The employees meet weekly for development. The employees are new, and the development is professional.

_____

_____

5. We need to replace the pipes that stretch across the ceiling. The pipes are rusty, and the ceiling is in the basement.

_____

_____

6. Investigators are searching for information. The investigators are persistent, and they are looking for reliable information.

_____

_____

7. Children who have had guidance are likely to become compassionate adults. The guidance is consistent.

_____

_____

8. The price of the hotel room includes breakfast and use of the swimming pool. The breakfast is continental, and the swimming pool is Olympic-sized.

_____

_____

_____

9. A bicycle repairman donated tires and rims to firefighters who rebuilt bikes for children. The firefighters were volunteers, and the children lived in the neighborhood.

_____

_____

_____

10. The informational interview is a meeting with a company expert to learn about opportunities. The meeting is informal, and you learn about opportunities for jobs.

_____

_____

_____

Indicating More _and_ Most

Most adjectives add _-er_ and _-est_ to show _more_ and _most_.

Adjective	More	Most
tall	taller	tallest
strong	stronger	strongest
fast	faster	fastest
warm	warmer	warmest

A few adjectives change spelling rather than adding _-er_ and _-est_.

Adjective	More	Most
good	better	best
bad	worse	worst

The adjectives in the _more_ column are used to indicate that one item has _more_ of a quality than one other item. Use them to compare two items.

Janice is _taller_ than Peggy.

October's storm was _worse_ than September's storm.

The adjectives in the _most_ column are used to indicate that one item is, in some way, above all other similar items; it is the _most_. Use them to compare three or more items.

Janice is the _tallest_ child in the second grade.

December's storm was the _worst_ on record.

The _-er_ ending indicates the meaning of _more_; _-est_ indicates the meaning of _most_. Therefore, do not repeat the meaning by writing _more better_ or _most kindest_.

The trip was ~~more~~ longer than we had expected.

Life has taught us that the ~~most~~ wealthiest people are not always the ~~most~~ happiest people.

Most adjectives with two or more syllables (pronounceable parts) do not add -er and -est because the word would become difficult to say. When adjectives have two or more syllables, the words *more* and *most* are used instead of the endings -er and -est.*

> Algebra was *more* challenging than geometry, but trigonometry was the *most* challenging math course I ever took.

Adjective	More	Most
sensitive	more sensitive	most sensitive
careful	more careful	most careful
famous	more famous	most famous
difficult	more difficult	most difficult
beautiful	more beautiful	most beautiful

PRACTICE 5   In the following sentences, some of the adjectives are used correctly; others are not. Correct where necessary.

1. Traffic is worst going into the city than it is going out of the city.

   _____

   _____

2. Children ask the most curious questions.

   _____

3. Knowing that I have done my best is the most greatest feeling.

   _____

4. The salesperson who helped us today was more pleasanter than the previous one.

   _____

   _____

5. When we shopped for living room furniture, we discovered that the comfortablest couch was also the most expensive one.

   _____

   _____

*The exception to this rule is adjectives that end in -y. If an adjective ends in -y, change the -y to -i and add -er or -est, as in *sunny, sunnier, sunniest.*

Verb Forms Used as Adjectives

Think of the many roles you play: student, employee, family member, friend. You often change roles, depending on where you are and what you are doing. Words are like that. They change roles, depending on where they are and what they are doing in a sentence. Verb forms ending in *-ing* and *-ed* are usually verbs. Yet these words can also be used as adjectives.

EXAMPLE 1

The <u>fans</u> <u>motivated</u> their team.

- The word *motivated* is used here as a verb. Asking yourself, "Who did what?" or "What is happening?" will help you find the subject and verb of a sentence. Applying these questions to the sentence above tells us that the subject is *fans* and the verb is *motivated*.

The *motivated* <u>team</u> <u>won</u> the NBA Championship.

- The word *motivated* is used here as an adjective. (Who did what? What's happening?) The subject is *team* and the verb is *won*. We know that the team is motivated, but now *motivated* is an adjective describing the team. The subject-and-verb structure of this sentence is <u>*team*</u> <u>*won*</u>.

EXAMPLE 2

The <u>plaster</u> <u>is crumbling</u> all over the carpet.

- The word *crumbling* is used here as a verb: Who did what? What is happening? The subject-and-verb structure is <u>*plaster*</u> <u>*is crumbling*</u>.

<u>We</u> <u>will replace</u> the *crumbling* plaster.

- The word *crumbling* is used here as an adjective. We know that the plaster is crumbling, but in this sentence the subject is *we* and the verb is *will replace*. *Crumbling* is an adjective describing *plaster*.

-ed Adjectives

The motivated team won the NBA Championship.

The *-ed* adjectives are in italics. They look and sound like this:

unexpected news	*relaxed* students
satisfied customers	*discounted* merchandise
skilled mechanics	*confused* tourists

- An *-ed* adjective often goes before the noun it describes.

- Although we may not hear the *-d* or *-ed* pronounced at the end of these words, that is how *-ed* adjectives are spelled. As you edit your writing, check to make sure you have added the necessary *-d* or *-ed*.

Notice how these writers use *-ed* adjectives, which are in boldface type.

1. Scores of **interconnected** rooms line the cliffs of the canyon.

—David Roberts,
"The Old Ones of the Southwest"

2. Lennie's face broke into a **delighted** smile.

—John Steinbeck, *Of Mice and Men*

3. Mabel's worn face has the texture of **crinkled** cotton, but suddenly she

looks pretty.

—Bobbie Ann Mason, "Shiloh"

4. He crept to the door and squinted through the **fogged** plate glass.

—Richard Wright, "The Man Who
Lived Underground"

5. Our scientific power has outrun our spiritual power: We have

guided missiles and **misguided** men.

—Martin Luther King, Jr.

PRACTICE 6   In the five previous sentences, draw an arrow from the *-ed* adjective to the noun it describes. The first one has been done for you.

PRACTICE 7

SENTENCE COMBINING In each of the following pairs of sentences, condense the information in the second sentence into one *-ed* adjective. Then place the adjective in the first sentence, before the noun being described. The first one has been done for you.

EXAMPLE: The employee smiled and shook the administrator's hand. The employee was promoted.

The promoted employee smiled and shook the administrator's hand.

1. We were impressed with the interviewer's approach. The approach was relaxed.

_____

_____

© 2000 Houghton Mifflin Company

2. The students needed a break from classes. The students were exhausted.

_____

_____

3. The customer service increased sales and boosted employee morale. The customer service was improved.

_____

_____

4. The union workers left the negotiations. They were relieved.

_____

_____

5. The surgery on his arteries was successful. His arteries were blocked.

_____

_____

6. A police car sat on the shoulder of the southbound lane. The car was unmarked.

_____

_____

7. The band will begin its major promotional push in August. The band has been reorganized.

_____

_____

8. The doctor submitted an explanation of the patient's treatment to the insurance company. The explanation was detailed.

_____

_____

_____

9. New car models are entering a market. The market is saturated.

_____

_____

10. Miles of wires and telephone cords ran along the walls, under desks, and on the floor. The wires and telephone cords were intertwined.

_____

_____

_____

-ing Adjectives

We will replace the crumbling plaster.

The *-ing* adjectives are in italics. They look and sound like this:

sparkling eyes	*convincing* argument
confusing chapter	*squeaking* brakes
smiling children	*escalating* prices

• An *-ing* adjective goes before the noun it describes.

Notice how these writers use *-ing* adjectives, which are in boldface.

1. I was a **listening** child, careful to hear the very different sounds of Spanish and English.

—Richard Rodriguez, "Aria"

2. A haze rested on the low shores that ran out to sea in **vanishing** flatness.

—Joseph Conrad, *Heart of Darkness*

3. He stared at the **singing** faces with a **trembling** smile.

—Richard Wright, "The Man Who Lived Underground"

4. We squeezed through the narrow, **chattering**, jam-packed bar to the entrance of the big room, where the bandstand was.

—James Baldwin, "Sonny's Blues"

5. **Splashing** waves and **squawking** seagulls surrounded us.

—Florence Ladd, *Sarah's Psalm*

PRACTICE 8 In the five previous sentences, draw an arrow from the *-ing* adjective to the noun it describes. The first one has been done for you.

PRACTICE 9

 SENTENCE COMBINING Condense the information in the second sentence into an *-ing* adjective and place that adjective in the first sentence, before the noun it describes. The first one has been done for you.

EXAMPLE: The man looks as if he knows something we don't. The man is smiling.

The smiling man looks as if he knows something we don't.

1. Our vacation is over. It was relaxing.

_____

2. Everyone respects the supervisor. He is an encouraging person.

_____

_____

3. Ellis supported his family by working two jobs. His family was growing.

_____

_____

4. Rosita not only survived the interview, she got the job. The interview was agonizing.

_____

_____

5. The men were moved by the speaker's testimony. The testimony was inspiring.

_____

6. After listening to his mom's words, the kindergartner left for his first day of school. His mom's words were reassuring to him.

_____

_____

7. The jury listened intently to the defense attorney's evidence. The evidence was overwhelming.

_____

_____

8. The team wears uniforms splashed with purple, green, and gold. The team is high-scoring.

_____

_____

9. Environmentalists hope to preserve the prairie as a habitat for native grasses and birds. The birds are migrating.

_____

_____

_____

10. Industries are using a variety of strategies to attract and retain capable staff. The industries are competing.

_____

_____

Review: Writing with Adjectives

- Use adjectives to add specific description to your writing.
- Consider using *-ing* and *-ed* verb forms as adjectives. They add vivid detail to sentences.

 REVIEW PRACTICE The following details are taken from "Wilderness Rafting Siberian Style," by Michael McRae. Individually or in groups, condense each sentence in italics into an adjective and place the adjective in the previous sentence.

Yuri was in trouble. *The trouble was serious.* The river had seized

his boat and sent it cartwheeling over a waterfall. *The waterfall*

was a ten-foot one. Yuri ended up far downstream and was obviously

dazed. His teammates tried throwing him rescue lines, but he was

too weak to grasp them. The current grabbed him once again and

swept him away like a rag doll. *The current was swirling.* He disappeared

around the bend. *The bend was sharp.* When the teammates finally

found him, he was gasping for air on the shore. *The shore was rocky.*

EXTRA CHALLENGE   Individually or in groups, use the following sentences as models and replace each adjective in italics with an adjective of your choice. Be creative; the adjective you choose need not have the same meaning as the one being replaced. The first one has been done for you.

EXAMPLE: In a *clear, fine* voice, she sang ballads of the *old* days in her country, and the child was always caught in their magic.

                                    —José Antonio Villareal, "Poncho"

In a ___*mysterious, enchanting*___ voice, she sang ballads of the ___*festival*___

days in her country, and the child was always caught in their magic.

1. She wrote once a week, the *labored* writing of a seven-year-old.

                                    —Tillie Olsen, "I Stand Here Ironing"

She wrote once a week, the _____ writing of a seven-year-old.

2. The *brief* day drew to a close in a *long, slow* twilight.

                                    —Jack London, "To Build a Fire"

The _____ day drew to a close in a _____ ,

_____ twilight.

3. So we must see that peace represents a *sweeter* music, a *cosmic* melody that is far superior to the discords of war.

                                    —Martin Luther King, Jr., *Where Do We Go*
                                    From Here: Community or Chaos

So we must see that peace represents a _____ music,

a _____ melody that is far superior to the discords

of war.

4. He walked with the *creeping* movement of the *midnight* cat.

                                    —Stephen Crane, "The Bride Comes to Yellow Sky"

He walked with the _____ movement of the

_____ cat.

5. Cicadas rasped in the *brittle* leaves of the *dry* season, and a cluster of stingless bees hummed softly just above our heads.

—Noel Grove, "The Many Faces of Thailand"

Cicadas rasped in the _____ leaves of the

_____ season, and a cluster of stingless bees

hummed softly just above our heads.

Chapter 13

Writing with Adverbs

◆ Adverbs

◆ Beginning with an Adverb

Adverbs

"How often do you go to the bookstore?"

"Occasionally"

Occasionally is an adverb.

Adverbs are words that look and sound like this:

quietly	noisily	persistently	quickly
anxiously	obviously	skillfully	tirelessly
silently	aggressively	smoothly	fearfully
foolishly	understandably	nervously	enthusiastically

An adverb gives additional information about a verb, an adjective, or another adverb. Most adverbs end in *-ly*. Adverbs that do not end in *-ly* include *now, seldom, never, then,* and *often*.

Notice how these writers use adverbs, which are in boldface.

1. The wind blew **mournfully**.

—Bernard Malamud, "The Presence of Death"

2. She had fought **valiantly** to keep me from knowing her secret.

—William Carlos Williams, "The Use of Force"

3. I remember **vividly** the soft light of dawn and the gentle quiet that settled on the birthing room moments after my daughter was born.

—Thomas Moore,
The Re-Enchantment of Everyday Life

4. Moonbeams splash and spill **wildly** in the rain.

—Virginia Woolf, "A Haunted House"

5. She **immediately** jumps forward, places one hand on her hip in the manner of a fashion model, juts out her chest, and flashes me a toothy smile.

—Amy Tan, "A Pair of Tickets"

PRACTICE 1   Add specific detail to the following sentences by adding adverbs. You can select adverbs from the previous pages or create your own. The first one has been done for you.

EXAMPLE: The musician's fingers danced across the keyboard.

The musician's fingers danced *playfully* across the keyboard.

1. The witness spoke.

_____

2. He stood with his hands stuffed in his pockets.

_____

3. The child stuttered as he recited the poem.

_____

4. We loaded the van with furniture.

_____

5. Airline employees worked to reschedule flights for the snowbound customers.

_____

_____

Beginning with an Adverb

Carefully, they closed the door and left their past behind.

Beginning a sentence with an adverb changes the rhythm of a core sentence. As you edit your writing, see if all of your sentences begin with the subject. For an occasional change in rhythm, you can begin a sentence with an adverb. The pattern looks like this:

> Adverb , core sentence .
> *Carefully*, they closed the door and left their past behind.

Here is the core sentence pattern:

The kindergarten teacher gently took the frightened child's hand.

- If we move the adverb to the beginning of the sentence, we create a change in rhythm. Move the adverb *gently* and place it at the beginning of the sentence.

Gently, the kindergarten teacher took the frightened child's hand.

- A comma is placed after *gently* to let readers know we are not beginning with the subject of the sentence. Commas are used to set off introductory words, and in that sentence, *gently* is an introductory word.

Notice how the following writers use adverbs, which are in boldface. Read the sentences aloud to hear how beginning with an adverb changes the rhythm of a sentence.

1. **Finally**, my mother came ashore.

   —Jamaica Kincaid, *Annie John*

2. **Eventually**, writing in my head spilled over onto scraps of paper in the middle of the day.

   —Susan McBride Els, *Into the Deep*

3. **Gradually**, I became comfortable in her company.

   —Florence Ladd, *Sarah's Psalm*

4. **Stiffly**, they sat on the blue living room sofa.

   —Richard Rodriguez, "Aria"

5. **Ultimately**, scientists would like to figure out how genetic defects cause depression, and then to design drugs to correct whatever has gone awry.

   —Judith Hooper, "Targeting the Brain"

PRACTICE 2

 SENTENCE COMBINING   Combine each of the following sentence pairs into one sentence by condensing the second sentence into an adverb. When you need to change the form of the word by adding *-ly*, that change is noted in brackets. You can place the adverb either within the sentence or at the beginning. The first one has been done for you, giving two possibilities.

EXAMPLE: The fog rolled over the city streets. It was slow and silent. [Add *-ly*.]

The fog rolled slowly and silently over the city streets.

or

Slowly and silently, the fog rolled over the city streets.

1. Jake's face crinkled into a smile. This was sudden. [Add *-ly*.]

   _____

2. Our dinner was interrupted by old friends who were driving through town. The interruption was unexpected. [Add *-ly*.]

   _____

   _____

3. The relationship had changed. That was obvious. [Add *-ly*.]

   _____

4. The tourists sidestepped motorcycles driven by teenagers in love with speed. The tourists were nervous. [Add *-ly*.]

   _____

   _____

5. The new school superintendent launched an early-education program and capped class size at twenty-eight in the elementary schools. The superintendent did this immediately.

   _____

   _____

6. The mountain climbers wedged their swollen feet into the frozen cracks. They wedged their feet repeatedly.

   _____

   _____

7. Scratches can be removed from an automobile windshield by polishing it with cerium oxide. This works on occasion. [Add *-ly*.]

_____

_____

8. The family waited in the emergency room for someone to call their name. They were anxious. [Add *-ly*.]

_____

_____

9. His free time is interrupted to help another person in need. The interruptions are frequent. [Add *-ly*.]

_____

_____

10. The agents combed through the boxes of court records. The agents did this slowly and meticulously.

_____

_____

Review: Writing with Adverbs

- Use adverbs to express your ideas clearly, concisely, and vividly.

- Read your writing aloud, listen for the rhythm of your sentences, and see if beginning a sentence with an adverb will give your writing the sentence variety it needs.

 REVIEW PRACTICE Individually or in groups, read the following paragraph and circle the adverbs.

My mother taught me that what you sow you will surely reap. She believed that the good that we do will eventually bear fruit. My mom consistently gave to others. She cooked extra helpings to share with friends and other families. She drove friends who needed transportation and listened to neighbors who needed support. At times, the people my mother helped treated her indifferently. But she continued to help others because she believed the seeds she sowed would bear fruit in her life and in her children's lives. She was right. I am reaping today from her sown seeds. When I am rejected, I remember my mom's words. When I feel like quitting, I remember my mom's actions. I value myself, and I know that I did not learn to do that on my own. I am reaping the harvest from the seeds my mom carefully planted.

—Student Writer

 EXTRA CHALLENGE Individually or in groups, fill in the blanks with adverbs of your choice. Be creative; your adverb does not need to have the same meaning as the adverb you replace. The first one has been done for you.

EXAMPLE: She sat at a side window sewing *furiously* on a sewing machine.

—Kate Chopin, "The Storm"

She sat at a side window sewing _quietly_____ on a sewing machine.

1. The wind blew *mournfully*.

—Bernard Malamud, "The Presence of Death"

The wind blew _____.

2. Sykes poured out a saucer full of coffee and drank it *deliberately* before he answered her.

—Zora Neale Hurston, "Sweat"

Sykes poured out a saucer full of coffee and drank it _____

before he answered her.

3. Moonbeams splash and spill *wildly* in the rain.

—Virginia Woolf, "A Haunted House"

Moonbeams splash and spill _____ in the rain.

4. *Gradually,* I became comfortable in her company.

—Florence Ladd, *Sarah's Psalm*

_____ , I became comfortable in her company.

5. *Stiffly,* they sat on the blue living room sofa.

—Richard Rodriguez, "Aria"

_____ , they sat on the blue living room sofa.

Chapter 14

Writing with Prepositional Phrases

◆ Prepositional Phrases
◆ *Focus on Fragments*

Prepositional Phrases

"Where did you go last night?"

"To the movies"

To the movies is a prepositional phrase.

Prepositional phrases look and sound like this:

during summer vacation	with a curious expression	behind us
through the front door	past the second light	within one week
in the night's blue silence	across the parking lot	before dinner
along the riverbank	against our advice	over the fence
down the slippery steps	throughout the rainy season	without stopping
from their experiences	up the dusty road	at me

© 2000 Houghton Mifflin Company

A prepositional phrase is an idea that begins with a preposition. A simple, though not exact, way to identify a preposition is by deciding whether the word would make sense after the words *The dog ran.* (The dog ran *under . . . over . . . behind . . . through. . . .*) Although this sentence does not work for the prepositions *of* and *except,* it will help you identify other prepositions.

Common Prepositions		
about	by	past
above	during	through
across	except	throughout
after	for	to
against	from	toward
among	in	under
around	inside	underneath
at	into	until
before	like	up
behind	of	with
below	off	within
beneath	on	without
beside	outside	
between	over	

A prepositional phrase begins with a preposition and ends when the idea the phrase expresses is completed. To find the end of a prepositional phrase, repeat the preposition and ask yourself, "What?" The answer will tell you where the phrase ends.

Our mailbox is stuffed with bulk mail advertisements.

- The preposition in this example sentence is *with.* In order to find out where the phrase ends, we need to repeat the preposition in the question "*With* what?" The answer will identify the prepositional phrase *with bulk mail advertisements.*

Hot sun and cool breezes reminded them of summer vacations in the mountains.

- Sentences often have more than one prepositional phrase. The question technique remains the same. In this example, the first preposition is *of.* "*Of* what?" The answer identifies the prepositional phrase *of summer vacations.* The second preposition is *in.* "*In* what?" The answer identifies the prepositional phrase *in the mountains.*

Notice how the following writers use prepositional phrases, often putting a series of them together. The prepositional phrases are in brackets.

1. Insects click [**in the fields**].

—Richard Rodriguez, "To the Border"

2. Window sashes shuddered [**in a blast**] [**of winter air**].

—Toni Morrison, *Beloved*

3. The waves came [**without snarling**].

—Stephen Crane, "The Open Boat"

4. Spit coagulated [**into little white gobs**] [**at the corners**] [**of her mouth**].

—Arundhati Roy, *The God of Small Things*

5. His smile was a two-line checkerboard [**of white and gold**].

—Maya Angelou, *Gather Together in My Name*

Subjects, Verbs, and Prepositional Phrases

Subjects and verbs are never inside prepositional phrases. Prepositional phrases are details added to the subject-and-verb skeleton.

 PRACTICE 1 Individually or in groups, add prepositional phrases to the following skeleton sentences. Select prepositional phrases from the previous pages or create your own. See how many you can add without making the sentence confusing.

1. The tracks led.

_____

2. My friend looked.

_____

3. The car swerved.

_____

4. The train whistled.

_____

5. Students relaxed.

_____

Prepositional phrases are often placed after the subject of a sentence. In the sentence *Students in the cafeteria relaxed*, the subject is *students*, not *cafeteria*. We have noted that the subject of a sentence is never inside a prepositional phrase. Knowing this is important when you check your sentences for subject-verb agreement. Because subjects should agree with their verbs, look for prepositional phrases around the subject. Isolate them so that you can clearly identify the subject.

The skill (of the doctors) is evident in the emergency room.

- When we circle the prepositional phrase *of the doctors*, the subject of the sentence is clear: *skill*. The verb of a sentence needs to agree with the subject. Because the subject *skill* is singular, the verb must be singular: *is*. (The subject cannot be *doctors* because it is in a prepositional phrase.)

PRACTICE 2   In the following sentences, the prepositional phrases are circled. Underline the subject once and the verb twice. The first one has been done for you.

EXAMPLE: The manufacturer (of these appliances) guarantees them for only one year.

1. Tickets (for the late movie) are on sale now.

2. The price (of repairing our telephone and answering machine) exceeds the cost of a new machine.

3. The taillights (of a single car) guided our way through the fog.

4. Breakfasts and lunches (at the new coffee shop) are inexpensive.

5. A powerful network (of ties among family, friends, and neighbors) nurtures everyone in the community.

PRACTICE 3   Circle each prepositional phrase that follows the subject. Then underline the subject once and the correct verb twice. As you select the verb, remember how present tense verbs work. If the subject is a singular noun, the verb ends in *-s*. If the subject is a plural noun, the verb does not end in *-s*. The first one has been done for you.

EXAMPLE: The books (on the top shelf) (has, have) not been dusted in years.

1. The cars in the driveway (was, were) dented by hailstones.

2. The signatures on the petition (indicates, indicate) that Americans are concerned.

3. The stained glass windows in the sanctuary (radiate, radiates) light.

4. The bag of groceries (was, were) on the back porch all day.

5. The voter turnout in November's elections (was, were) high.

6. All files on the hard drive (need, needs) to be backed up on a floppy disk.

7. A list of rules (is, are) on the back of the insurance form.

8. The stereo speakers in the record store (is, are) mounted under an acrylic dome.

9. Arthritis in both hands (limits, limit) her flexibility.

10. A complete set of encyclopedia volumes (is, are) available on one compact disc.

Beginning with a Prepositional Phrase

Over a petty disagreement, they destroyed a valuable friendship.

Effective writing includes sentences that occasionally vary the typical subject-verb sentence pattern. One of the ways you can achieve sentence variety is to begin with a prepositional phrase. The pattern looks like this:

> <u>Prepositional phrase</u> , <u>core sentence</u> .
> *Over a petty disagreement*, they destroyed a valuable friendship.

Here is the core sentence pattern:

They destroyed a valuable friendship over a petty disagreement.

- If we move a prepositional phrase to the beginning of the sentence, we create a change in rhythm. Let's move the prepositional phrase *over a petty disagreement* to the beginning of the sentence.

Over a petty disagreement, they destroyed a valuable friendship.

- A comma is placed after *over a petty disagreement* to show readers that we are not beginning with the subject of the sentence. Commas are used to set off introductory words, and *over a petty disagreement* is now a group of introductory words.

PRACTICE 4   Circle each of the prepositional phrases that begin the following sentences. Notice that the comma tells readers when the extra information is over and the core sentence begins. The first one has been done for you.

EXAMPLE: (At the first gesture) (of morning), flies began stirring.

—Charles Frazier, *Cold Mountain*

1. In that place , the wind prevailed.

—Glendon Swarthout, *Bless the Beasts and Children*

2. With a wry smile on her lips , she listened to the sound of his

retreating steps.

—Henry Roth, *Call It Sleep*

3. In the midst of the children's laughter , I turned pale.

—Yasunari Kawabata, "The Man Who Did Not Smile"

4. In Pueblo country , throughout the yearly growing season , the

corn dances take place.

—Linda Hogan, "Thanksgiving"

5. With no theater, no recreation center, and no restaurant in town ,

the schools and churches were the focal point for social activities.

—Jimmy and Rosalynn Carter, *Everything to Gain*

PRACTICE 5 Rewrite each of the following sentences by moving a prepositional phrase to the beginning of that sentence. When a sentence begins with a prepositional phrase, use a comma to separate it from the core sentence. The first two have been done for you.

EXAMPLE: The finalist for a split second considered dropping out of the race.

For a split second, the finalist considered dropping out of the race.

EXAMPLE: A variety of seafood is available at the outdoor restaurant on the pier.

At the outdoor restaurant on the pier, a variety of seafood is available.

1. The president announced additional layoffs during his press conference.

_____

_____

2. It looked as if nothing had changed on the surface.

_____

_____

3. She is unbeatable on the basketball court.

_____

_____

4. He swam toward the sinking boat with fierce determination.

_____

_____

5. Students can register for classes by phone or computer on some campuses.

_____

_____

6. The amendment to the Senate bill was approved without hearings or formal debate.

_____

_____

7. The team felt pressured with four state titles in four years.

_____

_____

8. Beth scored a driving layup to give her team the lead with less than three minutes left.

_____

_____

9. The local hospital offers classes in cardiopulmonary resuscitation (CPR) on the second Monday of each month.

_____

_____

10. The group doubled its membership for the first time in three years.

_____

_____

Focus on Fragments

A prepositional phrase or a series of prepositional phrases cannot stand alone as a sentence. A sentence needs both a subject and a verb.

Fragment: At the last possible moment
Sentence: _We paid our bills_ at the last possible moment.

Fragment: The trailer on the next lot
Sentence: The trailer on the next lot _is for sale._

Review: Writing with Prepositional Phrases

• Use prepositional phrases to add specific details to your writing.

• When editing your writing, look for prepositional phrases around the subjects of your sentences. Remember to isolate the prepositional phrases so you can identify the subject. Then check for subject-verb agreement.

• For sentence variety, begin a sentence with a prepositional phrase.

 REVIEW PRACTICE In the following paragraph, the details of the prepositional phrases have been deleted. Individually or in groups, complete the prepositional phrases by creating your own details.

A soft fall rain slips down through _____ ,

and the smell of _____ is so strong that it can

almost be licked off _____ . Trucks rumble along

_____ , and men in _____ stained with

_____ shout to _____ from the

_____ . Beneath them, the ocean swells up against

_____ and sucks back down to _____ .

Beer cans and old pieces of_____ rise and fall, and

pools of _____ undulate* like _____ .

The boats rock and creak against _____ , and

seagulls complain and hunker down and complain some more.

—Adapted from Sebastian Junger, *The Perfect Storm*

EXTRA CHALLENGE Individually or in groups, use the following highlighted sentences as models and replace the prepositional phrases in italics with your own prepositional phrases. Be creative; your prepositional phrases do not need to have the same meaning as the ones you replace. The first one has been done for you.

EXAMPLE: *Underneath the wagon, between the hind wheels,* a lean and rangy mongrel dog walked sedately.

—John Steinbeck, "The Chrysanthemums"

Before daylight, outside the closed restaurant _____ ,

a lean and rangy mongrel dog walked sedately.

1. *With a wry smile on her lips,* she listened to the sound of his retreating steps.
   —Henry Roth, *Call It Sleep*

_____ , she listened to the

sound of his retreating steps.

2. *In Pueblo country, throughout the yearly growing season,* the corn dances take place.
   —Linda Hogan, "Thanksgiving"

_____ , the corn dances take

place.

---

* The verb *undulate* means "to move in waves."

3. Wet snow drifted *in the black night.*

—Vladimir Nabokov, *Pnin*

Wet snow drifted _____.

4. Waves *of relief* ripple *down my spine.*

—Jon Krakauer, "Straight Up Ice"

Waves _____ ripple _____.

5. All the years that have passed have not dimmed my memory *of that first glorious autumn.*

—Willa Cather, *My Antonia*

All the years that have passed have not dimmed my memory of _____

_____.

Chapter 15

Writing with Relative Clauses

◆ Relative Clauses
◆ *Focus on Fragments*

Relative Clauses

"I need a friend . . .   who understands computers."

Who understands computers is a relative clause.

Relative clauses look and sound like this:

who works part-time

who works part-time and attends college full-time

which she unwrapped carefully

which was sooner than we expected

that we want for our future

that is on sale

Ideas that begin with *who, which,* or *that* and describe a noun are called relative clauses. Notice how the second example in the list expands the first example. These clauses can expand until the idea is complete.

As you write with relative clauses, keep these facts in mind:

1. A relative clause is not a sentence. It is an addition to a sentence.

2. A relative clause describes a noun in the sentence and follows the noun it describes.

3. *Who* is used about people. *Which* is used about things. *That* is used about things and sometimes about people.

Notice how these writers use relative clauses, which are in boldface.

1. The farmers **who used to gather around the courthouse square on Saturday afternoons to play checkers and spit tobacco juice** have gone.

—Bobbie Ann Mason, "Shiloh"

2. An old lady **who lived alone in one of the back rooms** was the first absolutely toothless person I had ever seen.

—Ernesto Galarza, *Barrio Boy*

3. The sky was filled with a floating white mist **which clung to the street lamps.**

—Bernard Malamud, "Spring Rain"

4. The amount **that appears later on your credit card bill** may not match the amount charged at the location.

—Colwell and Shulman, *Trouble-Free Travel*

5. The ties **that ordinarily bind children to their homes** were all suspended in my case.

—Frederick Douglass, *Narrative of the Life of Frederick Douglass, an American Slave*

PRACTICE 1   A relative clause gives additional information about a noun in a sentence. In each of the five previous sentences, draw an arrow from the relative clause to the noun it describes. The first one has been done for you.

PRACTICE 2   A relative clause is not a sentence. An idea beginning with *who, which,* or *that* can give additional information about another word in a sentence, but the additional information cannot stand alone as a sentence. There must be a core sentence supporting the relative clause. Return to the same sentences you worked on in Practice 1 and underline each core sentence. The first one has been done for you.

PRACTICE 3   Complete each of the following sentences by finishing the relative clause. Make sure you have a core sentence that supports the addition.

1. The person who _____

   will succeed.

2. Lisa likes movies that _____.

3. The final exam, which _____ , was easier

   than we had expected.

4. The clothes that _____ were first

   quality.

5. Employees who _____ sometimes

   start their own businesses.

 PRACTICE 4   Individually or in groups, circle all the relative clauses in the following two selections.

I, who had never been a soldier , who had never fought in battle , who had never fired a gun at an enemy , had been given the task of starting an army.

—Nelson Mandela,
The Autobiography of Nelson Mandela

I want a wife who will plan the menus , do the necessary grocery shopping , prepare the meals , serve them pleasantly , and then do the cleaning up while I do my studying . I want a wife who will care for me when I am sick and sympathize with my pain and loss of time from school .

—Judy Brady, "I Want a Wife"

PRACTICE 5

 SENTENCE COMBINING Writing with relative clauses is a valuable way to combine two sentences into one compact sentence. Condense the information in the second sentence into a relative clause beginning with *who, which,* or *that* and place the addition after the noun it describes. The first two have been done for you.

EXAMPLE: Hurricanes are approaching Florida's coastline. Hurricanes form over warm ocean water.

Hurricanes, which form over warm ocean water, are approaching Florida's coastline.

EXAMPLE: The customer left his credit card on the counter. He was just here.

The customer who was just here left his credit card on the counter.

1. Every day at the hospital I work with patients. They have taught me how to replace anger with understanding.

_____

_____

_____

2. A soft-spoken fisherman told us the history of the town. He ran the country store and post office.

_____

_____

_____

3. The ice storm toppled the generators. The generators supplied electricity for the county's homes and businesses.

_____

_____

_____

4. My cousin connects with her office daily through the Internet. My cousin lives three miles from her nearest neighbor.

_____

_____

_____

5. Part-time jobs are the answer for many workers. These workers need flexible hours.

_____

_____

_____

6. The newspaper reporter put the details in perspective. The reporter understood the historical background of the story.

_____

_____

_____

7. The annual conference lasts five days. The annual conference is held at company headquarters.

_____

_____

_____

8. Computer programmers are creating new programs. These programs offer quick access to the World Wide Web.

_____

_____

_____

9. The dilapidated building was saved and recently renovated for theaters and restaurants. The building had been headed for demolition.

_____

_____

_____

10. An outdoor sculpture garden will open to the public in July. The sculpture garden features human and wildlife figures made of bronze.

_____

_____

_____

Using Commas

Relative clauses are punctuated in varying ways. Relative clauses beginning with the word *that* are never set off by commas. Those beginning with *which* usually are. Those beginning with *who* sometimes have commas.

That Clauses Never Have Commas

Remembering this rule will help you avoid many comma errors. Do not use a comma when writing with a *that* clause.

> The planning committee has scheduled a series of events *that promote jazz and classical music.*

Which Clauses Usually Have Commas

> Staffing agencies place college graduates in short-term assignments, *which often lead to full-time employment.*

Who Clauses Sometimes Have Commas

> Doc Brown, *who volunteers at the boys' club,* plays basketball like a star.
> The people *who are sitting in the back row* cannot see the stage.

Deciding whether or not to use commas with *who* clauses involves judging how necessary that information is to the meaning of the sentence. If the *who* clause only gives extra information that is *not* necessary for the sentence to make sense, use commas to separate the information from the rest of sentence.

> Doc Brown, who volunteers at the boys' club, plays basketball like a star.

- Can you leave out *who volunteers at the boys' club* and still keep the meaning of the sentence? Yes. *Doc Brown plays basketball like a star* does not need the information about volunteering at the boys' club in order to make sense. Therefore, commas are used.

If the information in the *who* clause is essential to the sentence's meaning, do not use commas.

> The people who are sitting in the back row cannot see the stage.

- Can you leave out *who are sitting in the back row* and still keep the meaning of the sentence? No. If you leave this information out, the sentence says that all the people cannot see the stage. That is not the intended meaning of the sentence. The addition is necessary to identify who cannot see the stage. Therefore, there are no commas.

Maintaining Agreement

All parts of a sentence need to fit together smoothly. Therefore, an addition must fit the word it describes. When writing with relative clauses, make sure the verb in the addition agrees with the noun it refers to.

© 2000 Houghton Mifflin Company

Correct: People *who are investing in their futures* take advantage of opportunities in the present.

• The addition *who are investing in their futures* describes *people*. Because *people* is plural, the verb in the addition is plural: *are investing*.

Incorrect: People who ~~is~~ investing in their futures take advantage of opportunities in the present.

Correct: The history exam *that was postponed* is now rescheduled for Wednesday.

• The addition *that was postponed* describes *exam*. Because *exam* is singular, the verb in the addition is singular: *was postponed*.

Incorrect: The history exam that ~~were~~ postponed is now rescheduled for Wednesday.

PRACTICE 6   In each of the following sentences, circle the relative clause, draw an arrow to the noun it describes, then underline the correct verb inside the relative clause. The first one has been done for you.

EXAMPLE: The brothers (who (is, <u>are</u>) renting the apartment next door) are quiet neighbors.

1. The groceries that (is, are) loaded in the wire basket are discounted .

2. The bolt of lightning , which (was, were) about twenty feet from us , split the tree in two .

3. Her eyes , which (was, were) hidden by sunglasses , were hard to see .

4. The restaurant uses fresh ingredients that (is, are) prepared in front of customers .

5. The new gallery , which (open, opens) this weekend , features local contemporary artists .

6. Companies that (support, supports) their employees benefit from employee loyalty .

7. Many companies offer career-development programs that (help, helps) employees plan and prepare for future positions .

8. The low-budget film , which (has, have) been praised for its originality and unique story line , continues to attract audiences around the country .

9. Free seminars are available for individuals who (want, wants) help with completing Medicare forms .

10. The computer company invested in technology that (use, uses) satellites to transmit data .

Focus on Fragments

A relative clause is not a sentence. A relative clause can give additional information about another word in a sentence.

Fragment: Which helped create a blockbuster movie.

Sentence: *The film studio bought three days of national television advertising,* which helped create a blockbuster movie.

Fragment: The salesperson who gets the highest commission.

Sentence: The salesperson who gets the highest commission *is usually the one who works the most hours.*

Review: Writing with Relative Clauses

- Use relative clauses to add specific detail to your sentences.

- Use a relative clause to combine two sentences into one compact sentence.

- Place the relative clause after the noun it describes.

- Use *who* with people, *which* with things, and *that* with people and things.

- Do not use commas with *that* clauses.

 REVIEW PRACTICE Individually or in groups, rewrite the following paragraph by replacing the relative clauses in italics with relative clauses of your own.

Some families deliberately use hurtful language in their daily communication. "What did you do all day around here?" can be a red flag to a woman *who has spent her day on household tasks that don't show unless they're not done.* "If only we had enough money" can be a rebuke to a husband *who is working as hard as he can to provide for the family.* "Flunk any tests today, John?" only discourages a child *who may be having trouble in school.*

—Delores Curran, "What Good Families Are Doing Right"

Some families deliberately use hurtful language in their daily

communication. "What did you do all day around here?" can be a

red flag to a woman _____

_____ .

"If only we had enough money" can be a rebuke to a husband who

_____ .

"Flunk any tests today, John?" only discourages a child who

_____ .

 EXTRA CHALLENGE Individually or in groups, read the following paragraph and circle the relative clauses.

There is great satisfaction in being able to make a difference for someone who needs help . The tiredness that comes from any physical activity is all worthwhile . Working with Habitat for Humanity has made our spirits soar . It has been inspiring to help build a home for people who have never lived in a decent place and never dreamed of owning a home of their own . We have seen the joy it can bring both to the one who is giving time and energy and to the one who is receiving the new home . Soon after we began our work with Habitat for Humanity , we asked Tom Hall , who had come to the international headquarters for brief volunteer service and had already stayed five years , "Why do you keep on staying?" His answer was , "I see the faces of those who receive the homes ." We have seen the faces too.

—Adapted from Jimmy and Rosalynn Carter,
Everything to Gain

Chapter 16

Writing with Definition Additions

- ◆ Definition Additions
- ◆ *Focus on Fragments*

Definition Additions

"Who's Vanessa?"

"A loyal and trustworthy friend"

A loyal and trustworthy friend is a definition of Vanessa.

Definitions look and sound like this:

the student in the back row   the worst day of the week

a hard-working parent   the best-priced CD player on the market

an opportunity I don't want to miss   a dedicated instructor

We can add a subject and a verb and use a definition as part of a core sentence: *Vanessa is a loyal and trustworthy friend.* We can also use the definition as an addition to a core sentence: *Vanessa, a loyal and trustworthy friend, supports our decision.* In this chapter we focus on writing with definition additions, which in some situations are called appositives.

Definition additions are added to a core sentence. They give additional information about a noun in a sentence, and they are placed either after or before that noun.

EXAMPLE 1

A core sentence: *Vanessa supports our decision*.
The sentence with the definition addition, first after and then before *Vanessa*:

Vanessa, **a loyal and trustworthy friend**, supports our decision.
A loyal and trustworthy friend, Vanessa supports our decision.

EXAMPLE 2

A core sentence: *The refugees fled toward the border*.
The sentence with the definition addition, first after and then before *refugees*:

The refugees, **hungry for peace**, fled toward the border.
Hungry for peace, the refugees fled toward the border.

Notice, in Examples 1 and 2, how commas are used to separate the definition from the rest of the sentence. It is important to remember that commas set off (1) introductory words at the beginning of a sentence and (2) words interrupting the flow of thought in a sentence. When we put an addition at the beginning of a sentence, we use a comma to set off these introductory words. When we put an addition at the middle or end of a sentence, we use commas to set off these words that interrupt the flow of thought.

Definition Additions After the Noun

Vanessa, a loyal and trustworthy friend, supports our decision.

Read the following five sentences aloud to hear the rhythm of definition additions, which are in boldface. The commas show us where the addition begins and ends.

1. The pawnbroker, **a red-bearded man with black horn-rimmed glasses**, was eating a whitefish at the rear of the store.

    —Bernard Malamud, "Idiots First"

2. Mama, **the fearless one**, suddenly became afraid of dogs.

    —Henry Louis Gates, Jr., "Change of Life"

3. Patience, **something Denver had never known**, overtook her.

    —Toni Morrison, *Beloved*

4. All her friends, **young and old**, call her Mama.

    —Toshio Mori, "The Woman Who
    Makes Swell Doughnuts"

5. A crowd of young men, **some in jerseys and some in their shirt-sleeves**, got out.

    —Ernest Hemingway, *The Sun Also Rises*

PRACTICE 1   Definition additions are extra information added to a core sentence. In the five previous sentences, underline each core sentence. The first one has been done for you.

PRACTICE 2   In each of the following sentences, underline each core sentence and circle the definition addition. The first two have been done for you. Notice that in the second example, the addition has been placed at the end of the sentence.

EXAMPLE: <u>Crater Lake</u> , (the deepest lake in the United States) , <u>was formed 7,700 years ago from a volcano in what is now Oregon</u> .

EXAMPLE: <u>Pat raised four children</u> , (a rewarding and challenging experience) .

1. Harriet Tubman , a famous guide on the Underground Railroad , became known as "Moses ."

2. The youngest child, a sleepy four-year-old , tried to concentrate on their conversation .

3. Faxing , the transmission of a document or photograph over a telephone network , has been in use since 1986 .

4. Nikko wants to major in geology , the study of the earth's crust .

5. The musicians' performances are funded by Meet the Composer , an organization that puts artists in touch with their communities .

PRACTICE 3   Select definitions from your imagination or from the list below and add them to the sentences that follow.

Definitions	
a small woman with fire in her eyes	my cousin's best friend
the only sibling who remained at home	an elderly man with twelve grandchildren
a veteran of both Vietnam and the Gulf War	
someone I have learned to trust	
a student I met in the bookstore	

1. Richard, _____ , listened carefully before responding.

   _____

   _____

2. Juan, _____ , has a positive attitude.

   _____

   _____

3. The patient, _____ , accepts life with grace and dignity.

   _____

   _____

   _____

4. Stacy, _____ , took responsibility for running the family farm.

   _____

   _____

   _____

5. The four-star marine general, _____ , contributed to the
   morale of the armed forces.

   _____

   _____

PRACTICE 4   Create your own definition addition for each sentence.

1. The home team is happy about the new quarterback, an athlete who

   _____ .

2. Sabrina, a _____ , gives me a ride to school each day.

3. My car, _____ , is parked outside.

4. My most difficult course, _____ ,

   is also my favorite.

5. The governor, a _____ ,

   launched a three-year fundraising drive for cultural programs.

Definition Additions Before the Noun

A loyal and trustworthy friend, Vanessa supports our decision.

Although definition additions are usually placed after the noun they explain, you can also place them before the noun. You can begin the sentence with a definition addition when it defines the subject of your sentence. Remember to place a comma at the end of the addition to let readers know where the core sentence begins.
Notice how these writers start a sentence with a definition addition:

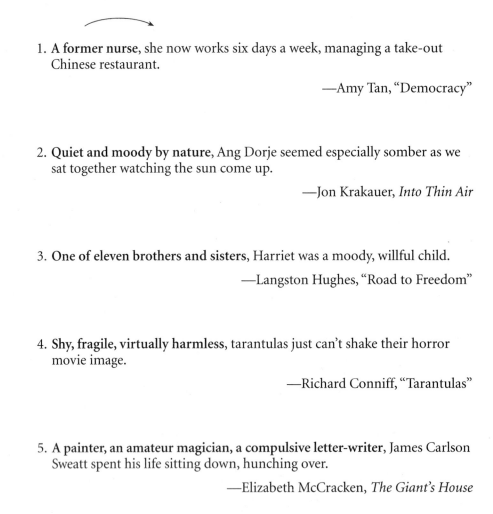

1. **A former nurse,** she now works six days a week, managing a take-out Chinese restaurant.

   —Amy Tan, "Democracy"

2. **Quiet and moody by nature,** Ang Dorje seemed especially somber as we sat together watching the sun come up.

   —Jon Krakauer, *Into Thin Air*

3. **One of eleven brothers and sisters,** Harriet was a moody, willful child.

   —Langston Hughes, "Road to Freedom"

4. **Shy, fragile, virtually harmless,** tarantulas just can't shake their horror movie image.

   —Richard Conniff, "Tarantulas"

5. **A painter, an amateur magician, a compulsive letter-writer,** James Carlson Sweatt spent his life sitting down, hunching over.

   —Elizabeth McCracken, *The Giant's House*

PRACTICE 5   In the five previous sentences, draw an arrow from the addition to the noun it defines. The first one has been done for you.

PRACTICE 6   The definition additions in the following sentences are placed after the noun. Rewrite the sentences by moving the addition and placing it before the noun. Remember to mark the end of the addition with a comma to let readers know where it ends and the core sentence begins. The first one has been done for you.

EXAMPLE: The volunteers, strong and determined people, spent a week hauling lumber and climbing ladders.

Strong and determined people, the volunteers spent a week hauling lumber and climbing ladders.

1. Girfaldi's, a noisy and popular restaurant, is already booked for New Year's Eve.

_____

_____

_____

2. The park, a small patch of land tucked into one corner of the city, is a magnet for water birds.

_____

_____

_____

3. Habitat for Humanity, a nationwide volunteer program, builds homes for families who need assistance.

_____

_____

_____

_____

4. The note, difficult to read but impossible to ignore, captured our attention.

_____

_____

_____

5. The saguaro, a cactus that grows in Arizona and California, can reach 50 feet in height, weigh 9 tons, and live 200 years.

_____

_____

_____

PRACTICE 7

 SENTENCE COMBINING Writing with definition additions will help you create concise sentences with varied rhythm. In the following sentence pairs, condense the second sentence into a definition addition. Then place the addition either before or after the noun it describes in the first sentence. Make sure you mark the additions appropriately with commas. The example shows you two options, but you need to write only one sentence.

EXAMPLE: The principal announced his retirement yesterday. The principal is a respected person in the community.

A respected person in the community, the principal announced his retirement yesterday.

or

The principal, a respected person in the community, announced his retirement yesterday.

1. Tom discovered his freedom in the mountains. Tom was a city man.

   _____

   _____

2. Shannon and Katrice drove me to the airport. Shannon and Katrice are my brother's best friends.

   _____

   _____

3. The conference participants were able to rest and relax. They were free from outside distractions.

   _____

   _____

4. The cease-fire was announced last night. The cease-fire is an agreement that promises an end to violence.

   _____

   _____

5. Aspirin helps prevent the formation of blood clots and reduces fever and inflammation. Aspirin is a compound found in the bark of willow trees.

   _____

   _____

6. The Anasazi lived for more than two thousand years in what is now Colorado, Utah, Arizona, and New Mexico. The Anasazi are ancestors of modern Pueblo Indians.

_____

_____

_____

_____

7. Ralph Ellison writes from his experience as an African American in his book *Invisible Man*. Ralph Ellison is one of the most celebrated and influential writers in America.

_____

_____

_____

_____

8. Participants in the photography workshop learn to notice the small details of daily life. The photography workshop is a weekend class for all age groups.

_____

_____

_____

9. Acupuncture involves inserting special needles just under the skin to rebalance the body's flow of energy. Acupuncture is a 5,000-year-old Chinese medical practice.

_____

_____

_____

_____

10. Women's basketball now receives national recognition. Women's basketball is a fast-paced game of quick passing and accurate shooting.

_____

_____

_____

Focus on Fragments

Definition additions need to be part of a sentence. The following definition lacks the subject-verb structure of a sentence and is therefore a fragment.

Fragment problem: Full of life and in search of their own identity.

You can correct fragments such as this in either of two ways:

Solution 1: Add a subject and a verb.

The children were full of life and in search of their own identity.

Solution 2: Use the words as a definition addition and add a core sentence.

The children, full of life and in search of their own identity, *saw a future filled with opportunities to succeed.*

Review: Writing with Definition Additions

- When you edit your writing, look for sentences that tell who or what someone or something is. Often, you can take this definition, condense it into a definition addition, and place it in another sentence.

- Place definition additions next to the nouns they describe.

- Use commas to let readers know where the addition begins and ends.

 REVIEW PRACTICE In the following excerpt, two sentences are in italics. Individually or in groups, condense each italicized sentence into a definition addition and add it to the previous sentence.

Time was running out. It was our 43rd day on Trango Tower.

Trango Tower is a 3,000-foot tooth of granite that rises like a bad dream out of the Karakoram Range in Pakistan. Clouds to the south were as black as oil. Winter was closing in.

"Man, this storm looks scary. Let's vamoose," said Mike Lilygren. *Mike was the most levelheaded climber on our team.* Together with Bobby Model and Jeff Bechtel, Mike and I were stuffed into hammock-like tents hanging off the rock face. There was nothing between us and the ice 2,000 feet below.

—Adapted from Todd Skinner, "Storming the Tower"

EXTRA CHALLENGE Individually or in groups, use the following sentences as models, create your own definition additions, and fill in the blanks. Be creative; your additions do not need to have the same meaning as the ones you replace. The first one has been done for you.

EXAMPLE: Patience, *something Denver had never known,* overtook her.

—Toni Morrison, *Beloved*

Patience, *no longer a choice but a necessity* , overtook her.

1. My father, *a fat, funny man with beautiful eyes and a subversive wit,* is trying to decide which of his eight children he will take with him to the county fair.

—Alice Walker, "Beauty: When the Other Dancer Is the Self"

My father, _____ , is trying to decide which of his eight children he will take with him to the county fair.

2. His ranch, *an island of cleared, grassy meadows in an immense forest tract near Canada,* happens to be the hub of half a dozen overlapping wolf territories.

—Douglas H. Chadic, "Return of the Gray Wolf"

His ranch, _____ , happens to be the hub of half a dozen overlapping wolf territories.

3. *Quiet and moody by nature,* Ang Dorje seemed especially somber as we sat together watching the sun come up.

—Jon Krakauer, *Into Thin Air*

_____ , Ang Dorje seemed especially somber as we sat together watching the sun come up.

4. He was a handsome man, *tall and distant.*

—Edna O'Brien, "Sin"

He was a handsome man, _____ .

5. They were a mountain people, *a mysterious tribe of hunters whose language has never been positively classified in any major group.*

—N. Scott Momaday, *The Way to Rainy Mountain*

They were a mountain people, a _____

_____ .

Chapter 17

Writing with -ing Verb Forms

- ◆ *-ing* Verb Forms: Overview
- ◆ *-ing* Nouns
- ◆ *-ing* Additions
- ◆ *Focus on Fragments*

-ing Verb Forms: Overview

"What is Chris doing?"

"Relaxing after a long day"

Relaxing after a long day is an idea beginning with an *-ing* verb form.

Verb forms ending in *-ing* change roles, depending on where they appear in a sentence. Most of the time, you will know by the rhythm of the sentence what role an *-ing* verb form is playing. In previous chapters, we used *-ing* verb forms with helping verbs in a sentence. We also used *-ing* verb forms as adjectives describing someone or something.

As the main verb in a sentence:

Chris *is relaxing* after a long day.

As an adjective:

We look forward to a *relaxing* weekend.

In this chapter, we use *-ing* verb forms as nouns and as additions to a core sentence. An *-ing* verb form can be a noun (verbal noun). It is often used as the subject of a sentence. This verb form can also be used as an addition to a sentence.

As a noun:

Relaxing helps people cope with stress.

As an addition to a sentence:

Relaxing after a long day, Chris watched the evening news.

-ing Nouns

Relaxing helps people cope with stress.

In the above sentence, the writer is referring to the act of relaxing. The name of this act is a noun. Although *-ing* nouns can be used anywhere in a sentence, we will concentrate on using them as subjects because they are effective ways to condense your ideas.

Notice how these writers use an *-ing* noun as the subject of the sentence.

1. **Writing** is a struggle against silence.

—Carlos Fuentes

2. The thick **ticking** of the tin clock stopped.

—Bernard Malamud, "Idiots First"

3. **Growing** older seemed to agree with him.

—Len Deighton, *Funeral in Berlin*

4. **Working** together on a project that we felt strongly about ignited a part of

us we did not know existed.

—Elvira M. Franco, "A Magic Circle of Friends"

5. The **swaying, shuddering, thudding, flinging** stops, and the furniture of

life falls into place.

—Nadine Gordimer, *July's People*

PRACTICE 1   In the following sentences, underline each subject once and the verb twice. The first two have been done for you.

EXAMPLE: <u>Driving</u> without sunglasses <u>hurts</u> my mother's eyes.

EXAMPLE: <u>Maintaining</u> a normal body weight, <u>increasing</u> consumption of fruits

and vegetables, and <u>reducing</u> fat intake <u>reduce</u> cancer risk.

1. Reading good literature will improve a person's vocabulary.

2. Completing my education is important to me.

3. Understanding ourselves helps us to understand others.

4. The outpouring of personal support exceeded our expectations.

5. Awarding large contracts to coaches and players is part of professional sports.

PRACTICE 2

 SENTENCE COMBINING Using an *-ing* noun as the subject of a sentence will help you avoid writing awkward sentences. It replaces the talking style of using the word *you* with a more direct statement. Rewrite each of the following sentences by changing the verb in the subordinate clause to an *-ing* subject. Then make sure the verb of your sentence agrees with this singular subject. The first two have been done for you. Notice how the *-ing* subject eliminates the need to use *you* in any part of the statement.

EXAMPLE: If you focus on your future goals, it helps you put present responsibilities in perspective.

Focusing on future goals helps put present responsibilities in perspective.

EXAMPLE: When you eat highly saturated fats, you can clog your arteries.

Eating highly saturated fats can clog arteries.

1. When you make decisions, it is not always easy.

_____

2. If you think that bills will simply disappear, this solves nothing.

_____

3. If you procrastinate, you waste time.

_____

4. When you exercise three times a week, you speed up your metabolism.

_____

5. If you wax the car, this will probably take all afternoon.

_____

6. If you laugh, that eases tension.

_____

7. When you give a speech in front of a large audience, this can be frightening.

_____

8. If you live in a large city, you have both advantages and disadvantages.

_____

9. If you break the speed limit, you are gambling for a ticket.

_____

10. When they include the parental advisory label on CD's, they are warning parents that the lyrics contain profanity or violence.

_____

_____

-ing Additions

We have just practiced using an *-ing* verb form as the subject of a sentence. An *-ing* verb form can also begin an idea used as an addition to a core sentence.

Relaxing after a long day, Chris watched the evening news.
Relaxing after a long day is an *-ing* addition.

These additions look and sound like this:

Walking across campus   Coasting down Interstate 94
Peering through a streaky windshield   Debating both sides of the issue
Waiting for the right moment   Running down the street

An *-ing* addition can go either before or after the noun it describes. Let's take this core sentence: *The people heard the wind stop.* We will place an *-ing* addition first before and then after the noun, *people.*

Before the noun:
Lying in their beds, the people heard the wind stop.

After the noun:
The people, *lying in their beds,* heard the wind stop.

—John Steinbeck, *The Grapes of Wrath*

-ing *Additions Before the Noun*

Lying in their beds, the people heard the wind stop.

The pattern looks like this:

> *-ing* addition , core sentence .
> *Lying in their beds,* the people heard the wind stop.

One of the most effective ways to use an *-ing* addition before a noun is by beginning your sentence with it. Starting a sentence with an *-ing* addition is an excellent way to occasionally change the rhythm of your sentences. Just make sure the subject of the sentence follows the addition.

Read these sentences aloud, so that you hear the rhythm of beginning a sentence with an *-ing* addition. Also, notice that the addition is followed by the subject of the sentence.

1. **Holding the damp white sheets against her chest**, she was picking meaning out of a code she no longer understood.

   —Toni Morrison, *Beloved*

2. **Distrusting the world**, they approached everything timidly.

   —Oscar Hijuelos, "Visitors, 1965"

3. **Shrugging**, Kiowa pulled off his boots.

   —Tim O'Brien, *The Things They Carried*

4. **Holding his hand and hearing him tell it**, I did not believe a word of it.

   —Ernest Hemingway, "A New Kind of War"

5. **Licking the dirt off their fingers along with the sausage grease**, the boys watched the conflict with detached interest.

   —Nadine Gordimer, *July's People*

PRACTICE 3   In the five previous sentences, draw an arrow from the *-ing* addition to the subject of the core sentence. The first one has been done for you.

An *-ing* addition cannot stand alone. It needs to be connected to a core sentence. In the following practice, the subjects and verbs in the core sentences have been underlined as a reminder that these additions need the support of a complete sentence.

PRACTICE 4   Choose *-ing* additions from your imagination or from the list below and add them to the core sentences. Place each addition before the person or thing it describes.

Examples of *-ing* Additions

Deciding to leave work early

Hoping to maintain an A in the course

Flying down the dirt road at 60 miles an hour

Wandering through the central train station

Remaining open to new possibilities

Developing rapidly

---

1. _____ , the <u>driver</u> suddenly <u>remembered</u> a sharp blind turn just ahead.

   _____

   _____

2. _____ , <u>I</u> <u>skipped</u> my lunch hour.

   _____

   _____

3. _____ , <u>we</u> <u>studied</u> late into the night.

   _____

   _____

4. _____ , the <u>storm</u> <u>ripped</u> across the open field.

   _____

   _____

5. _____ , the <u>children</u> <u>stared</u> in awe at the mosaic ceilings.

   _____

   _____

PRACTICE 5   Each of the following sentences begins with an *-ing* addition, but because the writer did not mark where the addition ends, the ideas are confusing. Correct each sentence by placing a comma at the end of the *-ing* addition. The first one has been done for you.

> EXAMPLE: Repeating the directions to himself, the child began walking to his uncle's house.

1. Not understanding a word of Russian Craig hoped to get by with hand gestures.

2. Knowing we might change our minds later we did not succumb to the salesperson's pressure.

3. Substituting hard work and community spirit for money they renovated the gymnasium.

4. Recognizing the need to communicate its position the committee began a grass-roots campaign.

5. Visiting remote sites in Utah's Capital Reef National Park we discovered sagebrush, songbirds, and solitude.

-ing *Additions After the Noun*

> The people, lying in their beds, heard the wind stop.
>
> —John Steinbeck, *The Grapes of Wrath*

Notice how these writers use the *-ing* addition after the noun. Read these sentences aloud to hear the rhythm.

1. Bernard, **wearing a black turtleneck sweater, dirty flannels, and slippers, was waiting on the landing outside.**

   > —Brian Moore, *The Lonely Passion of Judith Hearne*

2. The withered moon, **shining on his face**, awakened him.

   > —John Steinbeck, "Flight"

3. His mind, **desperately craving some kind of mooring**, clung to details.

   > —Arundhati Roy, *The God of Small Things*

4. He slowed down as he walked, **watching her as if spell-bound.**

   > —D. H. Lawrence, "The Horse-Dealer's Daughter"

5. Pedro, **sitting in his hammock,** was eating a slice of watermelon and thinking of Tita.

   > —Laura Esquivel, *Like Water for Chocolate*

PRACTICE 6   Underline the core sentence in the five previous sentences. The first one has been done for you.

PRACTICE 7   In the following sentences, the -*ing* addition has been placed before the noun(s) it describes. Move that addition and place it after the noun(s) it describes. Remember to use commas to let readers know where the addition begins and ends. The first two have béen done for you.

> EXAMPLE: Gazing through the morning mist, the sleepy campers saw deer in the distance.
>
> The sleepy campers, gazing through the morning mist, saw deer in the distance.
>
> EXAMPLE: Looking for a fracture, the technician and the radiologist examined the x-rays.
>
> The technician and the radiologist, looking for a fracture, examined the x-rays.

1. Flickering in the distance, the lights let us know that our friends were expecting us.

   _____

   _____

2. Outlining the company strategies, the board of directors presented the plan.

   _____

   _____

3. Erupting with enormous force, volcanoes and earthquakes have created the earth's mountains.

   _____

   _____

4. Recognizing possibilities for growth, the sales department recommended an aggressive advertising campaign.

   _____

   _____

5. Considering the financial benefits of healthy employees, the human resource department initiated an employee fitness program.

   _____

   _____

   _____

PRACTICE 8

 SENTENCE COMBINING Writing with *-ing* additions is an excellent way to combine sentences. In each pair of sentences that follows, condense the information in one of the sentences into an *-ing* addition and place it either before or after the noun it describes. Many of the following pairs of sentences can be combined in a variety of ways. The example shows you two of the options, but you need to write only one sentence.

EXAMPLE: Giant bulldozers tore up the damaged road. They blocked traffic for miles.

Blocking traffic for miles, giant bulldozers tore up the damaged road.

or

Giant bulldozers, tearing up the damaged road, blocked traffic for miles.

1. My dad sat on the steps with a cup of coffee in his hands. He explained what had happened.

   _____

   _____

2. Mattie waved at the crossing guard. Mattie turned the corner in her pickup truck.

   _____

   _____

3. The fathers hoisted their children on their shoulders. The fathers made sure no one missed a moment of the game.

   _____

   _____

4. The corporation brought jobs and security to the city. The corporation employed 2,000 people.

   _____

   _____

5. Smith rummaged through his papers. He searched for the credit card receipt.

   _____

   _____

6. The president and the vice president motivated and inspired the employees. They focused on the long-term goal.

   _____

   _____

7. No one is allowed to bring food or drink into the park. That is according to the rules.

   _____

   _____

8. Charles and Marissa persuaded the community to organize a neighborhood outreach program. They explained their vision for the future.

   _____

   _____

9. The ambassador to the United Nations defended his country's human rights record. The ambassador read from a prepared text.

   _____

   _____

10. The five world championship banners commemorated the team's victories. The banners hung from the stadium rafters.

   _____

   _____

Focus on Fragments

An *-ing* addition by itself is not a sentence. If you are writing fragments that begin with *-ing,* use one of these solutions:

> Solution 1: Add a subject and a helping verb.
>
> Solution 2: Use the *-ing* idea as an addition and add a core sentence.
>
> Solution 3: Use the *-ing* idea as the subject of a sentence.

Fragment problem: Standing on a ladder.

> Solution 1: Add a subject and a helping verb.
>
> *My sister was* standing on a ladder.
>
> Solution 2: Use the *-ing* idea as an addition and add a core sentence.
>
> Standing on a ladder, *my sister was able to paint the ceiling.*
>
> Solution 3: Use the *-ing* idea as the subject of a sentence.
>
> Standing on a ladder *can be dangerous.*

Review: Writing with -ing Verb Forms

• Use -*ing* verb forms as the subjects of sentences.
• Write compact sentences with varied rhythm by using -*ing* additions.

REVIEW PRACTICE   The following selection has sentences with -*ing* additions coming before nouns and after nouns. Circle the -*ing* additions.

After a meal of soup , salami and cookies , I settle in to sleep , wondering whether the dire reports I had heard from the Japanese researchers had overstated the dangers of the area . A few minutes later , I awake, feeling an insect on my finger . Flicking it off , I feel another take its place , and then suddenly thousands of bugs seem to bite me at once . Seconds later , I hear a strangled cry from Karen as she is attacked as well . Stumbling blindly over roots and a massive column of ants , we tear down a path and dive into the river.

Stamping , slapping and at a loss , I rouse Fay , whose tent is out of the line of attack . Surveying the insects that still cover my legs , he says drowsily , "Driver ants can really be a problem ; they can kill a tethered goat , " and then goes back to sleep . Moving my hammock away from the column of ants , I wince with pain as I drive a spiky vine clear through my thumb and watch blood spurt out.

—Eugene Linden, "The Last Eden"

 EXTRA CHALLENGE Individually or in groups, use each numbered sentence as a model, create your own -*ing* addition, and fill in the blank. Be creative; your additions do not need to have the same meaning as the additions you replace. The first one has been done for you.

EXAMPLE: He slowed down as he walked, *watching her as if spell-bound.*
—D. H. Lawrence, "The Horse-Dealer's Daughter"

He slowed down as he walked, <u>*searching the driveway for his keys*</u> .

1. *Sitting cross-legged on the quilt,* we ate chicken sandwiches and cucumber salad with red onion.

—Anna Quindlen, *One True Thing*

_____ , we ate chicken

sandwiches and cucumber salad with red onion.

2. Bernard, *wearing a black turtleneck sweater, dirty flannels, and slippers,* was waiting on the landing outside.

—Brian Moore, *The Lonely Passion of Judith Hearne*

Bernard, _____ , was waiting on

the landing outside.

3. The people, *lying in their beds,* heard the wind stop.

—John Steinbeck, *The Grapes of Wrath*

The people, _____ , heard the wind

stop.

4. His mind, *desperately craving some kind of mooring,* clung to details.

—Arundhati Roy, *The God of Small Things*

His mind, _____ , clung to details.

5. The withered moon, *shining on his face,* awakened him.

—John Steinbeck, "Flight"

The withered moon, _____ , awakened him.

Chapter 18

Writing with -ed Additions

- ◆ *-ed* Additions
- ◆ *Focus on Fragments*

-ed Additions

"How's Pat feeling about tomorrow's game?"

"Determined to win"

Determined to win is an idea beginning with an *-ed* verb form.

Ideas beginning with an *-ed* verb form look and sound like this:

Encouraged by my grades

Respected as a leader in the community

Praised for their performance

Convinced that the weather would change

Surrounded by family and friends

Assured that the problem was minor

An *-ed* verb form is similar to an *-ing* verb form: it changes roles, depending on where it is in a sentence. Most of the time, we use it as the past tense verb in a sentence. In this chapter, we focus on using an *-ed* verb form in an addition to a core sentence.

This addition is formed by using the form of the verb called the past participle. The form will end in *-ed* when the verb is regular: *asked, enjoyed,* and *believed.* The form will end in *-d, -t, -en,* or *-n* when the verb is irregular: *found, fought, eaten,* and *begun.* As you write with *-ed* additions, keep these two points in mind:

1. The *-ed* addition is an addition to a core sentence.
2. The addition can go before or after the noun it describes.

Let's take this core sentence: *The folk songs celebrate the river town's character.* We will place an *-ed* addition first before and then after *folk songs.*

Before the noun:

> **Repeated for generations**, the folk songs celebrate the river town's character.

After the noun:

> The folk songs, **repeated for generations**, celebrate the river town's character.

-ed *Additions Before the Noun*

Repeated for generations, the folk songs celebrate the river town's character.

The pattern looks like this:

> *-ed* addition , core sentence .
> *Repeated for generations*, the folk songs celebrate the river town's character.

Beginning a sentence with an *-ed* addition is an effective way to change sentence rhythm. Because readers expect the subject to come first, use a comma to let them know you are beginning with an addition, not with the subject.

Read these sentences aloud to hear the different rhythm of beginning with an *-ed* addition. Notice that the addition is followed by the subject of the sentence.

1. **Enchanted,** <u>he</u> <u>groped</u> toward the waves of melody.

   —Richard Wright, "The Man Who Lived Underground"

2. **Empowered by our incredible mind,** <u>we</u> <u>explore</u> what drives us, constrains us, and inspires us.

   —Susan A. Greenfield, *Human Mind Explained*

3. **Crammed into cattle trains by Hungarian police,** <u>they</u> <u>wept</u> bitterly.

   —Elie Wiesel, *Night*

4. **Entranced,** <u>I</u> <u>listened</u> to his every word.

   —Florence Ladd, *Sarah's Psalm*

5. **Flushed and breathless,** <u>he</u> <u>let</u> himself drop onto a mound and <u>took</u> his head in his hands.

   —Yashar Kemal, "A Dirty Story"

PRACTICE 1   An *-ed* addition must be separated from the core sentence with a comma. The following sentences have not been punctuated correctly. Correct them by placing a comma after the addition. The first one has been done for you.

EXAMPLE: Frayed at the edges the rope snapped in the storm.

Frayed at the edges, the rope snapped in the storm.

1. Surrounded by jungle the river is inaccessible.

2. Unoccupied for years the cabin needed cleaning.

3. Scattered across seven states the family kept in touch in spite of the distance.

4. Inspired by the movie's message we left the theater feeling good about human nature.

5. Compressed into one calendar year the master's degree program uses the classroom, e-mail, and faxes for instruction.

PRACTICE 2   Select *-ed* additions from your imagination or from the list below and use them to begin the sentences that follow.

Examples of *-ed* additions

Asked about next season   Gutted with potholes

Blinded by the blizzard   Established in 1922

Released last January

Designed and developed by college students

---

1. _____ , the solo album balances studio precision with concert stage power.

_____

_____

2. _____ , the computer games have captured the market.

_____

_____

3. _____ , the local savings and loan institution continues to
serve the community.

_____

_____

4. _____ , the athlete grinned and sidestepped the question.

_____

_____

5. _____ , the expressway was closed for spring repairs.

_____

_____

-ed *Additions After the Noun*

The folk songs, repeated for generations, celebrate the river town's character.

Placing an *-ed* addition after a noun gives a sentence a different kind of rhythm.
Notice how the following writers use the *-ed* addition, which is in boldface.

1. <u>Her eyes</u>, **shadowed and confused,** <u>finally settled on his face.</u>

> —Flannery O'Connor, "Everything
> That Rises Must Converge"

2. He paused, **stunned by their disbelieving eyes.**

> —Richard Wright, "The Man Who
> Lived Underground"

3. Dozens of family photos, **framed in dull brass or varnished wood,** stood
on an ivory lace runner.

> —Ann Tyler, *Saint Maybe*

4. So today my face is plain, **unadorned except for a thin mist of shiny sweat
on my forehead and nose.**

> —Amy Tan, "A Pair of Tickets"

5. Two stocky women, **bare-headed and bare-footed,** went by carrying a
bucket of milky water between them.

> —John Steinbeck, *The Grapes of Wrath*

PRACTICE 3   In the five previous sentences, underline the core sentence. The first one has been
done for you.

PRACTICE 4

 SENTENCE COMBINING Writing with *-ed* additions is an effective way to write compact sentences and change the rhythm of your sentences. In each pair of sentences that follows, condense the information in the second sentence into an *-ed* addition and place it either before or after the noun it describes. The example shows you the two options.

EXAMPLE: The old wooden door refused to open. It was warped by the weather.

Warped by the weather, the old wooden door refused to open.

or

The old wooden door, warped by the weather, refused to open.

1. Our first apartment was our castle. It was cramped and cluttered with old furniture.

   _____

   _____

2. Anna's parents left the teacher's conference and celebrated. Her parents were pleased with the report.

   _____

   _____

3. Their particle-board bookcase sagged in the middle. It was loaded with books and magazines.

   _____

   _____

4. The videogame industry adopted ratings and warning labels. The videogame industry was pressured by Congress.

   _____

   _____

   _____

5. Keith joined a twelve-step program that saved his life. He was incarcerated for armed robbery and drugs.

   _____

   _____

   _____

6. This national park offers 140 miles of hiking trails. The park is located six miles below the rim of the crater.

_____

_____

7. The group met in New York City to discuss its future. It had been forced to cancel its European tour.

_____

_____

8. Our local theater hired several young directors. The theater was determined to diversify its programming and broaden its audience.

_____

_____

9. The hot dog stand is thriving. It is located at the intersection of Route 1 and Traverse Drive.

_____

_____

10. One television news station is trying to redefine its image. It was criticized for engaging in tabloid television.

_____

_____

Focus on Fragments

An -*ed* addition is not a sentence. If you are writing fragments that begin with -*ed*, use one of these solutions:

    Solution 1:   Add a subject and a helping verb.

    Solution 2:   Use the -*ed* idea as an addition and add a core sentence.

Fragment problem: Prepared for the interview.

    Solution 1:   Add a subject and a helping verb.

    Andrea had prepared for the interview.

    Solution 2:   Use it as an addition and add a core sentence.

    Prepared for the interview, *Andrea confidently entered the room.*

Review: Writing with -ed Additions

• Use -ed additions to write compact sentences with varying rhythm.

• Place these additions next to the nouns they describe.

 REVIEW PRACTICE The following information is taken from "Database" in *U.S. News & World Report*. Individually or in groups, condense the information given in the first sentence into an -ed addition. Then use the addition to start the second sentence.

Mosquitoes are attracted by perspiration, breath, and body heat. They fly in for the kill. They can smell human beings 65 to 115 feet away. The females are the problem. They need the protein found in both human and animal blood to reproduce. Female mosquitoes produce 100 to 300 eggs at a time and, over the course of a 30-day life, lay as many as 3,000 eggs.

 EXTRA CHALLENGE Individually or in groups, read the following paragraph. After you have an overview of what the paragraph is about, go back to each sentence in italics. Condense each sentence in italics into an -ed addition and add that addition to the beginning of the sentence that follows. When you have completed this activity, the paragraph will have excellent sentence variety. The first sentence of the paragraph has been done for you.

EXAMPLE: *Visitors are attracted to clear waters and peaceful surroundings.* Visitors come to paddle the Shenandoah River as it flows through Virginia and West Virginia.

Attracted to clear waters and peaceful surroundings, visitors come to paddle the Shenandoah River as it flows through Virginia and West Virginia.

Visitors are attracted to clear waters and peaceful surroundings. Visitors come to paddle the Shenandoah River as it flows through Virginia and West Virginia. *The river is bordered by mountains a quarter of a billion years old.* The river ripples and rolls gently into the misty light. Outfitters rent canoes to those who want to paddle along its grassy banks. Some come to paddle the gentler waters and fish for smallmouth bass; others choose to challenge the crashing rapids, called white waters. I have done both. Last spring, when I paddled the white waters, a frothy wave smacked the canoe side-on and we flipped. Yet I soon regained my footing. *I was chilled and refreshed.* I stood hip-deep in the rushing Shenandoah and looked up at the mountains. *I was reminded that this land and these waters have seen thousands of years of struggle.* I gazed across the valley with its pale green promise of another summer. Then, I did the only thing I could do in that situation: I simply smiled. The canoe is a simple boat that leaves no trace when it's gone, leaving the Shenandoah to roll on, week after week, millennium after millennium.

—Adapted from Angus Phillips,
"Simple Gifts of the Shenandoah"

_____

_____

_____

_____

_____

_____

_____

_____

_____

_____

_____

_____

_____

_____

Chapter 19

Changing Rhythm Review

◆ Starters
◆ Interrupters

Starters

In condensing ideas and working with different sentence rhythms, we have practiced using a variety of additions with the core sentence. We have placed those additions at the beginning and in the middle of a sentence. Additions at the beginning are often called *starters* because they start the sentence. Additions placed in the middle of a sentence are called *interrupters* because they interrupt the flow of the sentence. First, we will review the *starters*.

PRACTICE 1   Read the following sentences aloud to hear their rhythm; then answer the question that follows.

> Because he wanted to prove that he could succeed, Daryl ran the marathon.
> Consistently and effortlessly, Daryl ran the marathon.
> Over steep hills and past cheering crowds, Daryl ran the marathon.
> A seasoned long-distance runner, Daryl ran the marathon.
> Giving it the best he had, Daryl ran the marathon.
> Determined to finish, Daryl ran the marathon.

What do the sentences in the list have in common?

Those six sentences all have the same core sentence, *Daryl ran the marathon,* and they all begin with an addition. Although the additions vary, they all follow the same pattern: they are added to the beginning of a core sentence. They are called *starters* and follow this pattern.

Starter , core sentence .

Use Commas

Using starters is an excellent way of changing the rhythm of your sentences. When you begin a sentence with any starter, mark the end of the starter with a comma to show readers where the core sentence begins.

PRACTICE 2 In small groups, create your own sentences in the <u>Starter, core sentence</u> pattern. An example of each type of starter is provided. Use that example as a guide and create your own starter. You may use *Daryl ran the marathon* as the core sentence or create your own core sentence. The first one, the subordinate clause, has been done for you.

SUBORDINATE CLAUSE (Turn to Chapter 11 for a review of subordinating conjunctions.)

> *Because he wanted to prove that he could succeed,* Daryl ran the marathon.

1. _*After he had trained for a year, Daryl ran the marathon.*_____

_____

ADVERB (Turn to Chapter 13 for a review of adverbs.)

> *Consistently and effortlessly,* Daryl ran the marathon.

2. _____

_____

PREPOSITIONAL PHRASE (Turn to Chapter 14 for a review of prepositional phrases.)

> *Over steep hills and past cheering crowds,* Daryl ran the marathon.

3. _____

_____

DEFINITION ADDITION (Turn to Chapter 16 for a review of definition additions.)

> *A seasoned long-distance runner,* Daryl ran the marathon.

4. _____

_____

-ING ADDITION (Turn to Chapter 17 for a review of *-ing* additions.)

> *Giving it the best he had*, Daryl ran the marathon.

5. _____

_____

-ED ADDITION (Turn to Chapter 18 for a review of *-ed* additions.)

> *Determined to finish*, Daryl ran the marathon.

6. _____

_____

Follow the Pattern

We have just reviewed a variety of sentence starters. Although they include different kinds of information, the starters follow the same pattern. First, they are added to the beginning of a core sentence. Second, they are marked with a comma to let readers know where the core sentence begins.

It is important to hear the rhythm of this pattern. You do not have to identify what specific starter you are writing because they all follow the same pattern. Recognizing the starter pattern will not only help you write well, it will help you read many different kinds of sentences.

PRACTICE 3   Read each of these sentences aloud to hear when the starter ends and the core sentence begins. Then, circle the starter. The first one has been done for you.

EXAMPLE: (A few miles south of Soledad), the Salinas River drops in

close to the hillside bank and runs deep and green .

> —John Steinbeck, *Of Mice and Men*

1. Almost sorry for him , Howe dropped his eyes .

> —Lionel Trilling, "Of This Time, Of That Place"

2. After nine claustrophobic days in our tents , we were tired of gin

rummy, disgusted with paperback novels , and intolerant of even

the best cowboy stories .

> —Todd Skinner, "Storming the Tower"

3. To study rare , mysterious animals , some biologists climb into

submersibles and plunge two miles down to the bottom of the sea .

> —John Fleischman, "Mass Extinctions Come to Ohio"

4. Unsmiling , ever watchful , my teachers noted my silence .

—Richard Rodriguez, "Aria"

5. Long thought to be a clean slate to which information could be added at any time , the brain is now seen as a super-sponge that is most absorbent from birth to about the age of twelve .

—Ronald Kotulak, *Inside the Brain*

Interrupters

Additions that are placed in the middle of a sentence are called *interrupters* because they interrupt the flow of the thought in the core sentence.

Read the following sentences aloud to hear their rhythm. Notice the variety of interrupters that have been added to the core sentence, *The parents participated in the video conference.*

The parents , who voiced their concerns about public education , participated in the video conference .

The parents , intelligent people from all walks of life , participated in the video conference .

The parents , gathering in the local town halls , participated in the video conference .

The parents , concerned about the future of our nation , participated in the video conference .

PRACTICE 4   In the four preceding sentences, circle the interrupter and underline the core sentence.

Use Commas

When you insert an addition that interrupts the flow of a core sentence, place commas on both sides of the interrupter to let readers know where it begins and ends. Commas act as handles allowing readers to mentally lift the addition out of the core sentence. All interrupters follow this pattern:

Core , interrupter , sentence .

PRACTICE 5 Individually or in small groups, create your own sentences with this pattern:

<u>Core, interrupter, sentence</u>. An example of each type of interrupter is provided. Use that example as a guide and create your own interrupter. You may use *The parents participated in the video conference* as the core sentence or create your own. The first one, the relative clause, has been done for you.

RELATIVE CLAUSE (Turn to Chapter 15 for a review of relative clauses.)

> The parents, *who voiced their concerns about public education,* participated in the video conference.

1. <u>*The parents, who wanted to become more active in their children's*</u>

   <u>*education, participated in the video conference.*</u>

DEFINITION ADDITION (Turn to Chapter 16 for a review of definition additions.)

> The parents, *intelligent people from all walks of life,* participated in the video conference.

2. _____

   _____

-ING ADDITION (Turn to Chapter 17 for a review of *-ing* additions.)

> The parents, *gathering in the local town halls,* participated in the video conference.

3. _____

   _____

-ED ADDITION (Turn to Chapter 18 for a review of *-ed* additions.)

> The parents, *concerned about the future of our nation,* participated in the video conference.

4. _____

   _____

Follow the Pattern

Interrupters, regardless of the kinds of information they include, follow the same pattern. They have commas on both sides to let readers know where the addition begins and ends. It is important to hear the rhythm of this pattern. You don't have to identify what specific interrupter you are writing because they all follow the same pattern.

As you write sentences with interrupters, make sure that you have a core sentence outside the interrupter. The sentence supporting this addition needs to be able to stand alone and make sense.

PRACTICE 6   Read the following sentences aloud to hear how they sound. Then, circle each interrupter and underline the core sentence. The first one has been done for you.

EXAMPLE: Illness , (especially when death is a possibility), makes us acutely aware of how precious life is and how precious a particular life is .

—Jean Shinoda Bolen, M.D., *Close to the Bone*

1. A broken-winged gull , hurled by the wind against the cliff , runs before me wearily along the beach .

—Loren Eiseley, "One Night's Dying"

2. Every one of us is called upon , probably many times , to start a new life .

—Barbara Kingsolver, *High Tide in Tucson*

3. The engagement of Martha and Sigmund , as far as their friends were concerned , remained about as secret as a July sun .

—Irving Stone, *The Passions of the Mind*

4. Hall , who had climbed Everest four times previously , understood as well as anybody the need to get up and down quickly .

—Jon Krakauer, *Into Thin Air*

5. Only the birds , brainlessly cheering and chattering in the sycamores , ignored the heat .

—William Styron, "A Tidewater Morning"

PRACTICE 7   At times, the interrupters are placed at the end of a sentence. Underline the core sentence and circle the interrupter. The first one has been done for you.

EXAMPLE: My grandmother had a reverence for the sun , (a holy regard that now is all but gone out of mankind).

—N. Scott Momaday, *The Way to Rainy Mountain*

1. The rain beat softly upon the shingles , inviting them to drowsiness and sleep .

—Kate Chopin, "The Storm"

2. I looked at him beside me , rolled in the red blanket on the white river sand .

> —Leslie Marmon Silko, "Yellow Woman"

3. It had been raining for a long time , a slow, cold rain falling out of iron-colored clouds .

> —James Thurber, "A Couple of Hamburgers"

4. The boy sat motionless , staring slantwise at the man .

> —Carson McCullers, "A Tree, a Rock, a Cloud"

5. Possibly all the generations of his ancestry had been ignorant of cold , of real cold , of cold one hundred and seven degrees below freezing point .

> —Jack London, "To Build a Fire"

Review: Writing with Starters and Interrupters

- Use commas to show readers where starters and interrupters begin and end.

- When you write with starters and interrupters, make sure you have a core sentence outside these additions.

 REVIEW PRACTICE Writing with starters and interrupters is an excellent way to combine sentences. Condense the information in the second of two sentences into either a starter or an interrupter and place it in the first sentence, next to the noun it describes. As you rewrite the following ten sentences, you will be following one of these sentence patterns:

> <u>Starter</u> , <u>core sentence</u> .
> <u>Core</u> , <u>interrupter</u> , <u>sentence</u> .

1. We studied late into the night. We knew that the final exam would determine our grades.

_____

_____

2. The thunder threatened to hold down the crowds. The thunder rumbled over the stadium.

_____

_____

3. A gift becomes a bribe when both the giver and the receiver recognize that some type of official duty will result. This is according to legal experts.

_____

_____

_____

4. Asthma affects 15 million people in the United States. Asthma is a chronic respiratory ailment.

_____

_____

5. Forest fires swept across the state. The fires were caused by lightning, drought, and human carelessness.

_____

_____

6. The IMAX is a major attraction at museums and science centers. The IMAX is an eighty-foot-high theater screen.

_____

_____

7. Hob Nob Junction is a favorite gathering place for families. It is the least expensive restaurant in town.

_____

_____

8. The leaders were willing to discuss the critical issues. They did this despite their differences.

_____

_____

9. Record companies are sending scouts abroad in search of new sounds. Record companies are hungry to latch on to new trends.

_____

_____

10. The utility company has become increasingly dependent on purchasing electricity from other states. The utility company is unable to run its nuclear plants efficiently.

_____

_____

_____

EXTRA CHALLENGE Individually or in groups, read the following paragraphs, which are based on "The Plant Hunter," an article by Christopher Hallowell published in *Time*. After you have an overview of what the paragraphs are about, go back to the sentences that are in italics. Each italicized section can be combined into one sentence. Using starters and interrupters, rewrite these ideas in compact sentences that connect smoothly with the surrounding sentences.

Nature is one of our most valuable sources for medicine. Nearly twenty-five percent of all prescription drugs are based on chemicals that are found in plants. Yet fewer than one percent of the world's plants have been tested for their effectiveness against disease. Therefore, scientists are searching the world's plants for undiscovered medicines.

Paul Cox is currently studying plants in Samoa. Paul is a world specialist in medicinal plants. Samoa is a small island in the South Pacific. A decade ago, Paul had witnessed traditional healers using local plants to heal their people. Many years later, after his mother died of cancer, Paul decided to return to Samoa. He explained his decision with these words, "I vowed I would do whatever I could to fight the disease that killed my mother." *Paul was determined to find a cure for cancer. Paul took his wife and four children and settled in an isolated village where he could learn from the local traditional healers.* These healers use the leaves, bark, and roots of local plants to treat conditions that range from high fever to appendicitis. *Paul watches them mix, prepare, and administer the plants. He does this on a day-to-day basis.* He studies their recipes and listens to their advice, learning the wisdom they have passed on from generation to generation. Paul has gained valuable information about potential medicines, which are now being tested in the United States. *Both parties are benefiting. They are benefiting through this sharing process.* Paul has located many medically promising plants, and the village has been able to take the proceeds from his research and build schools, clinics, and cisterns for catching rainwater to drink.

Paul Cox is not alone. *Drug companies and scientific institutions are working together, racing to study natural substances before the plants or the native people disappear. The companies and institutions are doing this all over the world.* Cox is one of many who believe that understanding how plants have been used for thousands of years is a valuable part of modern-day drug development.

_____

_____

_____

_____

_____

Chapter 20

Writing Parallel Ideas

◆ Parallel Patterns

◆ Paired Words

◆ Longer Parallel Ideas

Parallel Patterns

The manager guided, instructed, and encouraged the team.

When ideas are presented in parallel patterns, sentences flow smoothly. Writing in parallel patterns means putting similar ideas in similar forms. The words that are similar (parallel) in the sample sentence above are *guided, instructed,* and *encouraged*. They are all verbs, and they are all in the past tense. That sentence would not have a smooth rhythm if it read, *The manager guided, instructing, and encouraged the team*. In this case, *instructing* does not match because it is the *-ing* form, not the past tense form.

As you write your ideas in parallel patterns, keep the same balanced pattern for similar ideas. Place nouns with nouns, adjectives with adjectives, prepositional phrases with prepositional phrases, and so on.

The parallel items in the following sentences are in italics.

Pat is *kind, funny, cooperative,* and *intelligent*.

• Each item is an adjective.

The course in biomedical electronics gives students hands-on experience with *ECG monitors, defibrillators,* and *ECG recorders*.

• Each item is a noun.

© 2000 Houghton Mifflin Company

Our household chores include *folding laundry, cooking meals, washing dishes*, and *paying bills*.

• Each item consists of an *-ing* verb form and a noun.

The two major reasons cars break down on the road are *flat tires* and *overheated radiators*.

• Each item consists of an adjective and a noun.

PRACTICE 1 Each group has one item that does not match because it does not have the same form as the other items. Find the item and change it to parallel form. The first one has been done for you.

EXAMPLE: emotional, physical, ~~financially~~, spiritual

financial _____

1. danced, joked, smiled, laughing

_____

2. under the bridge, through the park, up the ramp, the driveway

_____

3. driving the van, waving our arms, play the stereo, weaving through traffic

_____

4. radiologist, electrician, teaching, computer analyst

_____

5. interesting books, optimistic movies, days that are sunny, home-cooked dinners

_____

When you are writing about a series of items, make sure that the items in the series are all alike. A parallel sentence looks like this:

Their children are   sensitive,
understanding,
kind, and
happy.

The basic setup, *Their children are*, fits each item. This sentence has parallel structure because every item fits with the setup:

Their children are sensitive.
Their children are understanding.
Their children are kind.
Their children are happy.

PRACTICE 2   Rewrite whichever part of each sentence needs to be parallel. The first one has been done for you.

EXAMPLE: Marcia is a good listener, loyal, and a trustworthy companion.

Marcia is a good listener, a loyal friend, and a trustworthy companion.

1. When on an interview, it is important to dress conservatively, shake hands firmly, speaking clearly, and answer questions directly.

   _____

   _____

2. His brother was in a bad mood because he lost his keys, locked himself out, and misses the bus.

   _____

   _____

3. He survived the fall, but he had a broken arm, several broken ribs, and one of his lungs was punctured.

   _____

   _____

4. As we left for the airport, the weather report predicted scattered thunderstorms, flash floods, and winds that would be high.

   _____

   _____

5. During finals week, we studied before school, during lunch break, and we also studied after work was over.

   _____

   _____

PRACTICE 3   Complete each of the following sentences by filling in the blanks with a parallel word or words.

1. I believe people should _____ and

   _____ one another.

2. My job responsibilities include _____ and

   _____ .

3. The ideal parent is _____ , _____ ,

    and _____ .

4. When I was younger, I _____ , _____ ,

    and _____ .

5. The two qualities I admire most in people are _____ and

    _____ .

Paired Words

Either . . . or, neither . . . nor, not . . . but, and *not only . . . but also* are words that work together. They set up ideas that need to be in parallel form.

Either . . . Or

When you write in the *either . . . or* pattern, the words following the word *either* and the word *or* must be in the same form.

> We should *either* **postpone** *or* **cancel** the party.
> They will stay *either* **at a motel** *or* **in a campsite**.

PRACTICE 4   Fill in the blanks with a parallel word or words.

1. We must either _____ or _____ .

2. For dinner we want either _____ or

    _____ .

Neither . . . Nor

Notice that the words *neither . . . nor* are just like the words *either . . . or* with an *-n* added. The *-n* makes the words negative. *Neither . . . nor* has a "not" meaning.

> Please order *either* tacos *or* burritos. (Order one of them.)
> Please order *neither* tacos *nor* burritos. (Don't order either of them.)

When you write in the *neither . . . nor* pattern, the words following *neither* and *nor* must be in the same form.

> *Neither* **money** *nor* **fame** lasts.
> Because we saw *neither* **Jerry** *nor* **Janet** at the party, we decided to leave early.

PRACTICE 5   Fill in the blanks with a parallel word or words.

1. Neither _____ nor _____ brings

happiness.

2. Neither _____ nor_____ will be open

on Memorial Day.

Not . . . But

When you write in the *not . . . but* pattern, the words following *not* and *but* must
be in the same form.

> They base their decisions *not* **on the facts** *but* **on their feelings.**
> Last night someone criticized me *not* **for making noise** *but* **for being
> too quiet.**

PRACTICE 6   Fill in the blanks with a parallel word or words.

1. Today is not the time to _____

but the time to _____ .

2. I am kind not because _____

but because _____ .

Not Only . . . But Also

When you write in the *not only . . . but also* pattern, the words following *not only*
and *but also* must be in the same form.

> They are *not only* **good neighbors** *but also* **great friends.**
> It is important *not only* **to study hard** *but* **to study often.**

PRACTICE 7   Fill in the blanks with a parallel word or words.

1. Wilson is important not only to _____ but also to

_____ .

2. I am proud of myself not only because _____

but also because _____ .

© 2000 Houghton Mifflin Company

Longer Parallel Ideas

Writing in longer parallel patterns will give your sentences and paragraphs a flowing rhythm.

Parallel -ing Verb Forms

A series of words beginning with -*ing* verb forms produces a smooth pattern.

PRACTICE 8 In the following sentences, circle each group of words that begins with an -*ing* verb form. The first one has been done for you.

EXAMPLE: He looked at David , standing quietly beside him , gazing not at the jewels but at the people .

—Pearl S. Buck, *Come, My Beloved*

1. Sitting there in his American-style suit , puffing at a cigarette , he had seemed to her almost a stranger .

—Yukio Mishima, "Swaddling Clothes"

2. Getting a driver's license , needing a shave every morning , going to college , and reading the front page of a paper before the sports section — these all say a person is getting older .

—David Vecsey, "Old at Seventeen"

3. The stick sang through the air , catching the snake on the side of the head , sweeping him out of coil .

—Richard Wright, "Big Boy Leaves Home"

4. I sat in my bright kitchen wondering what to do , knowing I would never sleep .

—Alice Munro, "How I Met My Husband"

5. Among Native Americans , the Pueblo peoples have been especially successful at retaining their ties to the past , maintaining their ancestral religion , and keeping their communities intact .

—David Roberts, "The Old Ones of the Southwest"

Parallel Paragraphs

No practice: just experience fine writing.

1.

I teach first graders. I live in a world of skinned knees, double-knotted shoelaces, riddles that I've heard a dozen times, stale birthday cakes, hurt feelings, wandering stories, and one lost shoe ("and if you don't find it my mother'll kill me"). My work is dominated by six-year-olds.

My energy is spent in encouraging, supporting, consoling, and praising my children. In teaching, the inner rewards come from without. On any given day, quite apart from teaching reading and spelling, I bandage a cut, dry a tear, erase a frown, tape a torn doll, and locate a long-lost boot. The day is really won through matters of the heart. As my students groan, laugh, shudder, cry, exult, and wonder, I do too. I have to be soft around the edges.

—Daniel Meier, "One Man's Kids"

2.

Never shall I forget that night, the first night in camp, which has turned my life into one long night, seven times cursed and seven times sealed. Never shall I forget that smoke. Never shall I forget the little faces of the children, whose bodies I saw turned into wreaths of smoke beneath a silent blue sky. Never shall I forget those flames which consumed my faith forever. Never shall I forget that nocturnal silence which deprived me, for all eternity, of the desire to live. Never shall I forget those moments which murdered my God and my soul and turned my dreams to dust. Never shall I forget these things, even if I am condemned to live as long as God Himself. Never.

—Elie Wiesel, *Night*

3.

I have a dream that one day on the red hills of Georgia, the sons of former slaves and the sons of former slaveowners will be able to sit down together at the table of brotherhood.

I have a dream that one day even the state of Mississippi, a desert state sweltering with the heat of injustice and oppression, will be transformed into an oasis of freedom and justice.

I have a dream that my four little children will one day live in a nation where they will not be judged by the color of their skin but by the content of their character.

—Martin Luther King, Jr., "I Have a Dream"

Review: Writing with Parallel Ideas

- When you are writing in parallel patterns, keep the words in similar form so your sentences have a balanced rhythm.

- When you are writing with paired words, such as *either . . . or, not . . . but,* and *not only . . . but also,* make sure the words following them are in similar form.

REVIEW PRACTICE Individually or in groups, underline the parallel verbs in the following excerpt.

> I fought migraine then, ignored the warnings it sent, went to school and later to work in spite of it, sat through lectures in Middle English and presentations to advertisers with involuntary tears running down the right side of my face, threw up in washrooms, stumbled home by instinct, emptied ice trays onto my bed and tried to freeze the pain in my right temple, wished only for a neurosurgeon who would do a lobotomy on house call, and cussed my imagination.
>
> —Joan Didion, "In Bed"

 EXTRA CHALLENGE Individually or in groups, use the following sentences as models and replace the parallel words in italics with parallel words of your own. Be creative; your parallel words need not have the same meaning as the words you replace. The first one has been done for you.

EXAMPLE: She seemed to be vaguely *troubled*, vaguely *amused*.
                              —John Cheever, "Torch Song"

She seemed to be vaguely _surprised_, vaguely _confused_.

1. Those who do not know how to *weep with their whole heart* don't know how to *laugh either*.

    —Golda Meir

    Those who do not know how to _____ don't know

    how to _____ .

2. Wildly, Alfred bolted across the street, *sidestepping a taxicab by inches, ignoring the horns and curses of braking drivers*.

    —Robert Lipsyte, *The Contender*

    Wildly, Alfred bolted across the street, _____ ,

    _____ .

3. To be *the father of a nation* is a great honor, but to be *the father of a family* is a greater joy.

—Nelson Mandela

To be _____ is a great honor,

but to be _____ is a greater joy.

4. The difference between a *successful* person and others is not *a lack of strength,* not *a lack of knowledge,* but rather *a lack of will.*

—Vince Lombardi

The difference between a _____ person and others

is not _____ ,

not _____ , but rather

_____ .

5. The moment we *cease to hold each other,* the moment we *break faith with one another,* the *sea engulfs us* and the *light goes out.*

—James Baldwin, "Nothing Personal"

The moment we _____ ,

the moment we _____ ,

the _____ and

the _____ .

Part 4

Focusing on Words and Punctuation

Chapter

21

Reviewing Pronouns

◆ Pronouns and Antecedents

◆ Pronoun Agreement

◆ Pronoun Placement

◆ Indefinite Pronouns

◆ Pronouns Ending in *-self* and *-selves*

Pronouns and Antecedents

We use pronouns to refer to nouns we have already used so we don't have to keep repeating the same noun. Pronouns can be subjects or objects, or they can show ownership. Regardless of how you use a pronoun in a sentence, make sure readers will understand which noun the pronoun refers to.

Subjects, Objects, and Possessives

Pronouns can be subjects (they do the action), objects (they receive the action), or possessives (they refer to ownership).

PRONOUN CHART			
	Subject	**Object**	**Possessive**
Singular	I	me	my, mine
	you	you	your, yours
	he, she, it	him, her, it	his, her, hers, its
Plural	we	us	our, ours
	you	you	your, yours
	they	them	their, theirs

A pronoun can be the subject of a sentence: it does the action.

> *We* wondered when the weather would change.
> Throughout the night, *she* heard trees whipped by wind.

A pronoun can be the object of a verb: it receives the action.

> Alicia appreciates *him.*
> Wilson helps and supports *her.*

A pronoun can be possessive: it shows ownership.

> Milton opened *his* wallet and realized the credit card was gone.
> Milton and *his* wife called *their* credit card company immediately.

Antecedents

Pronouns are general words with little meaning unless we know what nouns they refer to. The word or words that a pronoun refers to are called *antecedents*. When you use pronouns in your writing, make sure the pronoun's antecedent is clear.

1. *Delia* never looked up from *her* work, and *her* thin, stooped shoulders sagged further.

> —Zora Neale Hurston, "Sweat"

- *Her* refers to *Delia.*
- *Delia* is the antecedent of *her.*

2. The wind sucked at the *windows* and released *them* suddenly to rattle in *their* metal frames.

> —Barry Holstun Lopez, "Winter Count 1973"

- *Them* and *their* refer to *windows.*
- *Windows* is the antecedent of *them* and *their.*

PRACTICE 1   The first sentence in the following paragraph introduces a toddler. Circle the pronouns in the paragraph that refer to the word *toddler*.

> In the ocean's shallows, a toddler dangles at the end of his mother's outstretched arms. As the waves cast the giggling child out toward sea and suck him back, he is grounded by his mother's firm stand on the earth under water. In time, the child will learn that the water itself supports him. He will wriggle free of his mother's fingers and swim, delighting in the freedom and gasping at the power of the waves.
>
> —Susan McBride Els, *Into the Deep*

Pronoun Agreement

Pronouns agree with the nouns they refer to, their antecedents. They agree in number (singular or plural) and in case (subject or object).

Agreement with Singular and Plural

If a noun is singular, the pronoun that refers to it must be singular (*he, him, his, she, her, hers, it, its, this, that*).

> *Linda* packed the boxes carefully. *She* wanted to make sure nothing would break.

If a noun is plural, the pronoun that refers to it must be plural (*they, them, their, these, those*).

> The *boxes* are standing in the kitchen. *They* are packed with memories and treasures.

A Common Error

A common error involves writing about a singular noun and referring to it with a plural pronoun.

Incorrect: When a *person* hurries, *they* will make mistakes.

- The writer mentions the noun *person*, which is singular, but the writer then uses the pronoun *they*, which is plural. The pronoun does not agree with its antecedent. This pronoun problem can be solved in either of two ways: changing the pronoun or changing the noun.

First Solution: Change the Pronoun

If you find yourself writing about a singular noun and referring to it with a plural pronoun, you can solve the problem by changing the pronoun.

EXAMPLE 1

Problem: If a *person* hurries, ~~they~~ will make mistakes.

- Here we need to change the plural pronoun *they* to a singular pronoun. We could choose either *he* or *she*. Be careful when the noun could name either a female or a male. If we write *he,* we could offend women. If we write *she,* we could offend men. We need to cover both possibilities and write *he or she.*

Solution: If a *person* hurries, *he or she* will make mistakes.

EXAMPLE 2

Problem: A *person* who does not wear ~~their~~ seat belt can get a ticket.

- A *person* is one; *their* refers to more than one. The pronoun *their* does not agree with the noun *person.* If we want to keep *person,* we need to recognize that a person may be either female or male.

Solution: A *person* who does not wear *his or her* seat belt can get a ticket.

Second Solution: Change the Noun

You can also solve an agreement problem by changing a singular noun to a plural noun. When we write with plural nouns, we don't have to be concerned about covering both masculine and feminine genders. Plural pronouns (*they, them,* and *their*) can refer to either masculine or feminine antecedents.

EXAMPLE 1

Problem: If ~~a person~~ hurries, *they* will make mistakes.

- If we write *people* instead of *person,* we do not have to be concerned with masculine or feminine gender. The word *they* refers to both.

Solution: If *people* hurry, *they* will make mistakes.

EXAMPLE 2

Problem: ~~A person~~ who does not wear *their* seat belt can get a ticket.

- If we write *passengers* instead of *person,* we do not have to be concerned with gender because *they* refers to both feminine and masculine.

Solution: *Passengers* who do not wear *their* seat belts can get a ticket.

PRACTICE 2 Correct the agreement problem in each sentence by changing the singular noun subject to plural. In most cases, you will also have to change the verb so the subject and verb agree. The first one has been done for you.

> EXAMPLE: A politician should forget sound bites and discuss their positions on the important issues.
>
> Politicians should forget sound bites and discuss their positions on the important issues.

1. A renter needs to make sure their landlord allows pets.

   _____

2. Before a student registers, they should know what classes are required for their major.

   _____

   _____

3. A writer can clarify their thoughts through freewriting.

   _____

4. If a person walks through those woods, they will see at least ten kinds of migrating birds.

   _____

   _____

5. A faithful friend is there when we need them.

   _____

6. Since a basketball player needs to be in excellent physical condition, they practice year round.

   _____

   _____

7. A working parent often has the responsibility of finding daycare for their children.

   _____

   _____

8. A physical therapist assists people in recovering from injuries and illnesses. They concentrate on helping patients regain muscle strength and mobility.

   _____

   _____

9. If a person is in close proximity to lightning, the electrical current can travel through the ground and into their legs.

_____

_____

10. A pet can provide valuable companionship, but they are time-consuming responsibilities.

_____

_____

Agreement with Subject and Object

Subject pronouns do the action: *I, you, he, she, we, they*. Object pronouns receive the action: *me, you, him, her, us, them*. Choosing the correct pronoun is not a problem when just one person is mentioned, but the choice can be confusing when more than one person is mentioned. There is an easy way to figure out the correct pronoun. If you are using a pronoun along with another person's name, temporarily remove that person's name from the sentence. The correct pronoun to use should then be clear.

EXAMPLE 1

Question: Which would you write?

Robert and *me* went to the game.

        or

Robert and *I* went to the game.

- To find out, temporarily take *Robert* out of the sentence.
- Which would you say? "Me went to the game" or "I went to the game."
- You would say *I*. Now put *Robert* back in and write:

Answer: Robert and *I* went to the game.

EXAMPLE 2

Question: Which would you write?

Corey wants to go to the game with Jackie and *I*.

        or

Corey wants to go to the game with Jackie and *me*.

- To find out, temporarily take *Jackie* out of the sentence.
- Which would you say? "Corey wants to go to the game with I" or "Corey wants to go to the game with me."
- You would say *me*. Now put *Jackie* back in and write:

Answer: Corey wants to go to the game with Jackie and *me*.

PRACTICE 3 Some of the following sentences are correct; others are not. Temporarily taking the "other person" out of a sentence will help you find and correct errors. The first two have been done for you.

EXAMPLE: We want to meet Natasha and he.

We want to meet Natasha and him.

EXAMPLE: Last night, my brother and me volunteered at the conference center.

Last night, my brother and I volunteered at the conference center.

1. Rick asked Maria and she to go out Saturday.

_____

2. I gave my last dollar to Lana and her.

_____

3. Edward and him gave us clear directions.

_____

4. Sheila and me will take care of the details.

_____

5. Few secrets exist between Scott and me.

_____

6. For my cousin and I, education is a passport to a secure future.

_____

7. We are looking for a doctor who will sit down with my mom and I and explain Mom's options.

_____

_____

8. In the middle of the movie, Fran and them decided to leave.

_____

9. Nick hopes that this job will give his wife and he the security they need.

_____

_____

10. When family members need anything, they always come to my husband and I.

_____

Pronoun Placement

Writing pronouns correctly involves two steps: choosing the correct pronoun and putting that pronoun in the right place. We have been looking at choosing the correct pronoun. Next, we will look at how to place that pronoun correctly. If you are using a pronoun along with a noun, put the noun first and the pronoun second.

Jeff took my *mother and me* out to dinner.

- (Not *me and my mother*.) The word *mother* is a noun. Therefore, *mother* is placed before the pronoun *me*.

Judy and he are gone for the day.

- (Not *he and Judy* are gone for the day.) *Judy* is a noun. Therefore, *Judy* is placed before the pronoun *he*.

PRACTICE 4 Some of the following sentences are correct; others have pronoun placement problems. Correct where necessary, keeping in mind that if the pronoun is used with another noun, you should put the noun first and the pronoun second. The first one has been done for you.

EXAMPLE: We chose her and Juan to be our representatives on the council.

We chose Juan and her to be our representatives on the council.

1. Cindy gave me and my family a ride to the airport.

_____

_____

2. After they had been honest with each other, she and Edward knew the relationship would last.

_____

_____

3. Robert is willing to help him and Gwen with the assignment.

_____

_____

4. When my friend and I left the store, I forgot to look for my sister.

_____

_____

5. Dan met him and Matthew in the parking lot.

_____

_____

PRACTICE 5   Rewrite the following sentences correctly by asking yourself two questions: *Do I have the right pronoun?* and *Is it in the right place?* The first two have been done for you.

EXAMPLE: Me and John went to the game yesterday.

John and I went to the game yesterday.

EXAMPLE: The uncertainty of the future hangs heavily on him and his wife.

The uncertainty of the future hangs heavily on his wife and him.

1. The decision was left up to Rosita and she.

   _____

2. Him and Gary went shopping for the day.

   _____

3. The registrar gave the last copies of the course listings to Michelle and I.

   _____

   _____

4. After leaving the restaurant, me and my son decided to eat out once a month.

   _____

   _____

5. When their children graduated, Ken and her celebrated with a trip to Jamaica.

   _____

   _____

Indefinite Pronouns

The pronouns we have been examining refer to definite people or things: pronouns such as *me, you, we, her*. Some pronouns, however, do not refer to a specific person or thing. Because they refer to something less definite, they are called *indefinite* ("not definite") *pronouns.*

Singular				
anybody	everybody	somebody	nobody	each
anyone	everyone	someone	no one	either
anything	everything	something	nothing	neither

Agreement Trouble Spot 1

The indefinite pronouns in the list are treated as singular and take a singular verb—that is, they take the same verb as *he, she,* or *it*. Notice that most of these words end in *-body, -one,* or *-thing*. Noticing the endings of these words is one way to remember that they are singular pronouns that take a singular verb.

> <u>Everybody</u> <u>is applauding</u>.
>
> <u>Everything</u> <u>is working</u> out well.
>
> <u>No one</u> <u>was sitting</u> down on the job.
>
> <u>Was</u> <u>everyone</u> <u>laughing</u>?

PRACTICE 6   Underline the correct verb in each sentence.

1. No one (is, are) complaining.

2. Nobody (was, were) interested.

3. Everything on the back shelves (is, are) for sale.

4. Everybody on the block (was, were) dancing.

5. Everyone (needs, need) a day off.

Agreement Trouble Spot 2

In the previous exercise, you selected a singular verb to match the singular subject. In addition, you need to make sure that other words in the sentence referring to the indefinite pronoun are also singular. You have two choices: either use singular pronouns or change the indefinite pronoun to a plural noun. The second solution is usually easier.

First Solution: Use Singular Pronouns

Problem: *Anyone* who wants to attend the ceremony needs to get ~~*their*~~ tickets early.

- *Anyone* is singular, but *their* is plural. We need to change the pronoun *their* to make it match *anyone*. One solution is to change *their* to singular pronouns and use *his or her*.

Solution: *Anyone* who wants to attend the ceremony needs to get *his or her* tickets early.

Second Solution: Change the Indefinite Pronoun to a Plural Noun

Problem: ~~*Anyone*~~ who wants to attend the ceremony needs to get *their* tickets early.

- If we change the singular pronoun *anyone* to a plural noun, we can keep *their*.

Solution: *People* who want to attend the ceremony need to get *their* tickets early.

PRACTICE 7 Rewrite each of the following sentences correctly by replacing the singular indefinite pronoun with a plural noun of your choice. In some cases, you will also need to change the verb from singular to plural form. The first one has been done for you.

EXAMPLE: When someone has been drinking, they are deadly on the road.

When drivers have been drinking, they are deadly on the road.

1. Everybody should receive their final grades in the mail.

_____

_____

2. Everyone must bring their own food to the picnic.

_____

_____

3. When anyone is traveling, they should buy traveler's checks and keep a copy of the check numbers at home.

_____

_____

_____

4. Each loan applicant must provide information about their credit history.

_____

_____

5. If anybody needs assistance on the Internet, they should take the weekend workshop offered on campus.

_____

_____

_____

Pronouns Ending in -self and -selves

Pronouns ending in -self and -selves are used in two ways: *reflexive* or *intensive*. *Reflexive* means that the action returns to the person or thing. *Intensive* means intensifying or emphasizing the person or thing.

REFLEXIVE AND INTENSIVE PRONOUNS		
	Person	**Pronouns: reflexive and intensive**
Singular	I	myself
	you	yourself
	he	himself
	she	herself
	it	itself
Plural	we	ourselves
	you	yourselves
	they	themselves

Reflexive Pronouns

When people do something to themselves, we use the pronouns in the list as reflexive pronouns.

> I taught *myself* Spanish by listening to tapes.

> David prepared *himself* for the difficult week ahead.

Intensive Pronouns

Sometimes pronouns ending in *-self* and *-selves* are used for emphasis.

> I *myself* want nothing to do with that project.
> Henry and I finished the project by *ourselves*.

- In the first sentence, *myself* emphasizes the point that I am someone who wants nothing to do with the project.

- In the second sentence, *ourselves* emphasizes the point that Henry and I finished the project alone, without help.

Be careful of how you use *myself*. *Myself* is often used incorrectly instead of *I* or *me*.

> *me*
> Lydia gave ~~myself~~ her class notes.

- Here, *myself* cannot act as a reflexive pronoun because Lydia did not give herself the notes. *Myself* also cannot act as an intensive pronoun here because Lydia is not emphasizing herself. The correct pronoun is *me*.

In addition, make sure you spell these words pronouns correctly. The words "theirselves," "their selves," and "hisself" are incorrect. Instead, write *themselves* and *himself*.

> *themselves*
> They were happy with ~~theirselves~~ when the grades arrived.

> *himself*
> After completing the course, he rewarded ~~his self~~ by taking a weekend vacation.

PRACTICE 8   Some of the following sentences have pronoun errors. Correct where necessary.

1. Please give the report to myself.

   _____

2. My neighbors locked theirselves out of their house.

   _____

3. The director honored both Sarah and me at the annual banquet.

   _____

4. They wanted to do a favor for myself, so they took care of the garden while I was gone.

   _____

   _____

5. While Michael was repairing the patio, he hammered hisself.

   _____

Review: Reviewing Pronouns

- Make sure each pronoun you use agrees with its antecedent. Singular nouns need singular pronouns.

   A *renter* needs to make sure *his or her* landlord allows pets.

- You can avoid having to cover both genders (*she and he, her and him, her and his*) by making the antecedent plural. Then you can use a plural pronoun (*they, them, their*).

   Renters need to make sure *their* landlord allows pets.

- When you are using a pronoun with a noun, you can determine the correct pronoun by temporarily removing the noun from the sentence.

   him

   Pete hopes that this job will give (his wife and) ~~he~~ the security they need.

- When you are using a pronoun with a noun, place the noun before the pronoun.

   My *friend* and *I* filled out the applications.

- When you are writing with indefinite pronouns (usually ending in *-one*, *-thing*, or *-body*), remember that these are singular pronouns. The easiest way to achieve agreement is by changing the indefinite pronoun to a plural noun.

   Students

   ~~Everybody~~ should receive *their* class schedules in the mail.

- Use *myself* only when stating that you did something to yourself or when you are emphasizing yourself.

   me

   The last two tickets were given to Phil and ~~myself~~.

REVIEW PRACTICE   Individually or in groups, edit the following paragraph for pronoun errors and correct where necessary.

Honesty is the foundation for every strong relationship. Me and my girlfriend are always honest with each other. If there is a problem, we talk about it. Two months ago, we faced a problem with a friend who was doing everything in his power to keep us apart. He filled her head with lies, lies which she then threw at I. We were both furious. She was angry at I because she thought that I was unfaithful to her. I was angry at she because she did not trust me. Finally, we started to talk, honestly and openly. Then the truth emerged. We were both angry at being betrayed. Only by being honest did we realize that there was only one person who had done the betraying, her friend. In the end, that friend taught us an important truth. Me and my girlfriend now know that honesty is the frame that supports our relationship.

—Student Writer

EXTRA CHALLENGE   The following excerpt is taken from an article in which the author describes what archaeologists have discovered about the Anasazi, Indians who lived in the Southwest over 2,000 years ago. Because the article is written from the point of view of the writer, he uses the pronoun *I*. Individually or in groups, rewrite the paragraph by changing the point of view to that of the third person, *he*. In other words, replace the pronouns *I, me, my,* and *myself* with the pronouns *he, him, his,* and *himself*.

I found my strongest links with the Anasazi by hiking into the back-country of Utah and discovering for myself the ruins of these ancient Pueblo Indians. In dozens of remote canyons, I visited hundreds of unrestored sites, admiring relics strewn in the dirt, taking care to leave them exactly as I found them. I clambered up to granaries built out of bound sticks covered with mud, where the Anasazi stored their beans and corn. I scaled frightening prehistoric trails that took me high above this sun-bleached land. Some of the ruins were simply beyond my reach, so I sat admiring these areas for hours through my binoculars. I slept under cottonwood trees, on stream banks where the Anasazi had hunted deer and rabbits. I drank from the same streams that had watered the ancients so long ago.

—Adapted from David Roberts,
"The Old Ones of the Southwest"

Chapter 22

Writing with Apostrophes

- ◆ Contraction
- ◆ Possession
- ◆ *Focus on Apostrophes*

Contraction

An apostrophe is used mainly for two reasons: to form a contraction or to show possession. We will first look at contraction, where an apostrophe indicates one or more missing letters.

Muscles contract when they squeeze together. Words also contract. Two words are squeezed together to form one word, and in the process, one or more letters drop out. The apostrophe marks where the letter or letters used to be.

could not = couldn't

should not = shouldn't

did not = didn't

you will = you'll

we are = we're

they are = they're

you are = you're

it is = it's

it has = it's (*It's* always means *it is* or *it has*.)

Please note: Contractions are considered casual. For formal writing and most college writing, use both words rather than the contraction.

PRACTICE 1   Write the contractions of the following words:

you are = _____   is not = _____

she is = _____   has not = _____

they are = _____   could not = _____

he is = _____   should not = _____

I will = _____   would not = _____

it is = _____   did not = _____

Possession

Each of the following sentences lets readers know that someone owns something.

Shantae owns a motorcycle, which is parked outside.

The motorcycle that Shantae owns is parked outside.

The motorcycle of Shantae is parked outside.

Another way to show ownership is by using a possessive form—that is, add an apostrophe and *-s* to the "owner."

Shantae's motorcycle is parked outside.

My *sister's* boyfriend tutors high school students.

Juanita's paycheck was mailed Friday morning.

Steps for Writing the Possessive

Writing the possessive involves a process. The first step is deciding if you are, in fact, dealing with ownership. If you are, draw a box around the owner and add *-'s* outside the box. If the name of the owner already ends in *-s*, you may drop the extra *-s*. We will now go through these three steps.

1. Decide If You Are Dealing with the Possessive

When a person or a thing owns something mentioned right after that owner's name, you are dealing with the possessive. Add *-'s* to the *owner*.

Let's look at the decision-making process. The first sentence is a question, followed by the thinking process that leads to the answer.

Question: Which is correct? *Bobby car is for sale* or *Bobby's car is for sale.*

• The word that comes after the name Bobby is *car*. Go backward. Ask yourself, "Do I mean the car of Bobby?" Yes. Therefore, put a box around *Bobby* and add *-'s* outside the box.

Answer: *Bobby's car is for sale.*

Question: Which is correct? *Bobby owns an expensive car* or *Bobby's owns an expensive car*.

• The word that comes after *Bobby* is *owns*. Ask yourself, "Do I mean the owns of Bobby?" No. The meaning of the sentence tells us that Bobby owns the car, but he does not own the word right after his name. There is no -'s.

Answer: *Bobby owns an expensive car*.

2. Draw a Box Around the Owner and Add -'s Outside the Box

If people or things own what comes right after their names, you are dealing with the possessive. Once you know you are dealing with the possessive, draw a box around the owner and add -'s outside the box.

The car 's battery is dead.

The college 's schedule is available in the lobby.

The plumber 's bill was more than we expected.

3. If the Name of the Owner Ends in -s, Omit the Extra -s

If the name of the owner already ends with -s, just add an apostrophe. The extra -s can be dropped so people do not have difficulty saying two -s sounds.*

Jerry Williams' courage carried the family through hard times.

• This sentence refers to the courage of Jerry Williams. When *Williams* is put in a box, we see that the name already ends in -s. Therefore, we can just add an apostrophe outside the box.

All students' papers are due on Friday.

• This sentence refers to the papers of all the students. When the word *students* is put in a box, we see that the name already ends with -s. Therefore, just add an apostrophe outside the box.

Writing Possessive Forms: Examples of the Process

Notice that the owner is placed in a box, and -'s is added outside the box.

the bottles of one baby = box around baby = baby's bottles

the bottles of three babies = box around babies = babies' bottles

the grades of one student = box around student = student's grades

the grades of many students = box around students = students' grades

the joy of one child = box around child = child's joy

the joy of two children = box around children = children's joy

---

*Some writers add an apostrophe and -s to one-syllable nouns that end in -s: bus's exhaust, Chris's car. This is acceptable.

PRACTICE 2   Rewrite the following phrases by using possessive forms. (Remember to put the owner in a "box.") The first two have been done for you.

      EXAMPLE: the schedule of my brother = my brother 's schedule

      EXAMPLE: textbooks for freshmen = the freshmen 's textbooks

    1. the proposals offered by the politician

      _____

    2. the proposals offered by the politicians

      _____

    3. the desk belonging to the secretary

      _____

    4. the success of the students

      _____

    5. the responsibilities of parents

      _____

    6. the sales in the store

      _____

    7. the concern of our friends

      _____

    8. the concern of our friend

      _____

    9. the spirit of the players

      _____

    10. the expectations of our group

      _____

PRACTICE 3   Rewrite each pair of short sentences as one sentence by using the possessive. The first two have been done for you.

      EXAMPLE: Jaryl has a daughter. The daughter is teaching in Kenya.

                Jaryl's daughter is teaching in Kenya.

      EXAMPLE: The president has advisers. They encouraged him not to sign the treaty.

                The president's advisers encouraged him not to sign the treaty.

1. Theresa has a car. It was just repainted.

   _____

2. Brian has a favorite sport. The sport is soccer.

   _____

3. The group has a new album. The album will be on the shelves in December.

   _____

4. Jill has a new job. The new job has given her self-confidence.

   _____

5. That student had a question. The question helped make the instruction clear to the rest of the class.

   _____

   _____

6. The employees have a new work schedule. The work schedule will take effect in January.

   _____

   _____

7. The mayor has a rule. It requires department officials to disclose any business ties to city contractors.

   _____

   _____

8. The company has objectives. Those objectives will change with the new president.

   _____

   _____

9. Elena has a sense of humor. Her sense of humor helps us smile even during the hard times.

   _____

   _____

10. Rodolfo has a straightforward approach. This approach impressed the audience.

    _____

    _____

Focus on Apostrophes

An apostrophe is used for contractions and possessives. Therefore, do not use apostrophes with verbs or with plural nouns.

> Incorrect: Marlene ~~run's~~ four ~~mile's~~ a week.
>
> Correct: Marlene *runs* four *miles* a week.

- The *-s* is on *runs* because present tense verbs end with *-s* when the subject is a singular noun.
- The *-s* is on *miles* because *miles* is a plural noun.
- Present tense verbs and plural nouns do end in *-s*, but they do not have an apostrophe.

An apostrophe is never used with pronouns. Therefore, do not add an apostrophe to pronouns such as *his, her, hers, its, my, mine, our, ours, your, yours, their,* and *theirs*.

> Incorrect: Phil packed up ~~his'~~ car and headed for the beach.
>
> Correct: Phil packed up *his* car and headed for the beach.

> Incorrect: We needed a driver's license for identification. I had remembered ~~mine's~~. My friends had forgotten ~~their's~~.
>
> Correct: We needed a driver's license for identification. I had remembered *mine*. My friends had forgotten *theirs*.

PRACTICE 4   Correct the errors in the following sentences. The errors involve omitting an apostrophe, omitting *-s,* or placing an apostrophe incorrectly.

1. We respected and appreciated Sheldon apology.

   _____

2. My sister now listen's to my advice.

   _____

3. Janie parents retired and moved to Florida.

   _____

4. Many adults' have high blood pressure, also known as hypertension.

   _____

5. The parents put their children needs before their own.

   _____

6. Experience's are great teachers.

   _____

7. The cut on Tobys front paw require's twelve stitches.

_____

8. The furniture store advertised weekend sale's that involved no money down, no monthly payments, and no finance charges.

_____

_____

9. The students backpack was stuffed with notes and textbooks.

_____

10. The trucks tire is flat.

_____

Review: Writing with Apostrophes

Writing with an apostrophe

- The apostrophe is used for two entirely different reasons: forming a contraction or showing possession.

  1. Contraction: indicating that one or more letters are missing.

     They're running late.

     You're the best friend I have ever had.

  2. Possession: indicating ownership.

     I left the *dog's* leash at home.

     We hope the *college's* schedule is changed next year.

Writing with -s

- The ending *-s* is used for three entirely different kinds of words: plural nouns, possessives, and present tense verbs that have *he, she, it,* or a singular noun as a subject.

  1. Plural nouns end in *-s* to show that there is more than one.

     Coupons and *rebates* attract *customers*.

     We want *hamburgers* and *fries* for dinner.

  2. Possessive forms of nouns have an apostrophe and an *-s* to show ownership.

     Barbara's dream is to graduate in May.

     The cable *company's* rates went up.

  3. Present tense verbs end with *-s* when the subject is *he, she, it,* or a singular noun.

     Robert *studies* in the library.

     The information booth *opens* at noon.

REVIEW PRACTICE In the following paragraph, the apostrophes needed for showing contraction and possession have been omitted. Individually or in groups, place the apostrophes where they belong.

Behind a dumpster sits a man who calls himself Red, enjoying the last drops of a bottle of wine called Wild Irish Rose. Its 1 A.M., and the thermometer hovers around 20 degrees with a biting wind. His nickname comes from a golden retriever his family once had back in Memphis, and a sparkle comes to his eyes as he recalls examples of the dogs loyalty. One day he plans to get another dog, and says, "Im getting to the point where I cant talk to people. Theyre always telling me to do something or get out of their way. But a dog is different."

—Jon D. Hull, "Slow Descent into Hell"

 EXTRA CHALLENGE Read the following excerpt from a student's essay about the Appalachian Trail. The paragraph has five apostrophes, but only one of them is used correctly. Individually or in groups, find and correct the four apostrophe errors.

Millions of people hike the Appalachian Trail annually. Following the clearly marked rectangular signs, which are neatly painted at eye level on prominent trees, the hikers walk along the path, soft with last season's leaves. They hike through virgin forests with towering trees, populated by song bird's whose singing echoes in the still of the forest. Their journey high up in the mountains occasionally offers a spectacular view of the valley below. They pass mountain streams and acres of wild flowers blooming in the shaded woods. When they tire after hours of walking through this majestic wonderland, they reach their campsite and light up the campfire. As the aroma of dinner fills the air, they sit and look at the beauty that surround's them. This is a magical time when every tree, shrub, and plant is sharply defined by the setting sun. When the sky blackens and millions of sparkling stars can be seen, the insect's begin their nightly chorus and the night birds harmonize. Sitting around the campfire, the hikers tell stories about their adventure's on the trail.

—Student Writer

Chapter 23

Focusing on Easily Confused Words, Spelling, and Vocabulary

◆ Easily Confused Words
◆ Spelling Guides
◆ Prefixes and Roots

Easily Confused Words

Many words are confusing only when we write. When we talk, we know which word we are using. The difficulty comes in knowing how that word is spelled. For example, say aloud, "We have two exams on Monday." The sound of *two* (meaning "2") is identical to the sound of *too* and *to* in "The pizza is too hot to eat." The words *two*, *too*, and *to* sound the same, so when we write, we need to be sure of how to spell the word we mean.

Some easily confused words are presented here in alphabetical order so you can use this list as a reference when editing your writing.

a an and

a: used before nouns that begin with a consonant sound (every letter but a vowel)

   A friend stopped by to talk.

an: used before nouns that begin with a vowel sound (*a, e, i, o, u*)

   An old friend stopped by to talk.

and: used to join words or ideas together
> We respect people who have integrity *and* compassion.

accept except

accept: to receive (verb)
> When we *accepted* them as they were, we became close friends.

except: but, other than (*Ex* means "out," as in *exit.*)
> Lisa threw away all her old hats *except* the one Eric had given her.

advice advise

advice: an opinion (noun)
> Because I needed *advice*, I talked with my grandmother.

advise: to give an opinion (verb)
> My grandmother *advised* me to accept the job.

affect effect

affect: to influence or make an impact on (verb)
> His positive attitude *affects* everyone around him.

effect: a result (noun)
> The *effects* of the tornado were featured on the ten o'clock news.

are our

are: a form of the verb *be*
> They *are* happy.

our: a pronoun showing ownership
> They want to borrow *our* vacuum cleaner.

brake break

brake: on a vehicle, a device used to slow down or stop (noun)
> The *brakes* failed after we drove through flooded streets.

break: to smash (verb)
> We tried not to *break* the china platter.

break: an interruption (noun)
> We need more than a coffee *break;* we need a vacation *break.*

breath breathe

breath: the air that goes in and out of lungs (noun)
Our *breath* smells like mint.

breathe: to inhale and exhale (verb)
It was so hot we could scarcely *breathe.*

buy by

buy: to purchase (verb) (Tip: The *u* in the middle can remind you of a U.S. dollar.)
We should *buy* groceries before the weekend.

by: near, before (preposition)
We need to leave *by* seven o'clock.

conscience conscious

conscience: a person's sense of right and wrong; an inner guide (noun)
She trusts her *conscience* to guide her.

conscious: awake, aware (adjective)
We were *conscious* of strange sounds coming from the alley.

desert dessert

desert: a hot, dry place (noun)
In July and August, this city feels like a *desert.*

desert: to abandon, leave (verb)
The family knew that friends would not *desert* them in their time of need.

dessert: food eaten after a meal (noun) (Tip: *Dessert* has two *s*'s. A dessert is something we would like two of.)
We ordered two *desserts* after dinner.

do due

do: to perform
When will you *do* your homework?

do: a helping verb, used for emphasis
They *do* like pizza.

due: payable; owed as a debt
The electricity bill payment is *due* on the first of the month.

due: expected
Their baby is *due* in July.

effect: See *affect*

except: See *accept*

find fine

find: to locate (verb)
>She cannot *find* her glasses.

fine: good (adjective)
>My English instructor said I wrote a *fine* paper.

fine: a sum of money to be paid as a penalty (noun)
>We paid a $50 parking *fine.*

fine: to impose a sum of money as a penalty (verb)
>The judge *fined* the defendant $500.

good well

good: describes a noun (adjective)
>Sarah is a *good* woman.

well: describes a verb (adverb)
>Calvin writes *well.*

have of

The way we sometimes say *could have, would have,* and *should have* makes the *have* sound like *of. Could of, would of,* and *should of* are incorrect.
>We *should have* made reservations.

hear here

hear: to pick up sound (verb) (Tip: Notice the word *ear* in *hear.*)
>I *hear* music.

here: in this place (adverb)
>Our relatives will be *here* for Thanksgiving.

hole whole

hole: a cavity, an opening (noun)
>The rusted muffler is full of *holes.*

whole: complete (adjective)
>Their *whole* argument is misleading.

it's its

it's: a contraction of *it* and *is*

I deleted two paragraphs from my writing, and now *it's* too short.

it's: a contraction of *it* and *has*

It's been a long time since we have relaxed on a weekend.

It's always means *it is* or *it has*. If you do not mean *it is* or *it has,* write the word without the apostrophe: *its*.

its: pronoun showing ownership

The company is reviewing *its* hiring practices.

knew new

knew: understood (past tense of *know*)

We *knew* the answer to every question.

new: unused, recent (adjective)

The *new* stadium will open in May.

know no now

know: to understand (verb)

I *know* they can be trusted.

no: a negative word

There are *no* quick solutions to this problem.

now: at the present time

We want to solve the problem *now* so we can move forward.

loose lose

loose: not fixed in place (adjective)

Steve's dog is running *loose* in the neighborhood again.

lose: to misplace something (verb)

Did you *lose* your car keys?

mind mine

mind: brain (noun)

I cannot make up my *mind*.

mind: to object (verb)
>> I don't *mind* if you leave early.

mine: pronoun showing ownership
>> You can borrow anything of *mine.*

new: See *knew*

no: See *know*

now: See *know*

our: See *are*

pass passed past

pass and *passed:* verbs showing action
>> We will *pass* this course.
>> He *passed* the ball to Randy.

>The past tense, *passed,* is also used to refer to death.
>> She *passed away* last week.

past: beyond (preposition)
>> We walked *past* the farmhouse.

past: time before the present moment (noun)
>> People who live in the *past* rob themselves of the present.

>Do not confuse *pass* and *passed* with *past*. *Past* is not a verb; it does not name any action. Another word in the sentence will name the action, and *past* will tell something about it.
>> <u>She</u> <u>lives</u> in the *past.*
>> <u>He</u> <u>walked</u> *past* the library.

peace piece

peace: calm, lack of disagreement
>> After they left, a sense of *peace* came over him.

piece: a portion or section
>> She ordered a *piece* of chocolate cake.

quiet quit quite

quiet: not noisy (adjective)
>We need a *quiet* place to study.

quit: to stop (verb)
>We both *quit* smoking in January.

quite: a bit, very, actually (adverb)
>Lillian said that her neighbors are *quite* friendly.

right write

right: correct (adjective)
>Arrogant people think they have to be *right.*

write: to put words on paper or on a computer screen (verb)
>We have to *write* two papers this weekend.

set sit

set: to put
>Please *set* (put) the box next to the kitchen table.

sit: to be seated, usually in a chair
>*Sit* down, relax, and enjoy the movie.

suppose supposed

When the word *to* follows the word *suppose,* write *supposed.*
>They were *supposed* to be here at noon.

than then

than: a word used in a comparison
>They like classical music better *than* country music.

then: next, at a certain time. *Then* refers to time.
>We worked until midnight and *then* collapsed.

their there they're

their: a pronoun showing ownership
>They celebrated *their* anniversary last weekend.

there: This word is used in two ways. It can refer to a location or introduce an idea.

there: a location

> When you get *there,* give me a call.

there: introducing a thought

> *There* are many career opportunities in computer sciences.

they're: a contraction meaning *they are.* When writing, ask yourself, "Can I substitute the words *they are?*" If you can, write either *they are* or *they're.*

> Janice hopes that *they're* working as hard as she is.
> *They're* kind people, and I enjoy being around them.

threw through

threw: a verb, the past tense of the verb *throw*

> Latasha *threw* the ball across the court.

through: from one side to the other (preposition)

> Commuters must walk *through* the tunnel to reach the train station.

to too two

To is either part of an infinitive or a preposition.

to: infinitive, such as *to see, to drive, to dance*

> They expect *to win* the game.

to: a preposition, as in *to the party, to St. Louis*

> We walked *to* the corner.

too: in excess, also (Tip: The additional *o* can remind you of *too much.*)

> The jacket is *too* small, and the pants are *too* large. (in excess)
> My little sister wants to go to the movies *too.* (also)

two: the number 2

> *Two* friends are taking us out for dinner.

use used

Whenever *use* is followed by *to,* write *used.*

> We *used* to waste time.

weather whether

weather: climate (snow, rain, sunshine, clouds)

> Rainy *weather* makes us sleepy.

whether: if; suggests a question

> Tell me before lunch *whether* you want to meet later.

well: See *good*

wear where

wear: to put on clothes (verb)
>   Children should *wear* mittens in winter.

where: refers to a place or location
>   *Where* did you put the mail?

we're were

we're: a contraction of *we* and *are*
>   *We're* happy that you decided to come with us.

were: past tense of the verb *be*
>   They *were* always available when we needed to talk.

whole: See *hole*

who's whose

who's: a contraction of *who* and *is*
>   *Who's* responsible for sending the invitations?

who's: a contraction of *who* and *has*
>   Do you know *who's* seen that movie?

If you don't mean *who is* or *who has,* write *whose.*

whose: a pronoun showing ownership
>   Don wants to know *whose* car is in the driveway.

write: See *right*

your you're

your: a pronoun showing ownership
>   Was this *your* idea?

you're: a contraction of *you* and *are*
>   *You're* expected to be on time for dinner.

If you do not mean *you are,* write *your.*

PRACTICE 1   Correct these sentences where necessary. A sentence may be correct, or it may have from one to three errors.

1. They need to no that there lives will change dramatically.

_____

_____

2. I have learned how to except insensitive remarks.

_____

_____

3. They changed there mines and did not right the letter.

_____

_____

4. Their have been to many accidents on Route 66.

_____

_____

5. Who's interested in auditioning for the play?

_____

_____

6. Its to hot to work in are yard.

_____

_____

7. Stephanie is use to studying late at night.

_____

_____

8. I never know weather they will listen or shut me out.

_____

_____

9. Ted and Tony were good friends in high school.

_____

_____

10. The jogger felt out of breathe and stopped to set on a park bench.

_____

_____

11. I don't want a peace of pie for desert.

_____

12. At the art fair, we walked threw all the exhibits an than bought a painting.

_____

_____

13. Whether they win or loose, we support are team.

_____

_____

14. We have no record of our purchases because we through out the receipts.

_____

_____

15. Class has been canceled, but were not sure why.

_____

_____

16. Some people find it hard to except when your right and there wrong.

_____

_____

17. I could of handled the situation better.

_____

18. When the grades were posted, we realized that everyone had pass the course.

_____

_____

19. After apologizing, I was able to leave with a clear conscious.

_____

_____

20. The babysitter warned the children, "Do not plan on leaving hear until you finish you're hole dinner."

_____

_____

Spelling Guides

Accurate spelling is important. You don't want your readers to stop at misspelled words and miss the strength of your ideas. The following suggestions can help you improve your spelling.

Learn Three Spelling Rules

Because English has adopted words from other languages, many words have irregular spellings that do not fit under a general rule. Still, there are three rules that will help you spell words correctly.

1. *-i* before *-e* rule

    I before *e*

    Except after *c,*

    Or when sounded like *a*

    As in *neighbor* or *weigh*.

    Repeating this rhyme will help you spell words like the following:

    relieve, believe, niece (*-i* before *-e*)

    receive, ceiling, deceive (except after *-c*)

    Some exceptions to this rule are *either, neither, foreign,* and *their*.

2. Rules for forming plurals

    Plural means "more than one." Although most nouns form the plural by adding *-s* (*one telephone, two telephones*), there are exceptions to that general rule.

    First exception: When the word you want to make plural ends in a consonant and *-y,* change the *-y* to *-i* and add *-es.*

Singular	Plural
party	parties
body	bodies
story	stories
theory	theories

    Second exception: When the word you want to make plural ends in *-s, -sh, -ch,* or *-x,* add *-es.*

Singular	Plural
dress	dresses
dish	dishes
church	churches
box	boxes

Third exception: When the word you want to make plural ends in -*f*, change the -*f* to -*v* and add -*es*.

Singular	Plural
scarf	scarves
thief	thieves
life	lives
knife	knives

Fourth exception: A few words do not follow any plural pattern. All you can do is memorize the forms.

Singular	Plural
child	children
man	men
woman	women
ox	oxen
mouse	mice
goose	geese
foot	feet
alumnus	alumni
deer	deer
moose	moose

3. **Rules for words ending in** -*y*

These rules involve recognizing vowels (*a,e,i,o,u*) and consonants (all the other letters).

When adding an ending to a word ending in -*y*, change -*y* to -*i* if a consonant comes before the -*y*.

try + ed =tried

happy + er =happier

apology + ize = apologize

lucky + ly =luckily

silly + est =silliest

lazy + ness =laziness

Do not change the -*y* if a vowel comes before the -*y*.

pay + ment =payment

buy + er =buyer

Keep a Personal Spelling List

Set aside a notebook where you can keep track of the words you misspell in your papers. Also list words you hear or read that you would like to use in future papers. Review these words when you have free time and when you are editing your papers.

Sound the Word Out

Concentrate on the words you misspell. Say each word aloud slowly as it is spelled, breaking it into parts. Seeing the parts will help you remember the problem areas, especially in words such as *Wed nes day, Feb ru ary,* and *lib rary.*

Sounding the word out is especially helpful if you are not putting *-ed* or *-s* endings on words. Because we often do not say these endings, we fail to write them. If you are making errors with word endings, correct the papers that have been returned to you and then read each paper aloud, emphasizing the ends of these words as you read.

Use the Word Processor's Spell Check Function

A word processor includes a spell check function that will locate many of your misspelled words. However, spell check will not find all errors. It ignores anything it recognizes as a word, whether or not that word is used correctly.

Consult a Dictionary or an Electronic Spell Checker

As you write a first draft, underline any words you think may be misspelled. Later, when writing the final draft, look up the underlined words in a dictionary or type them into an electronic spell checker that will give you a list of suggested spellings.

Prefixes and Roots

Many words in English come from other languages, especially Latin and Greek. Knowing Latin and Greek prefixes (beginnings of words) and roots (basic parts of the words) will improve your vocabulary. You will be able to figure out the meanings of many unfamiliar words in English.

Prefixes

A prefix is an addition to the beginning of a word; it often gives clues to a word's meaning. For example, *sub* is a Latin word that means *under.* Therefore, when a word begins with *sub*, you know that the word has an "under" meaning, as in *subway* and *submarine.*

PREFIX	MEANING	EXAMPLE
Dealing with *no*		
a-	not, without	amoral
in-	not	insensitive
non-	not	nonreturnable
mis-	wrongly	mistake
mal-	bad	malnutrition
anti-	against	antiabortion
ir-	not	irresponsible
un-	not	unnecessary
il-	not	illegal
contra-	against	contradiction
counter-	against	counterfeit
dis-	not	dishonest
Dealing with *time*		
pre-	before	prerequisite
post-	after	postoperative
retro-	backward	retroactive
Dealing with *numbers*		
uni-	one	uniform
bi-	two	bicycle
tri-	three	triangle
mono-	one	monologue
auto-	self	autonomous
multi-	many	multicultural
poly-	many	polygamy
cent-	one hundred	centennial
omni-	all	omnipotent
Dealing with *placement, amount*		
circum-	around	circumference
co-, com-	with, together	community
de-	away from	detract
ex-	out	exit
hyper-	too much, over	hyperventilate
hypo-	under	hypodermic
inter-	between	interstate
intra-	within	intravenous
macro-	big	macroeconomics
micro-	small	microscope
per-	through	perceive
re-	again	return
sub-	under	subconscious
super-	above	superior
trans-	across	transport
syn-	together	syndicate
semi-	half	semicircle
ultra-	beyond	ultrasound

Roots

A root is the most basic part of a word. For example, *aud* is a Latin root that carries the meaning of "hear." Therefore, when a word contains *aud*, that word usually means something about hearing—as in *audible, audio, auditorium*. If you know what a root means, you quickly have an idea of what a word with that root means.

ROOT	MEANING	EXAMPLE
anthro	human	anthropologist
ambul	walk, move	ambulatory
annus	year	annual
arthri	joint, skeletal	arthritis
aqua	water	aqueduct
aud	hear	auditory
biblio	book	bibliography
bene	good	beneficial
cardi	heart	cardiologist
chron	time	chronological
cred	believe	credibility
dict	say	dictate
equi	equal	equitable
finis	end	finish
graph	writing, drawing	photograph
hydro	water	hydrant
man	hand	manual
nom	name	nominate
osteo	bone	osteopathic
path, pathos	feeling, suffering	pathetic
ped	foot	pedal
phobia	fear	claustrophobia
psyche	mental	psychological
phon, phono	sound	phone
port	carry	portable
scrib, script	write	scribble
spec	see	spectacle
therm	heat	thermometer
tele	distant	television
vis	see	visual

Review: Focusing on Easily Confused Words, Spelling, and Vocabulary

- Review the list of easily confused words as often as necessary.

- Become familiar with prefixes and roots. These word parts will help you figure out the meaning of many unfamiliar words.

- Use these methods to improve your spelling:

  1. Review all corrected papers for spelling errors and keep a list of these words. Study the list whenever you have a free moment. Review it when you are writing a final draft.

  2. Say the correctly spelled word aloud slowly, emphasizing the sound of the troublesome section of the word.

  3. Look up easily confused words in the alphabetized section of this chapter or in a dictionary.

  4. Review the basic spelling rules.

  5. Use a dictionary, the spell checker in a word processor, or an electronic spell checker.

 REVIEW PRACTICE Individually or in groups, edit the following student paragraph for easily confused words errors.

Some friends are loyal; others are impostors. The way to tell

them apart is to see how they act in and emergency. Real friends

our there when their needed. Impostors find excuses for not helping

out. For example, when I was on my way to school, my car broke

down on Halsted Street. I found a pay phone and called a friend

collect, the same friend I had helped out numerous times. He didn't

even except the charges. Slamming down the phone in anger, I

tried another friend, who accepted the charges and picked me up

even though he had to drop the other things he was suppose to

do. When I got home, I called the first so-called friend too find

out why he could not help me. He said, "I had know time. I was

on my way out the door." What bothered me the most is that we

where both going to the same place. He could of easily picked me up. I learned that a friendship is only as good as the people involved. Impostors are for the moment; real friends are there when their needed.

—Student Writer

 EXTRA CHALLENGE Individually or in groups, refer to the previous charts to check the meaning of the following roots and prefixes. Then try to figure out the meaning of the words listed here.

1. Look up the meaning of *trans*. What do you think *transfer, translate, transmission,* and *transparent* mean?

2. Look up the meaning of *dict*. What do you think *dictionary, diction, dictate, dictation, dictaphone,* and *dictator* mean?

3. Look up the meaning of *scrib*. What do you think *inscribe, inscription, scribble, script,* and *scripture* mean?

4. Look up the meaning of *hydro*. What do you think *hydrant, hydroelectric, dehydrated,* and *hydraulic* mean?

5. Look up the meaning of *aud*. What do you think *audition, audience, audiovisual,* and *audit* mean?

Using Additional Punctuation

◆ Capital Letters and Periods
◆ Quotation Marks
◆ Colons
◆ Commas
◆ Numbers

Capital Letters and Periods

Capital letters and periods are signs for more than the beginning and ending of sentences. The following list summarizes the additional information these two signs give.

Abbreviations

Use capital letters and periods to indicate an abbreviation, which is a short version of a word or words. Listed below are examples of common abbreviations.

Titles

Notice that abbreviated titles include periods.

Mr.   Mrs.   Ms.   Jr.   Sr.   Dr.   Rev.   Ph.D.

Organizations

Notice that abbreviations for most organizations do not include periods.

USA or U.S.A.

FBI   CIA   NATO   NFL
CBS   NBC   UPS   CNN

Time

A.M. or a.m.   P.M. or p.m.

Latin Words

e.g.   Latin *exempli gratia,* "for example"

etc.   Latin *et cetera,* "and so forth"

i.e.   Latin *id est,* "that is"

P.S.   Latin *postscriptum,* "postscript"

cf.   Latin *confer,* "compare"

et al.   Latin *et alii,* "and others"

Internet Addresses

Periods are essential if you are writing e-mail messages or looking for information on the Internet (the Web). Both individuals and sites of information have addresses that include periods. If you fail to type a period, which in Internet language is called a *dot,* the computer responds that the address is unknown.

E-mail address for an individual: rrighter@ix.netcom.com

Web site address for an information site: www.travelweb.com

Direct Quotations

Capitalize the first letter of a sentence in a quotation.

He lives by the saying "What goes around, comes around."

The Pronoun I

Always capitalize the pronoun *I.*

Rico and I went to the movies last night.

Major Words in Titles

Capitalize the first, last, and all major words in titles of books and short stories, articles in magazines, and songs.

Irving Stone wrote *The Passions of the Mind.*
Eudora Welty wrote "A Worn Path."
The crowd sang "America the Beautiful."

Proper Nouns

The name of a specific person, place, or thing is capitalized. The general name is not capitalized.

I went to *high school* at *Linton High School.*

- *Linton High School* is capitalized because that is the specific name of the school, the name that would be inscribed above the front door. The first use of *high school* is not capitalized because it refers to high schools in general.

My friend needed her *mother* to baby-sit and pleaded, "Please, *Mother,* can you be here at noon?"

- The second use of *mother* is capitalized because it is used as a specific name, as you would use a name such as *Betty.* Substituting a name such as *Betty* will help you determine whether capital letters are needed. For example, in the first part of the sentence, we would not say, "My friend needed her *Betty* to baby-sit," but we would say, "Please, *Betty,* can you be here at noon?"

Our first question for the *doctor* was, "*Dr. Jameson,* when will the test results be back?"

- *Dr. Jameson* is capitalized because it is used as a specific name, as you would use a name such as *George.* Substitute *George* to test whether capital letters are needed. We would not say, "Our first question for the *George* was," but we would say, "*George,* when will the test results be back?"

Use the following chart as a reference tool when editing your writing.

CHART OF SPECIFIC AND GENERAL NOUNS

Specific Name	General Name
Dexter	my friend
God	a god
Dad, Father	my dad, his father
Mom, Mother	her mom, his mother
Aunt Louisa, Uncle George	my aunt, our uncle

Specific Name	General Name
Dr. Heath	her doctor
Professor Smith	the professor
President Lincoln	the president
Wal-Mart, Gap, Sears	the store
Pastor Rice	the pastor
Senator Simon	a senator
Monday, Wednesday	day
January, February	winter
April, May	spring
July, August	summer
October, November	fall
Christmas, Fourth of July	holiday
Grape Nuts	cereal
Waxman's Drugstore	drugstore
Buddhist, Jewish, Muslim, Protestant, Roman Catholic	religion
State Farm Insurance	insurance company
Calculus I, Literature 102	math course, literature class
Chicago, Los Angeles	city
State Street, Linder Avenue	street, avenue
English, Spanish, French	language
Maine, North Carolina, New Mexico	state
South, North, West, East, Midwest (areas of U.S.)	south, north, west, east (road directions)
Italy, Canada, Ethiopia, Ecuador	country
African American, Asian, Caucasian, Hispanic	people
Yellowstone National Park	park
Democrats, Republicans	political party
Miami University, Lakeland College	university, college
South Central High School	high school
Middle Ages	historical time
60 Minutes	television program
Newsweek	magazine
Close to the Bone	book
Federal Bureau of Investigation	organization

PRACTICE 1   Edit the following paragraph, placing capital letters where needed.

I was born in Duluth, minnesota, and returned there last summer to see what has changed and what has stayed the same. My old high school is there, but some of the teachers are now gone. My english teacher, Mr. Fairbanks, has retired, and my history teacher, Mrs. Richardson, has moved. Yet the halls of the building smell the same, and the neighborhood is just as I remember it. The insurance company is still on the corner of Main street and elm avenue. My favorite neighborhood store, johnson's deli, is still crowded with kids buying candy bars after school. I have decided that nothing in my hometown has changed as much as I have.

—Student Writer

Quotation Marks

Quotation marks let readers know the *exact* words someone said or wrote. The guidelines for punctuating spoken words and written words are similar. We will first look at how to punctuate spoken words.

Spoken Words

When you are writing about what another person said, you can write either the exact words or a summary. If you are writing the person's exact words, use quotation marks. If you are writing a summary or general idea of what the person said, do not use quotation marks.

EXAMPLE 1

Exact words: Trying to teach her cousins to be responsible, Joanna said, "Pay the bills or pay the consequences."

• Joanna's exact words are marked with quotation marks. Quotation marks tell readers that *Pay the bills or pay the consequences* is, word for word, what Joanna said.

Summary: Joanna urged her cousins to be responsible and pay their bills.

• No quotation marks appear in this sentence because Joanna's exact words are not being quoted. This is a summary of Joanna's exact words.

EXAMPLE 2

Exact words: Keith said, "My boss is paying me overtime."

Summary: Keith said that his boss is paying him overtime.

- Notice that the first sentence has quotation marks. Quotation marks signal readers that these are the person's *exact* words. If you had a tape recorder, the words in quotation marks would be the words on the tape.

- Notice the second sentence. These are not the exact words that Keith said because he would not refer to himself as *his* or *him*. The second sentence reports what Keith said; it gives the general idea of what he said. Therefore, there are no quotation marks. Look for the word *that* because it often announces a report of what someone said, not the exact words.

Guidelines for quoting spoken words:

1. Place the first quotation mark before the first word spoken; place the final quotation mark after the last word spoken. If someone says more than one sentence, do not mark each individual sentence. Mark the beginning and the end of the person's words.

   The financial adviser warned the audience, "Choosing the right credit card is like walking through a minefield. There are some good offers, but you need to read the fine print to sort through who charges exorbitant interest and who does not."

2. Separate the person talking from that person's words with a comma.

   Richard said, "Let's go out for dinner tonight." [The person speaking is written first.]
   "Let's go out for dinner tonight," Richard said. [The person speaking is written last.]

3. If someone's exact words are a question or an exclamation, let readers know by placing a question mark or exclamation point inside the quotation marks.

   Chris exclaimed, "I got the job?"
   Chris exclaimed, "I got the job!"

4. If what you are quoting is a sentence, begin the quoted sentence with a capital letter. It may seem strange to place a sentence inside a sentence, but you need to show readers that what is being quoted is a sentence.

   Diane explained, "My neighbors have been kind to us."

5. When you finish writing a quotation, place the period or the comma inside the quotation marks. [Notice the previous example.]

PRACTICE 2 Individually or in groups, translate the following reports to exact words by imagining what the person might have said. The first one has been done for you.

EXAMPLE: My mother announced that she would arrive on the 9:00 train.

My mother announced, "I will arrive on the 9:00 train."

1. Sonny said that he understands geometry but not algebra.

   _____

2. Samantha announced that she will rent a car in Boston.

   _____

3. Uncle Charles complained that his tooth hurts.

   _____

4. The fans encouraged the team to win.

   _____

5. Our neighbor told us if we want the best bargains, we should be in line at the sale an hour before it opens.

   _____

   _____

Written Words

Whenever you use someone else's written words in your writing, you need to copy the exact words, including the punctuation, and enclose the material in quotation marks.

Guidelines for quoting written words:

1. Put the first quotation mark at the beginning of what you are copying from the text. Put the final quotation mark at the end of what you are copying.

   John Steinbeck begins *The Grapes of Wrath* by describing the land: "To the red country and part of the gray country of Oklahoma, the last rains came gently, and they did not cut the scarred earth."

2. Place the period at the end of the quotation inside the quotation marks. (Notice the example in item 1.)

3. Separate the quoted sentence from your own words with a comma or a colon. A colon is more formal. (Notice the example in item 1.)

4. If you are typing, and the words you are quoting are four or more type-written lines, indent the whole section five spaces or use the tab key. Indenting the entire block of text is the sign of a long quotation; do not use quotation marks.

Frederick Buechner, in *Wishful Thinking,* describes anger:

> Of the seven deadly sins, anger is possibly the most fun. To lick your wounds, to smack your lips over grievances long past, to roll over your tongue the prospect of bitter confrontations still to come, to savor to the last toothsome morsel both the pain you are given and the pain you are giving back—in many ways it is a feast fit for a king. The chief drawback is that what you are wolfing down is yourself. The skeleton at the feast is you. (2)

The number 2 in parentheses means that the quotation can be found on page 2 of the book *Wishful Thinking.*

PRACTICE 3   Read the following paragraph and mark the exact words that Amelia Earhart wrote. Use a comma or a colon to introduce the quotation; use quotation marks to show where the quoted material begins and ends.

Just before her plane disappeared during her attempt to fly around the

world, Amelia Earhart wrote to her husband Please know that I am quite

aware of the hazards. I want to do it because I want to do it. Women must

try to do things as men have tried. When they fail, their failure must be

but a challenge to others.

Titles of Short Pieces of Writing

Quotation marks are also used around titles of short works.

Article in a newspaper or a magazine: "Simple Pleasures"
Poem: "Dream Deferred"
Short story: "Salvation"
Song: "Paradise Is Here"
Chapter of a book: "Market Influences"

Quotation marks are not used with the titles of longer literary works. Underline the title or, if you are writing with a word processor, put the title in italics.

Book: <u>The Man Made of Words</u> or *The Man Made of Words*
Book-length poem: <u>Paradise Lost</u> or *Paradise Lost*
Play: <u>King Lear</u> or *King Lear*
Movie: <u>Schindler's List</u> or *Schindler's List*
Magazine: <u>Time</u> or *Time*
Newspaper: <u>The New York Times</u> or *The New York Times*
TV program: <u>CNN News</u> or *CNN News*

Colons

Use a colon to introduce a quotation, a list, or an explanation or definition.

A quotation

> We remembered the words of John F. Kennedy: "Ask not what your country can do for you; ask what you can do for your country."

A list

> Vitamin A is found in a variety of fruits and vegetables: apricots, broccoli, cantaloupe, carrots, lettuce, parsley, spinach, and turnips.

An explanation or **a definition**

> There are two ways to do this job: the easy way and the right way.
>
> Two lizards found in the southwestern United States and western Mexico are poisonous: the Gila monster and the beaded lizard.

Commas

As explained in Chapter 10, use a comma to do the following things:

- Separate items in a series
- Connect two sentences with a coordinating conjunction (*and, but, or, so, yet, for, nor*)
- Set off introductory words
- Set off words interrupting the flow of thought in the middle of a sentence or at the end of a sentence

In addition, use a comma to do the following:

Address someone by name

> Connie, please call if you need our help.

Open and close a letter

> Dear Mr. Linn,
> Sincerely yours,

Set off parts of a date

> March 17, 1997, was our first anniversary.

Set off parts of an address

> Our neighbors are moving to 762 Smithfield Avenue, Albany, New York.

Set off numbers

> Our town's population grew from 9,000 to 17,000 in three years.

Numbers

The following guidelines will assist you in writing numbers correctly.

If the number consists of just one or two words, write it in words.

> Although we had room for only twenty people, we sent out twenty-six invitations.

If the number consists of three or more words, use numerals.

> We have 154 copies of old *National Geographic* magazines in the family room.

Be consistent within a sentence. If some of the numbers are in words and some of them are numerals, use numerals for all of them.

> A year consists of 12 months, 52 weeks, or 365 days.

If the number begins a sentence, write it in words.

> One hundred fifty people attended the weekend retreat.

Use numerals for street addresses, money, dates, scores, and time.

> Address: 18422 West 55th Street
> Money: $714.37
> Date: December 5, 1981
> Score: 15–7
> Time: 1:30 P.M.

Review: Using Additional Punctuation

- Use periods with abbreviations.
- Capitalize:
  - a. the first letter in names of specific people, places, and things
  - b. the pronoun *I*
  - c. the first letter of a sentence in a quotation
  - d. the first letter of the important words in a title
- Place quotation marks around someone's exact spoken or written words.
- Use quotation marks around titles of short pieces of writing.
- Underline or italicize longer pieces of writing.
- Use colons to introduce a quotation, a list, or an explanation or definition.
- Use commas to address a person by name, to open and close a letter, and to set off parts of dates, addresses, and numbers.

REVIEW PRACTICE In the following paragraph, some of the words are reports and do not need quotation marks. Other words are the exact words. Individually or in groups, punctuate the exact words as quotations by adding commas, capital letters, and quotation marks.

I bought an old Saab and thought I was getting a bargain. Within two months, the car broke down, and I realized that I had a money-hungry machine. I first took my car to Chuck's Auto where the mechanic told me you need a new motor. It's going to cost you $600. Today is Wednesday. By Saturday, we'll have your car ready. Not wanting to spend $600, I went to Ray's Auto Repair and waited three hours for them to tell me that they don't work on foreign cars. Frustrated, I stormed out and went to the mechanic my neighbor had suggested, Barry at Bodine's Repair. Barry checked out my motor and decided that the engine was fine. He said you have an electrical problem, but we don't fix electrical problems. Take it to a dealer. I am not taking it to a dealer because dealers are too expensive. Consequently, my car still does not work. I am running out of patience, and soon I'll be running out of money.

—Student Writer

 EXTRA CHALLENGE The following paragraph is based on "Memory," an article written by Geoffrey Cowley and Anne Underwood published in *Newsweek,* June 15, 1998. Individually or in groups, edit the paragraph for errors in using capital letters.

The power of memory is explored in "how memory works," an article by geoffrey cowley and anne underwood in *newsweek.* The authors summarize recent research about how we learn new information, include tips on how to increase our ability to remember, and conclude with an appreciation for the intricate workings of the mind. They refer to the insights of daniel schacter, a harvard psychologist, who observes in his book, *searching for memory*, that the simple act of meeting a friend for lunch requires a vast store of memory. We need to remember the day, the week, and the time. In addition, we must remember what the person looks like, the name of the restaurant and the street, how to get there, and how to put words together so we can talk once we meet. The wonder of memory is that we are able to retain as much as we do.

Part 5

Additional Resources for Writing

Chapter 25

Additional Ideas for Writing

◆ Ideas for Journal Writing
◆ Ideas for Paragraphs and Short Papers
◆ Ideas for Essays

Ideas for Journal Writing

Ideas from Life's Little Instruction Book

H. Jackson Brown, in *Life's Little Instruction Book,* gives 511 suggestions for living a happy and rewarding life. Some of his suggestions are listed below. Use them as a basis for journal writing, writing down the ideas they bring to your mind.

1. Be forgiving of yourself and others.

2. Take charge of your attitude. Don't let someone else choose it for you.

3. Never give up on anybody. Miracles happen every day.

4. Don't waste time learning the "tricks of the trade." Instead, learn the trade.

5. Stop blaming others. Take responsibility for every area of your life.

6. Admit your mistakes.

7. Remember that all news is biased.

8. Instead of using the word *problem,* try substituting the word *opportunity*.

9. Be bold and courageous. When you look back on your life, you'll regret the things you didn't do more than the ones you did.

10. Learn to listen. Opportunity sometimes knocks very softly.

11. Never deprive someone of hope; it may be all they have.

12. Give yourself an hour to cool off before responding to someone who has provoked you. If it involves something really important, give yourself overnight.

13. Strive for excellence, not perfection.

14. Pray not for things, but for wisdom and courage.

15. Be toughminded but tenderhearted.

16. Seek out the good in people.

17. Never give up on what you really want to do.

18. Loosen up. Relax. Except for rare life-and-death matters, nothing is as important as it first seems.

19. Don't waste time grieving over past mistakes. Learn from them and move on.

20. Spend less time worrying *who's* right, and more time deciding *what's* right.

21. Don't major in minor things.

22. Never cut what can be untied.

23. Never underestimate your power to change yourself.

24. Never overestimate your power to change others.

25. Instead of using the words *if only,* try substituting the words *next time.*

Additional Ideas for Journal Writing

1. Respond to a newspaper or magazine article. You could write about what you learned or what you agree or disagree with.

2. Choose a current controversy and select any of the following questions to spark your writing: What is your position? Who disagrees with you and why? Why is this issue important? What are the consequences of these varying positions?

3. Choose any of the following approaches:

   a. Close your eyes and describe everything you hear.

   b. Write down the lyrics of a favorite song and explain why you like them.

   c. Select a familiar object (toothbrush, sidewalk, tree, water, shoes . . .) and describe it from a new perspective.

   d. Describe a time when you wish you had said something but didn't— or a time when you said something that you later regretted.

   e. Select a character or situation in a movie or television program. Explain how the character or situation is realistic or unrealistic.

4. Choose any of the following first lines of poetry, use it as your first sentence, and write whatever ideas come to mind.

a. *When I was one-and-twenty*

   I heard a wise man say . . .

   —A. E. Housman, "When I Was One-and-Twenty"

b. *What happens to a dream deferred?*

   —Langston Hughes, "Dream Deferred"

c. *"Is there anybody there?" said the Traveller . . .*

   —Walter de la Mare, "The Listeners"

d. *I have done it again.*

   —Sylvia Plath, "Lady Lazarus"

e. *Yield.*

   No Parking.

   Unlawful to Pass.

   Wait for Green Light.

   —Ronald Gross, "Yield"

f. *A long time ago when I was a child . . .*

   —Howard Nemerov, "The Snow Globe"

g. *Something there is that doesn't love a wall . . .*

   —Robert Frost, "Mending Wall"

h. *Home's the place we head for in our sleep.*

   —Louise Erdrich, "Indian Boarding School: The Runaways"

Ideas for Paragraphs and Short Papers

Writing Idea 1

My memories of life in Paterson during those first few years are all in shades of gray. Maybe I was too young to absorb vivid colors and details, or to discriminate between the slate blue of the winter sky and the darker hues of the snow-bearing clouds, but that single color washes over the whole period. The building we lived in was gray, as were the streets, filled with slush the first few months of my life there. The coat my father had bought for me was similar in color and too big; it sat heavily on my thin frame.

—Judith Ortiz Cofer, "Silent Dancing"

Choose a color to describe an experience, a day, a week, a time in your life. Begin as Cofer begins: *My memories of . . . are all in shades of. . . .* Fill in the blanks and then include the details that explain or describe the color.

Writing Idea 2

What can your college do to improve students' college experience? Consider such things as the registration process, bookstore, library, computer labs, cafeteria, student support services, parking lots, and general atmosphere. In your main idea, state the needed improvement. Prove the need for the improvement with specific examples, and end with your suggestion(s) for bringing about the improvement.

Writing Idea 3

When do you feel happy, tired, bored, optimistic, or anxious? Choose a physical or psychological condition; describe a situation when you feel that way.

Writing Idea 4

Choose one of H. Jackson Brown's suggestions in *Life's Little Instruction Book,* listed earlier in the chapter under "Ideas for Journal Writing." Use the suggestion as your main idea and support it with an example from your experience.

Writing Idea 5

Why do a large percentage of students drop out of high school? Suggest one probable reason in the main idea. Then support that statement with specific details that will convince readers that your opinion is valid.

Writing Idea 6

Choose someone you like or respect and describe his or her most irritating or most admirable habit. In your main idea, name the habit. For instance, you might write, *My friend's most annoying habit is saying yes but meaning maybe.* Then give specific examples that will make the person's habit seem convincing to readers.

Writing Idea 7

Should colleges have required courses? Begin with a main idea stating that you do or do not think so. Support your main idea by explaining your reasons.

Writing Idea 8

Write about a person or an experience that has changed your life. Have your main idea name the person or experience; then explain the effect(s) that person or experience had on your life.

Writing Idea 9

Explain why a particular sports star, music star, or music group is popular. Include specific details, so readers who are not familiar with the star or group understand the reasons for your view.

Writing Idea 10

What wisdom would you like to share with others? What have you learned about yourself, others, or life? Finish the sentence *I believe that. . . .* That sentence will then be your main idea. Support it with one or more specific examples convincing readers that your belief is valid.

Ideas for Essays

Idea 1

Write about anything you believe needs to be changed. You can choose something personal, local, national, or international. For example, you could choose yourself, the job market, people's attitudes, the workplace, politics, television, welfare, credit cards, the educational system, the drug situation, laws, gun ownership, parenting, music, or America's role in the United Nations.

Option for organizing ideas: You will be writing about a problem. Name that problem in your thesis statement. Then, in the first section of your essay, describe the situation so that readers will recognize the problem. In the second section, tell why the problem exists or describe the effect that the problem has on others.

Idea 2

Cultural differences occur in a variety of ways and places. Describe a time when you were aware that people did things differently or thought differently—at a friend's house, with a fellow student, in an unfamiliar setting, or on a trip.

Option for organizing ideas: In the first section of your essay, describe the experience so readers understand your surprise or confusion. In the second section of your essay, explain what this experience taught you about yourself and others.

Idea 3

Time and maturity often change how we look at life and how we interpret past experiences. Think of something that happened to you in the past that you now see differently. Perhaps something you once saw as a dead end now looks more like an open door. Perhaps a person you once considered an enemy is now a friend. Write about any past experience that you now interpret differently.

Option for organizing ideas: In your thesis statement, name the experience or person and state that your perspective has changed. In the first section of your essay, describe the experience. In the second section, explain how you first interpreted it. In the third section, describe how you see that experience or person now.

Idea 4

Stereotyping exists only in the mind; it is a mental judgment. Stereotyping is putting people into boxes. Stephen L. Carter, in *Reflections of an Affirmative Action Baby*, writes:

> So I live in a box, not of my own making, and on the box is a label, not of my own choosing. Most of those who have not met me, and many of those who have, see the box and read the label and imagine that they have seen me.

Where have you seen stereotyping in your life? Consider not only how you may have been stereotyped but also how you have stereotyped others. Write about one kind of stereotyping: by age, sex, race, nationality, religion, or another factor. Describe the situation or the experience; then write about its effects.

Option for organizing ideas: In your introductory paragraph, quote Carter, restate Carter's meaning in your own words, and then write a thesis that states the kind of stereotyping you have seen or experienced. In the first section of your essay, describe the box you have been put into, the box you have seen other people put into, or the box you use to put other people into. In the second section of your essay, describe the effects of putting people into boxes, the effects of stereotyping.

Idea 5

In *Born for Love*, Leo Buscaglia writes about the significance of the little things we do:

> The majority of us lead quiet, unheralded lives as we pass through this world. There will most likely be no ticker-tape parades for us, no monuments created in our honor. But that does not lessen our possible impact upon the world, for there are scores of people waiting for someone just like us to come along: people who will appreciate our compassion, our encouragement, who will need our unique talents. Someone who will live a happier life merely because we took the time to share what we had to give.
>
> Too often we underestimate the power of a touch, a smile, a kind word, a listening ear, an honest compliment, or the smallest act of caring, all of which have the potential to turn a life around. (372)

Reread Buscaglia's paragraphs and think of something you did that made a difference, even if that difference was in how you felt about yourself. Or— rather than writing about something you did—you could write about a kind act or supportive words that you received.

Option for organizing ideas: In the first section of your essay, describe the situation so readers understand the background. In the second section, write about the effect of your actions on others and/or the effect on you.

Idea 6

Who we *are* is more important than what or how much we *own*. Personality traits determine our character, and our character runs through all that we do. Write about a personality trait that you admire in yourself or in others. You could choose honesty, joy, faithfulness, determination, willingness to listen, willingness to forgive, kindness, sensitivity, courage, dependability, creativity, dignity, energy, wisdom, faith, loyalty, optimism, persistence, or patience. These are big-sounding words, but these personality characteristics are seen every day in the "little things" we do and say.

Option for organizing ideas: You could approach the personality trait by looking at life stages, choosing a thesis such as "Courage is a quality I have been building through three stages of my life." Refer to the Student's Essay Map in Chapter 5 to see that writer's main points.

Idea 7

Below is a list of proverbs. Choose one that suggests a truth or insight that you can illustrate from your own experience. Use the proverb as your thesis, rewrite the proverb in your own words, and support it with examples from your experience.

A lie has speed, but truth has endurance.

—Edgar Mohn

Any fact facing us is not as important as our attitude toward it,
for that determines our success or failure.

—Norman Vincent Peale

As long as you keep a person down, some part of you has to be
down there to hold him down, so it means you cannot soar as you
otherwise might.

—Marian Anderson

Darkness cannot drive out darkness; only light can do that. Hate
cannot drive out hate; only love can do that.

—Martin Luther King, Jr.

Develop success from failures. Discouragement and failure are
two of the surest stepping stones to success.

—Dale Carnegie

Do not use a hatchet to remove a fly from your friend's forehead.

—Chinese proverb

Don't find fault. Find a remedy.

—Henry Ford

Don't go through life; grow through life.

—Eric Butterworth

Don't smother each other. No one can live in the shade.

—Leo Buscaglia

Drop by drop the ocean is filled.

—Swahili proverb

Everybody is looking for role models for their kids on television,
but the positive role models should be right there in the home.

—Kevin Teryl

Experience is not what happens to you. It is what you do with what
happens to you.

—Aldous Huxley

Hold fast to dreams, for if dreams die, life is a broken-winged bird
that cannot fly.

—Langston Hughes

I am only one, but still I am one. I cannot do everything, but still I
can do something. I will not refuse to do the something I can do.

—Helen Keller

If you want to accomplish the goals of your life, you have to begin with the spirit.

—Oprah Winfrey

I will prepare and someday my chance will come.

—Abraham Lincoln

In the middle of difficulty lies opportunity.

—Albert Einstein

It is never too late to be what you might have been.

—George Eliot

It's not whether you get knocked down; it's whether you get up.

—Vince Lombardi

My life, my real life, was in danger—and not from anything other people might do but from the hatred I carried in my own heart.

—James Baldwin

Never measure the height of a mountain until you have reached the top. Then you will see how low it was.

—Dag Hammarskjöld

No matter how long the night, the day is sure to come.

—Congolese proverb

No one can make you feel inferior without your consent.

—Eleanor Roosevelt

Not to know is bad; not to wish to know is worse.

—Nigerian proverb

Nothing good, nothing worthy, nothing creative can be born of hatred. Hatred begets hatred.

—Elie Wiesel

Obstacles are those frightful things you see when you take your eyes off the goal.

—Hannah More

Some people want to take curtain calls without being involved in the performance.

—Alton Maddox

The weak can never forgive. Forgiveness is the attribute of the strong.

—Mahatma Gandhi

There are no gains without pains.

—Benjamin Franklin

To be the father of a nation is a great honor, but to be the father of a family is a greater joy.

—Nelson Mandela

Read and Respond

Idea 8

Read "Mother to Son," a poem by Langston Hughes, an African-American poet who lived from 1902 to 1967. Then read the brief selection called "Abraham Lincoln Didn't Quit" on page 318.

Mother to Son

Well, son. I'll tell you:

Life for me ain't been no crystal stair.

It's had tacks in it,

And splinters,

And boards torn up,

And places with no carpet on the floor—

Bare.

But all the time

I'se been a-climbin' on,

And reachin' landin's,

And turnin' corners,

And sometimes goin' in the dark

Where there ain't been no light.

So boy, don't you turn back.

Don't you set down on the steps

'Cause you finds it's kinder hard.

Don't you fall now—

For I'se still goin', honey,

I'se still climbin',

And life for me ain't been no crystal stair.

Abraham Lincoln Didn't Quit

Adapted from *Chicken Soup for the Soul*
by Jack Canfield and Mark Victor Hansen

Born into poverty, Lincoln was faced with defeat throughout his life. He lost eight elections, twice failed in business, and suffered a nervous breakdown. He could have quit many times — but he didn't, and because he did not quit, he became one of the greatest presidents in the history of our country.

Lincoln was a champion, and he never gave up. Here is a sketch of Lincoln's road to the White House:

1816	His family was forced out of their home. He had to work to support them.
1818	His mother died.
1831	Failed in business.
1832	Ran for state legislature—*lost*.
1832	Also lost his job—wanted to go to law school but couldn't get in.
1833	Borrowed money from a friend to begin a business and by the end of the year was bankrupt. He spent the next seventeen years of his life paying off this debt.
1834	Ran for state legislature again—*won*.
1835	Was engaged to be married; his fiancée died, and his heart was broken.
1836	Had a serious nervous breakdown and was in bed for six months.
1838	Sought to become speaker of the state legislature—*defeated*.
1840	Sought to become an elector—*defeated*.
1843	Ran for Congress—*lost*.
1846	Ran for Congress again—*this time he won*—and went to Washington and did a good job.
1848	Ran for re-election to Congress—*lost*.
1849	Sought the job of land officer in his home state—*rejected*.
1854	Ran for Senate of the United States—*lost*.
1856	Sought the vice-presidential nomination at his party's national convention—got less than 100 votes.
1858	Ran for U.S. Senate again—*again he lost*.
1860	*Elected president of the United States.*

Writing Assignment

Both "Mother to Son" and "Abraham Lincoln Didn't Quit" deal with people's responses to life's challenges and obstacles. We all face challenges. Family members, friends, and co-workers cause difficulties; our personal attitudes and limitations cause difficulties; finances and limited time cause difficulties. Think of a particular challenge you have faced or are facing.

Option for organizing ideas: In your thesis statement, name the challenge. In the first section of your paper, describe the challenge so readers can see and hear what happened. In the second section, you might write about what caused this situation, the effect the situation had on you or others, how you overcame the challenge or what you need to overcome it, or what you have learned.

Idea 9

David Gelman, in "The Violence in Our Heads," writes:

> Teenagers don't invent violence; they learn it. To a considerable extent, they act out the attitudes and ethics of the adults closest to them. Thus, any study of the causes of teen crime might look first at the violence grown-ups have been carrying in their heads. In the last thirty years, Americans have developed a culture of violence surpassing in its pervasiveness anything we experienced before. It shows up in our speech, in our play, more than ever in the entertainments we fashion and fancy, and in business style. "There's an extraordinary degree of violence in the language, and it's the window to the actual feelings and mores of the culture," says Dr. Robert Phillips, director of forensic services for the Connecticut Department of Public Health.

Gelman maintains that teens do not invent violence; they learn it from our culture. Write about where violence can be seen in our culture. In addition to speech, sports, entertainment, and business, consider everyday life (traffic, families, communities). Is violence portrayed or accepted as the way to solve problems?

Option for organizing ideas: In your thesis statement, tell where violence is evident in our culture. In the first section of your essay, give specific examples of that violence. In the second section of your essay, you could discuss one reason for this violence or one way to change it. Quoting parts of Gelman's writing can be effective support for your argument.

Idea 10

Read "New Glimpse of an Old World," an article by Dan Stern in *U.S. News & World Report,* July 20, 1998.

New Glimpse of an Old World

Certain areas of the Amazon rain forest are like time warps to an earlier era in human history. A few months ago, while flying over a deeply secluded part of this jungle, Sydney Possuelo, who heads Brazil's federal Department of Isolated Indians, caught a glimpse of this old world, as he has several times before. Half-hidden beneath the thick canopy of trees was a village of about 200 members unknown to modern civilization, seemingly living in a hunter-gatherer society.

It's believed that when Portuguese navigator Pedro Cabral reached the South American coast in 1500, between 1 million and

11 million indigenous people (dubbed "Indians") lived in what is now Brazil. Nearly half a millennium later, there are only 300,000 surviving Indians. War, slavery, starvation, and disease—all primarily resulting from invaders—are to blame.

This latest discovery of an uncontacted tribe is another case in Brazil's ongoing political controversy over what to do with such groups. Brazil's government tries to find remote tribes, demarcate their territory, and then leave them alone. It creates guard posts to keep out farmers, loggers, gold miners, poachers, and other outsiders who might incite violence, degrade the tribal lifestyle, or bring diseases (against which the Indians have no inherited immunity). Nearly 200 million acres, roughly 11 percent of the national territory, have recently been promised to the remaining natives. Opponents of the move not only think this allotment is too much for so few people but want a return to Brazil's old policy of assimilation.

While assimilation has often been disastrous, some tribes do welcome interaction with the outside world; others want no change at all. As for this newly found tribe—of which almost nothing is known regarding its customs, language, or name—its remote location precludes any immediate threat from modern society. (It has yet to be photographed, except from the air.) The government has no plans to make contact. If and when the day of contact arrives, the government's policy is to let the group decide the level of acculturation.

Up to 55 uncontacted and undiscovered Indian groups are believed to live in remote pockets of the Amazon, which most anthropologists consider to be the last place on Earth where such tribes dwell.

Writing Assignment

Stern's article states that people take different sides on the issue of whether to contact undiscovered tribes. Some people believe that modern civilization can benefit these people and that therefore it would be wrong not to make contact with them. Others believe that modern civilization will harm, rather than help, these tribes. In small groups, discuss how modern civilization could both benefit and harm these people. Make a list of the ideas shared so you have ideas on paper to work with. After the discussion, clarify your position. Perhaps you take a clear position on one side or the other, or perhaps you see both sides of the issue and cannot decide which side to support. Clarify your position: for, against, or in between. Write a thesis statement that tells your position. Then develop your thesis by explaining and supporting your reasons.

Idea 11

Read the following paragraph taken from "The Magnetic Tube," an article by John Leland in *Newsweek*, Spring–Summer, 1997.

Of all the challenges a developing child faces, few are more problematic than the one we willingly bring into our homes: the television. It can be a godsend, especially when you're feeling one Pooh tape away from a really bad day. But the set also comes with its own sets of stories and mythologies, and its own values. It has ulterior motives. It captivates children sometimes when parents can't. And it teaches them things parents might not. From the moment children are born, researchers say, they learn to emulate what they see; that's how they learn. Television provides a whole universe of behavior to emulate, some desirable, some not. And the immersion begins early. By the age of two, American kids spend an average of twenty-seven hours per week in front of the set.

For any parent, that's a lot of competition. In nearly forty years of study, researchers have found a correlation between children's TV habits and their levels of creativity, aggressiveness, and social skills. As Peggy Charren, who heads the advocacy group Action for Children's Television, says, "The problem with television is that it's all educational." But just what is it teaching your child?

Writing Assignment

Peggy Charren states that all television is educational. The questions are: What exactly is television teaching children? What values are being taught? What messages are children receiving? As you answer these questions, consider both specific programs and advertisements. One way to clarify your thinking is by finishing the sentence *Television teaches children that. . . .*

Option for organizing ideas: In your thesis statement, say what you believe television is teaching children. Support your thesis with specific evidence, describing in detail what children see so that readers who have not seen the programs can visualize the content. Include, with each example, the message that the program is giving children.

Chapter 26

ESL Editing Information

- ◆ Nouns
- ◆ Determiners
- ◆ Verbs
- ◆ Verb Forms Used as Adjectives
- ◆ Prepositions
- ◆ Order of Adjectives
- ◆ Sentence Structure

If you are an ESL (English as a Second Language) student, you have many advantages that people who know only one language do not have. Along with your ability to communicate in another language, you have a broader understanding of culture and a richer appreciation of varying customs. Those are priceless gifts and gifts that are valuable in the working world. As you become increasingly proficient in English, you will find that English, just like your first language, has specific ways of putting words together. Some of those specific patterns are summarized in this chapter.

Nouns

Nouns are either countable or uncountable. You can find further information in either of two dictionaries: the *Oxford Advanced Learner's Dictionary* or the *Longman Dictionary of American English*.

Countable Nouns

Countable nouns refer to distinct items. These nouns have both singular and plural forms.

Singular	Plural
one *letter*	three *letters*
one *fact*	many *facts*

Uncountable Nouns

Uncountable nouns refer to a group or a general category of items. They are always considered singular and therefore have singular verbs. Many uncountable nouns refer to a mass or to abstract qualities.

Nouns that refer to a mass

mail	education	luggage
information	money	water
furniture	traffic	blood
equipment	garbage	milk

Our *mail* arrives daily before noon.
The *information* is important for us.

Nouns that refer to abstract qualities

advice	knowledge	health	happiness
fun	courage	honesty	success

Honesty is important in building stable relationships.

Uncountable nouns are never used with *a* or *an*. They are used alone, with the word *the*, with pronouns, or with quantity words such as *much, a great deal of, a little, some, any, less,* or *no.*

Alone	With a quantity word
We need *advice*.	We need *no advice*.
Luggage is expensive.	*Some luggage* is expensive.

You can use uncountable nouns in a countable sense by adding words or phrases that indicate quantity.

Their *words of advice* helped us make the right decision.

Our family drinks *three gallons of milk* a week.

Determiners

Every singular countable noun must begin with a determiner. Determiners are words that identify or quantify a noun.

Common Determiners

> a, an, the
> this, these, that, those
> my, our, your, his, her
> its, their
> whose, which, what
> all, both, each, every
> some, any, no, either, neither
> many, much, a few, a little
> several, enough

Other common determiners are possessive nouns (*Andrew's, people's*) and numerals (*one, two, three*, etc.).

Use *this* or *that* with singular countable nouns or uncountable nouns: *this chair, that furniture.*
Use *these, those, a few, many, both,* or *several* with plural countable nouns: *these stories, those shoes, a few problems, many solutions, both telephones, several friends.*

A, An, *and* The

A, an, and *the* are determiners called *articles.* Use *a* before a noun that begins with a consonant sound. Use *an* before a noun that begins with a vowel sound. Deciding which to use—*a, an,* or *the*—depends on whether the information is known to your readers or listeners.
Use *a* or *an* with a singular countable noun whose specific identity is not known.

> We want to read a *book.*
>
> • The readers or listeners will understand that you are referring to books in general, not to a specific book.

Use *the* if the identity is known or is about to be made known. *The* is used for all known nouns, whether they are countable, uncountable, singular, or plural.

> We want to read *the book.*
>
> • The readers and hearers will know what specific book you mean. You have previously mentioned this book in your paper or conversation.

> We want to read *the book* that was recommended in class yesterday.
>
> • Readers and hearers will know what book you mean because the sentence identifies the specific book.

© 2000 Houghton Mifflin Company

Verbs

Verbs are often followed by infinitives (*to* plus the base form) or the *-ing* verb form. Some verbs are followed only by the infinitive; some verbs are followed only by the *-ing* form; some verbs can be followed by either. Glance over the following lists for verbs you use often. You can practice saying them with the appropriate verb form.

Verbs Followed by an Infinitive

These verbs are commonly followed by an infinitive:

agree	manage
ask	need
beg	offer
bother	plan
choose	pretend
claim	promise
decide	refuse
expect	want
fail	wish
hope	

I *promise to call* you tonight.
They *offered to help* us with the work.
We *will need to study* this weekend.

Verbs Followed by an -ing *Verb Form*

These verbs are followed by an *-ing* verb form instead of an infinitive:

admit	imagine
appreciate	keep
avoid	miss
can't help	postpone
consider	practice
delay	quit
deny	recall
discuss	resist
dislike	risk
enjoy	suggest
finish	tolerate

We *enjoy cooking* Thai food.
I *will practice typing* during the weekend.
The elderly couple *avoided driving* after dark.

Verbs Followed by Either an Infinitive or an -ing Verb Form

You can use either the infinitive or the *-ing* verb form after some verbs; there is little or no difference in meaning.

begin   continue   hate   like   love   start

We began *to eat* dinner at 7:00.
We began *eating* dinner at 7:00.

- Both sentences have the same meaning.

With a few verbs, the meaning does change:

forget   remember   stop   try

We stopped *to buy* groceries.

- This sentence means that we bought groceries.

We stopped *buying* groceries.

- This sentence means we no longer buy groceries.

Verb Forms Used as Adjectives

The *-ing* and *-ed* adjectives give different information about the nouns they describe. An *-ing* adjective indicates that the noun produces a certain effect on others. An *-ed* adjective indicates that the noun itself feels the effect.

The *boring* speaker

- The speaker produces boredom in others. The people listening to the speaker are the ones who are bored.

The *bored* speaker

- The speaker feels the boredom. The speaker is the one who is bored.

Here are some other common *-ing* and *-ed* verb forms used as adjectives:

Noun Produces the Effect on Others	Noun Already Has the Effect
amazing	amazed
amusing	amused
annoying	annoyed
convincing	convinced
depressing	depressed
disappointing	disappointed
embarrassing	embarrassed
exhausting	exhausted
satisfying	satisfied
surprising	surprised

Prepositions

Prepositions, which are listed in Chapter 14, combine with verbs and adjectives in specific ways.

Prepositions with Verbs

Some verbs are used with specific prepositions. A list of the most common ones follows.

apologize *to* someone *for* something

apply *for* (a position)

arrive *at* (a building or an event)

arrive *in* (a country or city)

blame someone *for* something

call *off* a scheduled appointment

call *on* someone for a visit

complain *about*

concentrate *on*

congratulate someone *on* something

consist *of*

deal *with*

depend *on*

explain something *to* someone

fill *in* individual blanks (blank spaces) on a form

fill *out* an entire form

fill *up* a gas tank

insist *on*

interfere *with*

object *to*

reason *with*

rely *on*

reply *to*

smile *at*

specialize *in*

take advantage *of*

take care *of*

thank someone *for* something

throw something *at* someone (who is not expecting it)

throw something *to* someone (who is waiting to catch it)

worry *about*

Prepositions with Adjectives

Some adjectives are used with specific prepositions:

addicted *to*

afraid *of*

anxious *about*

ashamed *of*

aware *of*

confused *by*

content *with*

convenient *for*

excited *about*

fond *of*

full *of*

grateful *for* (something)

grateful *to* (someone)

happy *about*

interested *in*

jealous *of*

proud *of*

responsible *for* something

satisfied *with*

shocked *at*

similar *to*

sorry *for*

suspicious *of*

tired *of*

Order of Adjectives

When you use more than one adjective to describe a noun or a pronoun, use the following order.

1. judgment or opinion (*wonderful, beautiful, intelligent, terrible, strange*)

2. size (*small, large, big, tiny, tall, short*)

3. shape (*square, round, circular, flat*)

4. age (*ancient, old, middle-aged, young, new*)

5. color (*red, yellow, blue, green*)

6. nationality (*Italian, French, Chinese*)

7. material (*paper, wooden, iron, steel, plastic*)

Sentence Structure

In English, a subject must be included in every sentence, as was explained in Chapter 6. Other patterns that may differ from your native language involve using subordinating conjunctions, forming questions, and making negative statements.

Using Although *and* Because

The subordinating conjunctions *although* and *because* should not be combined with coordinating conjunctions (such as *but* or *so*) or with transition words (such as *however* or *therefore*).

Incorrect   Although we left early, ~~but~~ we did not arrive on time.

Correct   Although we left early, we did not arrive on time.

Incorrect   Because we knew company was coming, ~~therefore~~ we prepared extra food.

Correct   Because we knew company was coming, we prepared extra food.

Questions

To turn a statement into a question, move the helping verb in the statement and place it before the subject.

They *are* planning a surprise party for Patrick.
Are they planning a surprise party for Patrick?

If there is no helping verb, add a form of *do* and place it before the subject.

They filled out the application forms.

• Notice that *filled* indicates the past tense.

Did they fill out the application forms?

• Notice that *did* indicates the past tense.

Negatives

Use *one* of the following words to form a negative statement:

never	nobody	no one	nowhere
no	none	not	

When you are writing a sentence with *not*, place *not* after the first helping verb in a sentence.

Anne will sleep late on Saturday.
She will *not* sleep late on Sunday.

If there is no helping verb, add a form of *do*.

>   We finished our work.
>
>   • Notice that *finished* indicates the past tense.
>
>   We *did* not finish our work.
>
>   • Notice that *did* indicates the past tense.

Text Credits

Page 1: From THE LANGUAGE INSTINCT by Steven Pinker. Copyright © 1994 by Steven Pinker. By Permission of William Morrow Company, Inc.

Page 12: From *Conversations with Maya Angelou*. Literary Conversations Series, edited by Jeffrey M. Elliot. © 1989. Published by University Press of Mississippi.

Page 22: From *I Know Why the Caged Bird Sings* by Maya Angelou, p. 116. Bantam Books, 1996.

Page 24: From *The Color of Water* by James McBride, p. 57. Riverhead Books, 1996.

Page 24: From *No Free Ride: From the Mean Streets to the Mainstream* by Kweisi Mfume, p.16. Ballantine, 1996.

Page 25: From *Fish Cheeks* by Amy Tan. Originally appeared in *Seventeen*, December 1977.

Page 27: From *The Perfect Storm* by Sebastian Junger, p. 5. W.W. Norton & Company, 1997.

Page 27: From *Life on the Road* by Charles Kuralt. Putnam, 1990.

Page 30: Tim O'Brien, "On the Rainy River," from *The Things They Carried: A Work of Fiction*. Copyright © 1990 by Houghton Mifflin Company.

Page 30: From *Lives on the Boundary* by Mike Rose, p. 32. Penguin Books, 1989.

Pages 31, 161, 314: From BORN FOR LOVE, by Leo F. Buscaglia, Slack, Inc., 1992.

Page 32: From *Long Walk to Freedom: The Autobiography of Nelson Mandela* by Nelson Mandela, p. 144. Little, Brown and Company, 1994.

Page 39: Reprinted by arrangement with The Heirs to the Estate of Martin Luther King, Jr., c/o Writers House, Inc. as agent for the proprietor. Copyright 1958 by Martin Luther King, Jr., copyright renewed by Coretta Scott King.

Page 40: Reprinted by permission from Dr. Laura Schlessinger.

Page 42: Adapted from "The Decline of Neatness" by Norman Cousins, Copyright © 1990 by Time, Inc.

Page 42: Reprinted from *Journal of Psychosomatic Research*, 1967, "The Social Readjustment Rating Scale" by Holmes and Rahe, with permission from Elsevier Science.

Page 44: From *The Survivor Personality* by Al Siebert, p. 1. Perigee, 1996.

© 2000 Houghton Mifflin Company

Index